simply italian

simply italian

Sophie Braimbridge

MURDOCH
BOOKS

contents

Colourful antipasto platters are arranged with a selection of the local favourite *salumi* (cured meats), seafood or vegetables of contrasting flavours and textures, often served with fruit and country-style bread. The soups of Italy range from the hearty, warming, almost stew-like dishes from the north, thickened with beans, chestnuts and pearl barley, to the south's pappa al pomodoro, rich with tomatoes and soaked bread.

Italy's most famous export, pasta, comes in every shape and size under the hot Mediterranean sun. In the fiery south, dried pasta is dressed with chillies and tomatoes, the hallmark of that region's history of *cucina povera*. Rich Emilia-Romana is known for its many varieties of fresh golden egg pasta, simply dressed with butter or shaved truffles. The fame of Italy's pasta sauces—primavera, carbonara, basil pesto and Bologna's meat ragù—has now spread far beyond the country's borders.

The pasta of the north, the famous creamy arborio rice from Lombardy's Po valley, is flavoured and coloured with saffron, vegetables and squid ink and served thick or liquid enough to eat from a spoon, depending on where in Italy you are dining. Polenta, loved in Venice and the mountain regions, bubbles in huge pots and is served 'wet' to soak up rich game stews, or pressed into tins and then chargrilled.

There are very few landlocked regions of Italy, the coastline is abundant with fresh seafood and even inland areas have a rich supply of freshwater fish in their rivers and streams. Anchovies, mussels, crabs and fish can be bought daily from bustling port markets and are usually simply prepared, plainly fried or grilled or made into the favourite local fish stew.

The Italians are famed for the freshness of their ingredients: mushrooms and truffles are picked in the wild, herbs and vegetables carried swiftly from the ground to the plate. The game in the lush forests and hills of Tuscany and Umbria is treated no differently and the Italians are keen hunters. Birds are traditionally cooked in rich sauces of lentils and vegetables, balsamic vinegar and herbs, southern tomatoes or sun-ripened figs, or simply stuffed and roasted in a hot oven.

contents

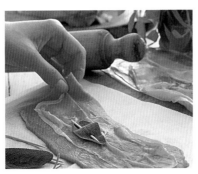

The Tuscans are the great meat-eaters of Italy, but the bistecca from Florence is rivalled in popularity by Venice's liver and onions, the saltimbocca of Rome and the bollito misto of the northern regions. Every Italian family has its own traditional recipe for veal meatballs and pork too is a favourite, with the *norcini* making use of all parts of the animal to prepare sausages, salami and cured meats.

The mainstay of Italian cooking, and certainly not seen as a mere accompaniment to meat or seafood, fresh vegetables are bought sometimes twice a day for lunch and dinner in local markets and chargrilled, grilled, fried, marinated or used for sauces, bakes and tossing through pasta. *Contorni* are vegetables served as side dishes with a meal.

When Queen Margherita visited Naples and asked to sample the city's famed thin crisp bread with topping, called 'pizza', she gave royal endorsement to a humble idea that has now become one of the world's favourite foods. Italy's country-style bread is used for crostini and bruschetta, while focaccia and white panini filled with salami or provolone are favourite cafe lunches.

The Arabs brought sugar to Sicily and the southern island is now the sweet-producing heart of the country: gelati, sorbets and granita are sold in cafes and at the roadside in an awe-inspiring array of colours and flavours. But Italy is renowned for more than its ices: the tiramisu of Treviso, Siena's medieval panforte, the dome-shaped zuccotto of Florence and, of course, biscotti and simple poached or grilled fruits are all perfect Italian endings to a meal.

South America produced the bean but it is Italy that embraced and perfected the art of coffee-making. Quick shots or long foamy drinks; strong or creamy; frothy milk, tall glasses or tiny cups; breakfast, lunch and dinner... the Italians have a coffee for every occasion. But coffee is not the only popular drink in Italy—grapes have been cultivated from very early times and today fine wines are produced throughout the country. It is easy to find a suitable wine to accompany any meal.

the Italians and their food

One thing all Italians have in common is their love of food, and especially their love of Italian food. I think only my Italian friend would go into a restaurant and talk about the cut of the steak he wanted to order and then chat further to the butcher next door before ordering it. But Italian food is really based upon home cooking, 'mama's food', and it is in the homes that you will discover its true essence. It is the ritual of buying local ingredients in the market, sometimes twice a day for both lunch and dinner, and taking them home to cook that makes food an essential part of Italian life. Italians pick their ingredients carefully: if something isn't in season or doesn't look at its best on the market stall they'll choose to cook something else instead. There is a great saying that defines Italian food more than any other and that is 'the best meal is first prepared in the market'.

It is hard to define an overall concept of Italian cooking, especially as, until late in the nineteenth century, Italy was not a complete country but a group of principalities and sovereign states. Italian food, traditional by nature, is still very much divided into different regions with each having its own distinct and unique cuisine.

As food production has always been fundamentally affected by landscape and climate, be it mountains or valleys, sea or meadows, sun or rain, to merely describe the landscape of Italy gives an idea of how the cooking varies across its length and breadth. The mountains and plains that chill in the cold wet winters of the north also grow luxurious green grass, feeding the cattle that produce rich cream and milk for butter. These are the dairy-eating areas. The hot dry south produces the vegetables, herbs and citrus fruit that love the sun: tomatoes, olives, lemons, chillies. Granitas and sorbets are essential for keeping cool. The landscape has also isolated parts of the country, with mountains or rivers separating different regions. It wasn't until communication advanced and roads improved that particular culinary favourites became known further than even a valley away. This is also why some foods have different names from town to town: for example the fresh eggless pasta *picci* served in Siena, Tuscany is the same pasta that is called *umbracelli* down the road in Orvieto, Umbria.

Outside influences have also left their mark on Italian food. The invading forces of the Greeks, Byzantines and Arabs, the close proximity of France and Austria and the Venetian spice traders of the Orient have all added to the cuisine, making it richer and more sophisticated. It was the spice traders who introduced a food that is now seen as the quintessential Italian ingredient, the tomato. This was first thought of as the evil golden apple of Eden, the *pomodoro*, as it was originally served green, before the southern Italians learnt to let it soften and ripen slowly in the sun.

In recent years Italian cuisine has become more unified throughout the country. With the migration of labour and general movement from country to city that has taken place since the Second World War, borders between areas have at last become blurred. Rice and meat are now eaten in the south and, for their part, southern labourers have taken their love of dried pasta to the industrial north, where the citizens of Milan or Turin would never have considered eating it previously. And that speciality of Naples, the pizza, is now loved worldwide.

antipasti e zuppa

Vegetable antipasto

Literally meaning 'before the meal' (*pasto*), and not 'before the pasta', as sometimes translated, antipasto can consist entirely of assorted vegetables, as here, or can include meat, seafood and cheese. This colourful vegetable antipasto can be made up using whatever is fresh or in season.

SERVES 6

INGREDIENTS

150 g cooked asparagus spears (see page 11), refreshed in cold water

½ quantity grilled vegetable salad (see page 180) or ready-prepared grilled peppers, aubergines and courgettes

6 slow-cooked tomatoes (see page 183) or 18 ready-prepared sun-dried tomatoes

6 stuffed artichokes (see page 186) or 6 ready-prepared marinated artichoke hearts

12 ready-prepared marinated mushrooms

12 ready-prepared marinated onions

6 arrancini (see page 84)

6 tapenade or red pepper crostini (see page 18)

a selection of marinated olives

lemon wedges, to serve

extra virgin olive oil, to serve

grissini (see page 207) or country-style bread, such as ciabatta, to serve

VEGETABLE antipasto plates can be as much or as little work as you like. You can either put together a collection of the suggested recipes from this book or you can buy ready-prepared ingredients from delicatessens or supermarkets. Alternatively, make some of the recipes and supplement these with some bought items.

CHOOSE from the suggested list, basing your selection on flavour, colour and compatibility. If you like crostini, then choose both types, or add a version of your own. If you don't have much time, pick easy things to make such as the asparagus or, quicker still, buy them. You can buy perfectly acceptable antipasto vegetables such as grilled peppers, aubergines, courgettes and sun-dried tomatoes at delicatessens, as well as marinated artichoke hearts, mushrooms, onions and olives.

TO make an attractive antipasto course, choose either one large platter or several small plates or bowls—it is better to spread things out rather than trying to cram them all in together. The crostini and grissini can be served on one plate, but if something is served in a sauce or if the individual vegetables have different herbs and flavourings they will probably be best served in individual bowls to prevent a confusion of flavours. Serve plenty of bread and grissini to accompany the antipasto (especially if you are serving it as a meal in itself) as well as extra olive oil and lemon wedges for dressing.

chargrilling

Chargrilling or using a barbecue gives the vegetables a more complex taste than simply grilling them. The marks created by the griddle look attractive and have a smoky flavour that permeates the food.

oven-roasting

Oven-roasting at a low temperature (slow cooking) means that the water evaporates out of food such as tomatoes as they cook. This gives them a richer, more intense flavour.

marinating

Marinating means combining food with aromatic ingredients so the food takes on the flavours of the marinade. It works particularly well with olives when they are cracked and mixed with chilli, garlic, orange peel and olive oil. Leave them in a jar in the fridge for a few days.

Seafood antipasto

Seafood antipasto is eaten in many coastal areas, though marinated sardines and anchovies are common all over Italy. Often the selection is regionally based, especially when a particular speciality, such as sea dates (a type of shellfish) or baby eels, is in season.

CHOOSE a selection of seafood from the list—you can serve as many or as few as you want, but four is probably a manageable number. If you are going to use fresh fish and grill them, make sure that they really are fresh. Heat the grill to its highest setting and brush each fish with olive oil. For extra flavour, put a small slice of lemon in the cavity of each one. Grill the fish on both sides until they are cooked through.

MARINATED fish can be bought in jars and tins or from delicatessens. Choose anchovies and sardines in salt or olive oil rather than vegetable oil. Rinse and pat them dry, then arrange in a dish and sprinkle them with lemon juice and chopped parsley (add a little chopped garlic if you like). Cooked prawns are best bought in their shells and peeled at home, or buy raw ones and cook them yourself if you prefer.

IF you have time, make a selection of the suggested recipes for your platter. If not, you can buy everything you need ready-prepared. Bear in mind that when you serve fish and shellfish you will need plenty of lemon to cut through any oil and lots of bread for mopping up juices.

TO make the fritto misto di mare, first make the batter. Sift the flour into a bowl and stir in ¼ teaspoon salt. Mix in the oil with a wooden spoon, then slowly add 75–100 ml warm water to make a smooth thick batter. Whisk the egg whites until stiff peaks form, then fold gently into the batter.

FILL a deep-fryer or large saucepan one-third full with oil and heat to 180°C (350°F), or until a piece of bread fries golden brown in 20 seconds. If the oil starts to smoke, it is too hot.

DIP the seafood into the batter, coating all sides. Fry in batches until the batter is crisp. Remove with a slotted spoon or tongs and drain on paper towel. Season with salt and serve immediately with lemon wedges.

cooking

Freshly grilled fish are one of the simplest and quickest antipasto to make at home. Make sure your grill is hot enough to brown and crisp the skins.

fritto misto

Fritto misto is often thought of as seafood but is traditionally a mixed platter that varies from region to region, featuring meat, vegetables, fruit or even chocolate. Deep-fry the seafood just before you serve the antipasto platter. The batter will become soggy if the cooked pieces are left to stand and its crispness should be a good contrast to the other dishes.

SERVES 6

INGREDIENTS

6 sardines or similar fish, gutted, scaled (see page 94) and grilled, or bought sardine fillets

6 salt cod fritters (see page 103)

1 quantity garlic prawns (see page 101) or bought cooked prawns

1 quantity octopus salad or ready-prepared marinated octopus

1 quantity prawn, cannellini bean and mint salad (see page 102)

1 quantity grilled mixed shellfish (see page 111)

1 quantity sfogie in saor (see page 105)

marinated anchovies (see page 98) or tinned anchovies

ready-prepared marinated mussels

FRITTO MISTO DI MARE

50 g plain flour

2 teaspoons olive oil

3 egg whites

600 g mixed cleaned prawns, squid rings and scallops (see page 96)

oil, for deep-frying

lemon wedges, to serve

finely chopped parsley, to serve

country-style bread; such as ciabatta, to serve

Meat antipasto

6 slices lardo

6 slices felino salami or
  1 or 2 cacciatore salami

6 slices coppa di parma

6 slices bresaola

6 slices prosciutto di Parma or San
  Daniele

6 plain olive oil bruschetta (see
  page 19)

6 slices mortadella

6 chicken liver crostini (see page 18)

black olives, in brine and unpitted

pickled baby onions (cipollini)

caperberries

sun-dried tomatoes

3 figs, halved

6 slices cantaloupe melon

country-style bread, such as
  ciabatta, to serve

extra virgin olive oil and lemon
  juice, to serve

Called *affettati misti* in Italian, the platter should be made up of a good selection of meats that contrast in flavour and appearance. Serve with fruit such as figs, olives and caperberries, or with slices of ripe melon or pear.

A meat antipasto plate is probably the quickest to put together. It is, however, very important that you choose a really good selection of meats. Buy the best quality you can afford: the fresher the meat is, the better it will taste. If you are planning on serving this dish often, you may want to buy a few whole salami and slice them yourself as you need them.

MEAT is best served with strong accompaniments such as caperberries, cipollini and olives, which cut through any fattiness, or with sweet fruit like figs and melon that enhance its flavours.

TO put together an attractive platter, cut the meat in different ways. The lardo needs to be sliced very thinly, almost shaved. The salami can be sliced according to your personal taste—generally the smaller salami such as cacciatore are cut into thicker slices than the large ones. Mortadella is often cut into cubes instead of slicing.

LAY out the meats on a platter, folding some and rolling others. Arrange a choice of the accompaniments on the platter with them so your guests can help themselves, and serve with plenty of bread. The bresaola should be sprinkled with a little olive oil and lemon juice just before you serve. Always serve a meat antipasto platter at room temperature—meat taken straight from the fridge will not have as much flavour.

shaving

Lardo is a piece of lard that has been salted, and sometimes flavoured on the sides with herbs or spices. It should be shaved very finely with a cheese slice, mandolin or potato peeler so it melts in the mouth, giving just a hint of flavour.

cubing

Mortadella is a very large cooked sausage from Bologna. It is either very finely sliced on a mechanical slicer or can be cut into cubes.

slicing

Larger salamis are best sliced on an electric slicer when you buy them. You can slice them at home with a sharp knife, but try to use one smooth cutting motion with a long blade rather than sawing backwards and forwards.

caperberries

These are the fruit of the caper bush preserved in brine. They are shaped like grapes and have a long stalk at one end and thin white stripes running along their length. They are similar in taste to capers, which are the unopened buds of the same bush, but the flavour is not as strong.

Crostini

Crostini are small pieces of bread toasted in the oven, rather than the larger grilled slices used for bruschetta, and, as an antipasto they are particularly associated with Tuscany. As an alternative to the toppings suggested here, you can also choose from those for the bruschetta (opposite).

MAKES 50

INGREDIENTS

CROSTINI

2 day-old ciabatta or pugliese

200 ml extra virgin olive oil

TAPENADE CROSTINI

250 g whole black olives, pitted

50 g anchovy fillets

1 tablespoon capers, drained

2 garlic cloves, crushed

15 g basil, finely chopped

grated zest and juice of 1 lemon

200 ml extra virgin olive oil

1 quantity crostini

RED PEPPER CROSTINI

3 tablespoons extra virgin olive oil

1 onion, finely chopped

2 red peppers, thinly sliced

2 garlic cloves, crushed

1 tablespoon capers, drained
and chopped

2 tablespoons balsamic vinegar

1 tablespoon roughly chopped
flat-leaf parsley

1 quantity crostini

CHICKEN LIVER CROSTINI

200 g chicken livers

3 tablespoons olive oil

1 small onion, finely chopped

2 garlic cloves, crushed

1 tablespoon finely chopped sage

2 tablespoons dry Marsala

2 tablespoons mascarpone

1 quantity crostini

TO make the crostini, preheat the oven to 180°C (350°F/Gas 4). Thinly slice the bread, cut each piece into quarters and drizzle olive oil over both sides. Lightly toast the bread in the oven until just crisp. The crostini will keep in an airtight container for at least a couple of days once completely cooled.

TO make the tapenade crostini, finely chop the olives, anchovies and capers together with a knife or food processor and put them in a bowl. Add the garlic, basil, lemon zest and juice, stir in the olive oil and season well. Spread on the crostini to serve. (The tapenade will keep in an airtight container in the fridge for up to a month if sealed with a layer of olive oil.)

TO make the red pepper crostini, heat the olive oil in a frying pan and cook the onion for a few minutes until soft. Add the peppers and cook for a further 15 minutes, stirring frequently. Season, then add the garlic and cook for another minute. Add the capers and vinegar and simmer gently for a few minutes to reduce the liquid. Add the parsley just before spreading onto the crostini.

TO make the chicken liver crostini, trim the chicken livers of any sinew. Heat the olive oil in a frying pan and gently cook the onion for 2 minutes until soft. Push the onion to the side, increase the heat and add the livers. Cook until they are lightly brown on both sides, then add the garlic and sage and cook for 1 minute. Add the Marsala and cook briefly to reduce the liquid. Season well. Chop to a paste in a food processor or by hand, then add the mascarpone. The chicken liver can be served warm or chilled on the crostini.

preparing

Crostini are best made with slightly stale bread. This will not only make it easier to slice but, as the bread will be drier, it will toast more quickly.

storing

Crostini can be made in advance but if you keep them for too long the oil will become stale. Store for two to three days in an airtight container and then crisp them up in a 180°C oven for 10 minutes before you use them. Bruschetta should be made to order.

Bruschetta

Bruschetta is a traditional Italian antipasto made using dense slightly stale bread that grills well. It is often served in its simplest form: rubbed with garlic while still hot and then drizzled with extra virgin olive oil. For variation, try these toppings of tomato, mushroom or aubergine.

TO make the basic bruschetta, grill, chargrill or toast the bread until it is light brown. Peel the garlic clove and rub over both sides of the bread, then drizzle a little extra virgin olive oil over each slice.

TO make the tomato and basil bruschetta, roughly chop the tomatoes and mix with the basil. Season well and pile onto the bruschetta.

TO make the wild mushroom topping, heat the olive oil in a large saucepan or frying pan. When the oil is hot, add just enough mushrooms to cover the base of the pan and cook them over high heat, stirring frequently. Season with salt and pepper. (Sometimes the mushrooms can become watery when cooked. Continue cooking until all the liquid has evaporated.) Add a little crushed garlic and thyme and cook for another minute. Remove from the pan and repeat with the remaining mushrooms. Spoon over the bruschetta and serve warm.

TO make the aubergine topping, heat a griddle on the stove and cook the aubergine slices, a few at a time, over moderately high heat until soft and cooked, turning once. Mix together the garlic, oil, lemon juice and mint and season well. Put the aubergine in a dish with the marinade and leave for 30 minutes. Place a couple of pieces of aubergine on each bruschetta and spoon the marinade over the top.

MAKES 12

INGREDIENTS

BRUSCHETTA

6 large slices country-style bread, such as pugliese or pan de campagne, halved
1 garlic clove
extra virgin olive oil

TOMATO AND BASIL BRUSCHETTA

4 ripe tomatoes
1 tablespoon shredded basil
4 pieces bruschetta

WILD MUSHROOM BRUSCHETTA

2 tablespoons extra virgin olive oil
400 g selection of wild mushrooms, particularly fresh porcini, sliced if large, or chestnut mushrooms
2 garlic cloves, crushed
1 heaped tablespoon chopped thyme
4 pieces bruschetta

AUBERGINE BRUSCHETTA

2 medium aubergines, sliced
2 garlic cloves, crushed
150 ml extra virgin olive oil
juice of 1 small lemon
3 tablespoons roughly chopped mint
4 pieces bruschetta

Deep-fried courgette flowers

SERVES 4

INGREDIENTS

12 courgette flowers

BATTER

50 g plain flour
2 teaspoons olive oil
3 egg whites

oil, for deep-frying
lemon wedges, to serve

Those who grow courgettes at home can make use of the yellow flowers that appear in steady supply throughout the summer or you can find them at your local greengrocer. If flowers aren't available, use the same batter and method with slices of courgette and aubergine.

CHECK the courgette flowers are clean and aren't hiding any insects. Trim the stems to about 2 cm (this gives you something to hold on to when dipping the flowers into the batter).

TO make the batter, sift the flour into a bowl and stir in ¼ teaspoon salt. Mix in the oil with a wooden spoon, then slowly add 75–100 ml warm water to make a smooth thick batter. Whisk the egg whites until stiff peaks form, then fold gently into the batter.

FILL a deep-fryer or deep pan one-third full with oil and heat to about 180°C (350°F), or until a piece of bread fries golden brown in 15 seconds. If the oil starts to smoke, it is too hot.

DIP the courgette flowers into the batter, coating them completely. Fry in batches until golden brown, turning once to cook on both sides. Drain on paper towels, sprinkle with salt and serve immediately with lemon wedges.

serving

Like many deep-fried foods, these courgette flowers will become soggy if you let them sit for too long before serving. If you want to prepare them a little in advance of serving, keep them warm on a tray lined with crumpled greaseproof paper in a low oven.

WHEN deep-frying, make sure that your oil temperature is correct, preferably by using a deep-fry thermometer or frying a piece of bread. Add the flowers in batches and cook until deep golden brown on both sides—if they aren't cooked for long enough, the centres will be raw and the batter pale and flabby. A sprinkling of salt after draining will add flavour and also help to soak up any excess oil.

anchovies

Tinned or bottled anchovies may be preserved in either salt *(acciughe sotto sale)* or oil *(filetti di acciuga)*. Some are filleted and some whole. The ones in salt need to be rinsed before use and the ones in oil, drained well.

Bagna caôda

A speciality of Piedmont, bagna caôda is a dip made of olive oil mixed with anchovies and garlic. Bagna caôda means 'hot bath' in the regional dialect: the 'hot' referring to the temperature at which the dish is served. Into it are dipped a selection of vegetables—whatever is fresh or in season.

TRIM, wash and dry the vegetables and cut them into suitably sized pieces for dipping.

PUT the oil, garlic and anchovies in a saucepan and place over medium heat. Cook gently, stirring once or twice, until the anchovies dissolve. Be careful that the garlic does not brown or it will taste bitter. Add the butter and leave over low heat, stirring once or twice until it has melted. Season with pepper.

TRANSFER the sauce to a bowl and keep it warm at the table by placing on a food warmer or over a burner or spirit stove (a fondue dish works well for this). Serve the vegetables and bread arranged on a platter.
To eat, dip your choice of vegetable into the hot bagna caôda and use a piece of bread to catch drips.

SERVES 4

INGREDIENTS

40 pieces assorted raw vegetables,
 such as carrot, celery, fennel,
 peppers and cauliflower florets
200 ml olive oil
6 garlic cloves, crushed
120 g anchovy fillets, finely chopped
90 g butter
country-style bread, such as ciabatta

SERVES 6

INGREDIENTS

700 g good-quality beef fillet

1 egg yolk

3 teaspoons Dijon mustard

3 tablespoons lemon juice

2 drops Tabasco

75 ml olive oil

1 tablespoon single cream

2–3 tablespoons capers, rinsed

Carpaccio

Carpaccio was created in the 1960s in Venice by the owner of Harry's Bar. It is thought to have been named in honour of the Italian Renaissance painter, Vittore Carpaccio, whose use of reds is reflected in the colour of the dish.

THE easiest way to slice your beef very thinly is to firm it up in the freezer first. Wrap the piece of beef tightly in clingfilm, keeping it in a nice block, and put it in the freezer for about half an hour or until it feels firm when you prod it.

USING a very sharp knife with a long blade or a mandolin, cut the beef into paper-thin slices. These slices should be so thin that you can almost see through them. Don't worry about the odd hole or tear.

AS you slice, lay the meat out on six serving plates, arranging the pieces in a thin even layer. Cover with clingfilm until you are ready to serve, making sure the clingfilm is pressed to the surface of the meat so it can't oxidise and turn brown.

BLEND together the egg yolk, mustard, lemon juice and Tabasco with a whisk, blender or food processor. Add the olive oil in a very thin stream, whisking or processing continuously until the mayonnaise thickens. When you have added all the oil, whisk in the cream. Season to taste with salt and white pepper.

DRIZZLE the dressing over the beef just before you serve and sprinkle each plate with capers.

beef

Italian beef tends to be very lean and is usually hung (matured) until it has a good strong flavour and is very tender. Beef is named according to its age: *bovino* refers to cows in general; *manzo* is meat from a three-year-old bullock; and *vitello* refers to veal. The names of beef cuts vary regionally and although countrywide standard cuts do exist, many people still prefer to use regional names.

HOLDING the beef firmly, cut down through it with a very sharp knife. You will find this easier if you use a long knife (such as a ham knife) and use the whole length of the blade to slide down through the meat. You should be able to cut a wafer-thin slice this way. Cutting with a short blade gives you less control.

ALTERNATIVELY, cut the beef into wafer-thin slices with a mandolin on its thinnest setting. This will only work if you have a wide mandolin and a piece of beef that will fit neatly against it (cut the piece of meat into thinner pieces if you need to).

Bottarga

Bottarga can be eaten thinly sliced and seasoned with lemon juice and olive oil but its strong flavour also works as a perfect foil for scrambled eggs or pasta. It can be kept in the fridge for some time or even frozen, but wrap it up tightly as it has quite a strong smell.

SLICE the bottarga with a sharp knife or mandolin. Cut it into enough slices to arrange a thin layer on four dinner plates.

TO serve the bottarga with olive oil, drizzle half a teaspoon of oil and squeeze a lemon wedge over each plate. Serve immediately (or the lemon will discolour the bottarga) with bread, olive oil and lemon.

TO serve the bottarga with scrambled eggs, lightly beat the eggs together, and season with pepper only (the bottarga is very salty). Preheat the serving bowls by filling them with boiling water. Leave to stand for a few minutes before drying. Slice half the bottarga, as above, and store the rest in the fridge, tightly wrapped.

HEAT the oil in a saucepan and add the eggs. Turn the heat down to low and gently scramble the eggs until they are creamy but not completely set. Tip the eggs into the serving bowls and put the bottarga on top where it will soften. Serve with the bread.

preparing

If you are using a knife to cut the bottarga, choose one with a long thin blade. This will give thinner slices than a short blade that has to be sawed backwards and forwards across the block.

SERVES 4

INGREDIENTS

BOTTARGA WITH OLIVE OIL

200 g bottarga

2 tablespoons extra virgin olive oil

4 lemon wedges

4 slices country-style bread

extra virgin olive oil and lemon wedges, to serve

BOTTARGA WITH SCRAMBLED EGGS

50 g bottarga

8 eggs

1 tablespoon olive oil

4 slices country-style bread

bottarga

Bottarga is made from either the roe of grey mullet *(bottarga di muggine)* or the roe of tuna *(bottarga di tonno)*, which is cured and then pressed into a solid block and dried. Tuna bottarga comes as a much bigger piece, usually without its skin, and mullet bottarga comes shaped in a neat block with its silvery skin still on. Bottarga is also sold as *botargue* and *poutargue*, the French versions of its name. Bottarga is thought to be an Arabic invention and is popular in Sicily, Spain, the south of France and North Africa.

Liguria

This predominantly coastal region is set in the north-east of Italy, overlooking the Ligurian Sea. Olives, grapevines, herbs and vegetables grow on the narrow stretch along the coast, while the hills just behind sustain a small dairy industry and the sea itself provides some fish and seafood. Liguria has always struggled to produce food: the land area available for farming is not large and the sea is colder than that of southern Italy and yields less fish. However, what is caught is prepared with great skill and the Ligurian fish stew has become one of the region's well-known dishes. Despite its relative paucity of produce, Liguria has a rich and varied cuisine based on small quantities of meat and cheese, with large amounts of herbs, vegetables and fragrant olive oil to dress pasta.

Liguria's most famous dish is pesto, made with basil and locally produced pecorino, and generally served with trenette or trofie pasta. This in itself sets Liguria apart from its northern neighbours: the food of the north is often dairy, rice or meat-based and basil is not a widely used ingredient. Other produce include walnuts (Ligurian walnut sauce is also famed), aubergines, purple artichokes and asparagus as well as renowned olives and olive oil. Focaccia also hails from Liguria, as does the light golden sponge cake, *torta Genovese*. Another speciality is *farinata*, a pancake of chickpea flour that is sold as street food. Chestnuts from the region are candied and eaten as a sweetmeat and *pandolce* is the golden sweet bread of Genoa.

Genoa, Liguria's capital city, is Italy's largest port and the Genoese are traditionally great seafarers. Many regional dishes are based on both fresh catch and *stocafisso* (air-dried cod). Preserved foods have a long tradition in the region: sailors who needed supplies to see them through long voyages carried dried ravioli and sardines in oil as well as dried cod.

Ligurian wine

Liguria does not grow a huge amount of grapes but, as its two largest neighbours are the well-known wine-producing regions of Tuscany and Piemonte, it does grow a large number of different varieties. In the area nearer Piemonte, wine is made using a single grape variety: *Pigato*, *Vermentino* and *Rossese* being the most popular. At the southern end of Liguria, wines are made from a blend of grapes as in Tuscany. Liguria's most famous wine is Rossese Dolceaqua, named after the town where it is made.

Minestrone alla Genovese

Nearly every region in Italy has its own style of minestrone. This version is served with a spoonful of pesto, which is stirred through at the end, and in some areas rice or pasta is added. Minestrone should always be accompanied by plenty of freshly grated Parmesan.

PUT the dried beans in a large bowl, cover with cold water and leave to soak overnight. Drain and rinse well.

TO make the soffritto (base flavouring) melt the lard in a large saucepan and add the onion, garlic, celery, carrot, parsley, sage and pancetta. Cook over low heat, stirring occasionally, for about 10 minutes, or until the onion is soft and golden.

ADD the potatoes and cook very gently for 15 minutes. Stir in the tomatoes, basil and borlotti beans. Season with plenty of pepper. Add the stock and bring to the boil. Cover and leave to simmer for 2 hours, stirring occasionally.

TO make the pesto, put the garlic and pine nuts in a mortar and pestle or food processor and pound or process until finely chopped. Add the basil and olive oil and pound or process until the basil is puréed. Season and mix in the Parmesan by hand. Put the pesto in a jar and cover the surface with a layer of olive oil to stop it discolouring.

IF the potatoes haven't already broken up, use a fork to roughly crush them against the side of the pan. Taste for seasoning and add the courgettes, peas, runner beans, cabbage and pasta. Simmer until the pasta is *al dente*.

SERVE with a spoonful of pesto and plenty of Parmesan.

SERVES 6

INGREDIENTS

220 g dried borlotti beans

50 g lard or extra virgin olive oil

1 large onion, finely chopped

1 garlic clove, finely chopped

2 celery stalks, halved then sliced

2 carrots, sliced

15 g flat-leaf parsley, finely chopped

2 sage leaves

100 g pancetta, cubed

3 potatoes, peeled but left whole

400 g tin chopped tomatoes

8 basil leaves

3 litres chicken or vegetable stock

PESTO

2 garlic cloves

50 g pine nuts

120 g basil, stems removed

9 tablespoons extra virgin olive oil

50 g Parmesan, grated

2 courgettes, sliced

220 g peas

120 g runner beans, cut into 4 cm lengths

¼ cabbage, shredded

150 g ditalini, avemarie or other small pasta

grated Parmesan, to serve

La ribollita

4 tablespoons olive oil

1 onion, finely chopped

1 large carrot

3 celery stalks

2 garlic cloves, crushed

250 g cavolo nero or savoy cabbage

1 courgette, finely chopped

400 g cooked cannellini or
   borlotti beans

400 g tin peeled tomatoes

1 whole dried chilli

200 ml red wine

1 litre chicken stock

75 g stale country-style bread, such
   as ciabatta or pugliese, crusts
   removed and broken into
   2.5 cm pieces

extra virgin olive oil, to serve

This hearty soup is a Tuscan speciality and should be thick enough to eat with a fork rather than a spoon. Traditionally it is made a day in advance, then reboiled—'ribollita'. The trick is to cook the vegetables gently and slowly so that they have time to infuse the flavour of the oil.

serving

Making the soup the day before (in this case, add the bread just before serving) allows the flavours to develop. When reheating, make sure it comes just to the boil but then remove it from the heat. Don't stir it too much or the bread will break up and alter the texture of the soup. Leave to cool for 5 minutes before serving in cold bowls. Ribollita should be served warm, rather than piping hot.

TO make the soffritto (base flavouring), pour the oil into a large saucepan and first add the onion. Cook the onion gently over low heat. While the onion is cooking, finely chop the carrot and celery and add them to the saucepan as you go along. Add the garlic, then leave to cook for a few minutes.

STRIP the leaves of the cavolo nero from the stems or cut away the thick stem of the savoy cabbage. Wash and finely chop the stems and roughly chop the leaves. Add the cabbage stems and courgette to the soffritto and cook, stirring occasionally, for about 5 minutes, or until the vegetables are translucent and have soaked up some of the olive oil.

STIR in the beans and cook for 5 minutes more, then add the tomatoes and chilli and cook for a further 5 minutes to reduce the liquid.

ADD the cabbage leaves and mix into the soup, stirring until just wilted. Add the wine and stock and gently simmer for about 40 minutes.

ADD the bread to the pan (if the bread is fresh, cut it into the pieces and then dry it out a little in the oven first to stop it disintegrating into the soup). Mix briefly and remove the pan from the heat. Leave for about 30 minutes to rest the soup and let the flavours mingle. Serve hot but not boiling with a generous drizzle of extra virgin olive oil (you may want to remove the chilli before you serve the soup).

cavolo nero

This cabbage has very long curly dark green leaves (though the name literally means 'black cabbage'). It is a classic ingredient of soups such as la ribollita, but can also be braised, steamed or baked and served as a vegetable accompaniment. Cavolo nero has a unique flavour, nuttier than regular cabbage, and can hold its own with stronger ingredients such as bacon, chilli and cheese. If it's not available, use dark green savoy cabbage instead.

Pappa al pomodoro

INGREDIENTS

900 g very ripe tomatoes or
  1 x 800 g tin chopped tomatoes
3 tablespoons olive oil
3 garlic cloves, finely sliced
200 g stale country-style bread,
  such as ciabatta or pugliese,
  crusts removed
15 g basil, torn into large pieces
50 ml extra virgin olive oil, plus
  extra to serve

In the Italian summer, when tomatoes are at their tastiest, there is great activity bottling, preserving, making sauces and soups. You need really ripe tomatoes for this recipe and, if you have the slightest doubt about their flavour, use a good chicken stock instead of the water.

YOU need to make sure the tomatoes are ripe for this recipe, both for flavour and colour. When you peel and chop the tomatoes they should be deep red. Pour on the boiling water but only leave it long enough to loosen the skins—not to cook the tomatoes.

BLANCHING the tomatoes in boiling water makes their skins much easier to peel off, although if they are really ripe they should come away easily anyway.

IF using fresh tomatoes, remove the stems and score a cross in the bottom of each one. Blanch in boiling water for 30 seconds. Transfer to cold water, peel the skin away from the cross (it should slip off easily) and chop the tomatoes.

POUR the olive oil into a large heavy-based saucepan, add the garlic and cook gently until light golden brown. Add the tomatoes, taking care as the oil may spit. Season with salt and pepper.

BRING the tomatoes to the boil and gently simmer, stirring occasionally so they don't stick. Simmer for about 10 minutes, stirring more frequently, until the mixture has thickened.

BREAK the bread into chunks and add to the pan. Remove from the heat and stir briefly to coat the bread with the tomato mixture. Scatter with the basil, season with salt and pepper and pour 500 ml boiling water over the bread. Add the olive oil and stir a little, being careful not to break up the bread too much.

LEAVE to rest for 5 minutes before serving. Serve in hot bowls with an extra drizzle of oil on top.

chestnuts

Chestnuts (castagna) grow in the mountainous areas of Italy and are in season in late autumn. As well as being roasted and eaten whole, they are ground into flour or used in soups and stews. If you can't get fresh ones, buy vacuum-packed, frozen or canned.

Chestnut, pancetta and cabbage soup

This soup takes its rich dark colour from the cavolo nero, a deep green cabbage that turns almost black when cooked. The soup is quite thick, but if you prefer it smoother and thinner, you can purée all of the soup and add a little more water.

REMOVE any thick stems from the cavolo nero and roughly chop the leaves. Wash well and cook in 1.5 litres of boiling water for about 10 minutes, or until the stems are tender. Drain in a colander over a large bowl to reserve the cooking water.

USING the same saucepan, heat the olive oil and cook the onion and pancetta over medium-high heat until the onion is soft and the pancetta lightly browned. Add the garlic and rosemary and cook for a few more minutes.

ADD the chestnuts and stir to infuse the flavours, then add the cabbage and season with salt and pepper. Add the wine, bring to the boil and cook for a couple of minutes. Finally add the reserved cabbage water, bring to the boil and then simmer for 10 minutes.

PUREE one-third of the soup, leaving the remainder unpuréed to give the dish a little texture. Serve the soup hot with crostini on top, drizzled with a little olive oil and sprinkled with Parmesan.

WHEN cleaning the cavolo nero, remove any thick or woody stems—these will remain rather tough and chewy in the finished soup. When you cook the cabbage until it is tender, it will lose its greenness and darken in colour.

SERVES 4

INGREDIENTS

200 g cavolo nero or savoy cabbage

2 tablespoons olive oil

1 onion, finely chopped

130 g pancetta or smoked bacon, diced

2 garlic cloves, chopped

2 tablespoons rosemary, finely chopped

200 g cooked, peeled chestnuts (see page 11), roughly chopped

200 ml red wine

4 crostini (see page 18)

extra virgin olive oil and grated Parmesan, to serve

barley

Barley *(orzo)* was once used to make an early version of polenta but now tends to be found only in soups. Most areas in the north have versions of barley soups, some thick, others more like minestrone. The barley used for all these soups is pearl barley.

SERVES 4

INGREDIENTS

200 g dried borlotti beans

2 tablespoons olive oil

1 small onion, thinly sliced

2 garlic cloves, crushed

1.5 litres chicken stock

1 tablespoon finely chopped thyme
 or sage

200 g pearl barley

100 g Parmesan, grated

1 tablespoon finely chopped parsley

4 teaspoons extra virgin olive oil

Bean and barley soup

An ancient grain crop, barley has long been used in the soups and stews of cold climate areas, as this is where it grows best. This soup, known as *minestra di orzo* in Italy, makes a hearty warming dish for winter.

SOAK the borlotti beans in cold water overnight. Drain off the water and put the beans in a large saucepan with plenty of cold water. Bring to the boil and simmer until tender (this will take about 1½ hours depending on the age of the beans—older drier beans may take longer to soften). Drain.

HEAT the olive oil in a large saucepan and cook the onion over low heat for 6 minutes, or until soft. Season with salt and pepper. Add the garlic and cook without browning for 20–30 seconds. Add the stock and thyme or sage and bring to the boil.

STIR in the barley a little at a time so that the stock continues to boil, then lower the heat and simmer for 15 minutes. Add the borlotti beans and simmer for 30 minutes, or until the barley is tender and the soup is thick.

PUREE one-third of the soup until smooth, leaving the remainder unpuréed to give the soup a little texture. Return to the saucepan and stir in the Parmesan and parsley. Season and stir in 125–250 ml hot water to give a spoonable consistency. Serve immediately, with a teaspoon of extra virgin olive oil stirred through each bowl.

cooking

If you need to make this soup quickly or you have forgotten to soak the dried beans overnight, use tinned borlotti beans instead. They don't need soaking or pre-cooking, simply rinse them well and add them to the barley when it is almost cooked.

Friuli-Venezia Giulia

The food of Friuli-Venezia Giulia has had many influences. The region is bordered on two sides by Slovenia and Austria and its Adriatic coastline has made it historically important. The Romans established the city of Aquileia, Attila the Hun swept through the area from the north and both the First and Second World Wars had a huge impact on the area, especially in the final division of land between Austria, Italy and the former Yugoslavia. Influences from all these cultures can be seen in the local food.

The region's most famous food is San Daniele ham, which some say rivals *prosciutto di Parma*, but it also produces Montasio cheese, a gnocchi called *cialzons*, *stinco* (braised veal or pork shin) and Slavic-style sausages called *cevapcici*. Gutsy soups such as *zuppa di farro* are made with beans, spelt or cabbage and the cooking is very much peasant-style, using lots of pork and wild animals in hearty stews. Flavourings tend to be more Slavic or Germanic than elsewhere in Italy, with dill and cinnamon being particular favourites, and many of the desserts, such as strudel, have a heavy Austrian influence. Pasta is not common to the area: instead polenta, risotto and gnocchi are eaten.

One of the region's most famous exports is coffee: the Illy factory is based in Trieste along with many other coffee companies. Beans arrive daily at the port to be roasted and sold onwards. Alongside the coffee served at the many cafes in the area, cakes and pastries are baked in quantity.

Wines of the region are not produced in large amounts but do tend to be of a very high quality, particularly the white wine, Tocai Friulano.

Coffee

Coffee in Trieste is said to be among the best in the world and the city boasts a huge number of cafes. As the beans arrive and are roasted daily the coffee is always very fresh. Trieste also has its own particular ways of serving coffee, different to other areas of Italy. A *cappuccino triestino* is served in an espresso cup or small glass and topped with a small amount of foam or whipped cream; a *cappuccino grande* is a typical cappuccino, a shot of espresso in a demi-tasse cup topped with foamed milk; and a *cappuccino viennese* in a similar cup is topped with whipped cream and chocolate.

pasta e gnocchi

fresh pasta

tortellini and cappelletti

Tortellini (pictured far right) originated in Bologna and can have a variety of fillings such as meat or spinach. Tortelloni is the larger version. Cappelletti is the traditional pasta of Emilia-Romagna and is usually filled with beef, pork or veal.

trenette

This flat long pasta is popular in Liguria and is most often served with pesto sauce. The same pasta may also be sold as bavette or linguine. Now also made as a dried pasta.

pappardelle

These wide flat pasta ribbons are served in the Veneto and Tuscany, often with rich sauces such as hare, duck or goose. In Tuscany, they are traditionally served *con la lepre*—with a hare sauce.

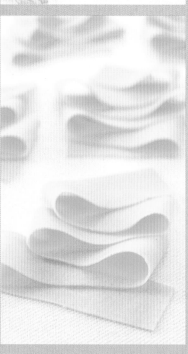

pizzoccheri

This thick noodle is made with a mixture of wheat and buckwheat flours. It is usually eaten with potato, winter greens, cabbage and cheese in a type of pasta bake. Pizzoccheri is a speciality of the Valtellina valley in Lombardy.

pansôti

This Ligurian stuffed pasta is traditionally filled with a mixture of *preboggion* (wild herbs and plants such as borage, dandelion and chicory) and Parmesan. The pasta is shaped into triangles and usually dressed with a walnut sauce.

lasagne

Lasagne is actually the name of the pasta sheet, rather than the actual dish. Most lasagne sheets are flat, but *lasagne riccia* has a frilled edge to incorporate more air and give a lighter dish. Green lasagne sheets *(lasagne verde)* are coloured by the addition of spinach. Lasagne sheets can also be rolled up and filled to make cannelloni.

ravioli

Smaller ravioli are eaten in soups, while larger ones are served with butter or a simple sauce. The filling is usually meat but wild mushroom or pumpkin are also popular. Ravioli are also known as agnolotti.

fettuccine

These long flat pasta ribbons are usually made with egg and served with delicate sauces. Fettuccine is popular in Rome and is similar to the tagliatelle that is more often eaten in the north.

dried pasta

penne rigate

These quill-shaped tubes are popular in Campania and Liguria, where they are served with chilli sauces in dishes such as *penne all'arrabbiata*.

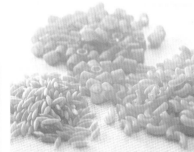

pastina

These tiny pastas of varying shapes are *pastina per brodo* (pasta for soups). They include farfalline (baby butterflies), stelline (stars), anellini (little rings) and diavolini (little devils).

spaghetti

Meaning 'little strings', spaghetti is made all over Italy, originally in lengths of up to 50 cm. It is eaten with a variety of sauces, often those containing oil, such as the simple garlic and oil sauce *(aglio e olio)*, or with clams *(vongole)*. Ironically, it would never be served in Italy with the meat ragù, bolognese. Spaghetti is sold in a variety of thicknesses including a thinner version, spaghettini.

rigatoni

The ribbing of this tube-shaped pasta helps it to pick up thick sauces such as meat ragù or tomato sauce. It is also suitable for pasta bakes.

bucatini

This long pasta is similar to a very thick spaghetti, but with a hole *(buca)* in the middle. It is the classic pasta used for amatriciana and carbonara sauces. Bucatoni is a thicker version.

orecchiette

Orecchiette, meaning 'little ears' is usually associated with Puglia. The shape is made by pressing the thumb onto small discs of pasta dough that are then left to dry. The resulting indentation 'traps' the sauce, which is often vegetable-based.

conchiglie

This shell-like pasta usually has a ribbed surface to help 'trap' sauces such as meat ragù or thicker vegetable sauces. The very large versions may be stuffed, often with ricotta and spinach, while the smaller conchigliette can be used in soups.

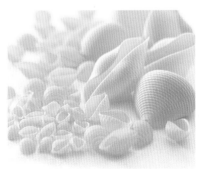

fusilli

A spiral-shaped pasta originally from Campania that is often served with tomato sauce or meat ragù.

making pasta

Making your own pasta always seems like one of those daunting tasks that is best left to the professionals. This is not so. It is not difficult to make fresh pasta at home and its quality (the pasta is generally much thinner and silkier) is unmatched by any store-bought varieties. When you are making pasta it can be difficult to measure the ingredients exactly. Variable egg sizes and the moisture content of the flour can affect how much of each you actually need. Just remember that the dough should be quite hard to knead and not too moist: simply add more flour or egg accordingly.

fresh egg pasta

Fresh egg pasta is made from eggs and *doppio zero* (00) flour, a soft wheat flour, sometimes with a little semolina added. This mixture gives a soft pliable pasta that can be easily shaped by hand. Fresh egg pasta is used to make lasagne sheets, can be cut into ribbons or folded into shapes such as tortellini. It is simple to make at home and has a lighter and more slippery texture than semolina pasta.

semolina pasta

Made from durum wheat (semolina) flour and water, semolina pasta is a tough dough that can be easily forced through dies to makes shapes such as spaghetti and rigatoni and then dried. It is sometimes eaten fresh in the south of Italy where it is formed into shapes such as orecchiette (little ears).

making fresh egg pasta

PUT 350 g doppio zero (00) pasta flour and 150 g fine semolina in a bowl. Make a well in the middle and add 10 egg yolks and 3 whole eggs.

MIX the eggs together briefly. Using a spoon, flick a little of the flour into the egg mixture.

USING your hands, start to blend in the eggs with the flour and semolina, eventually kneading to form a ball of hard dough.

KNEAD for about 5–10 minutes, or until the dough is smooth and velvety to the touch.

THE dough should not stick to your finger if pressed in the middle. If it does stick, add more flour and continue kneading.

COVER the dough with clingfilm and rest for 1–4 hours, depending on when you want to use it. You can leave the dough overnight but no longer or it will start to oxidise and black spots will appear.

rolling out fresh pasta dough

DIVIDE the pasta into six to eight flattened rectangular pieces and cover with clingfilm to prevent drying out.

DUST the work surface with semolina (flour will make the pasta heavier). Flatten the first segment of pasta so that it is easier to roll through the machine.

FEED the pasta through the rollers on the widest setting. Fold the flattened pasta in half or thirds, so that it fits across the rollers. Repeat this process three times to create a velvety texture.

cutting fresh pasta dough by machine

ATTACH the cutting blades to your machine: the wide one for tagliatelle and the narrower one for linguine.

FEED a sheet of pasta into the machine and carefully collect the cut pasta as it comes out at the other end.

EITHER hang up the pasta to dry over a broomstick or on a pasta dryer or coil it into wide nests. To keep the nests from sticking, toss them in a little semolina.

cutting fresh pasta dough by hand

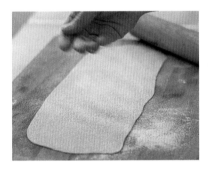

ROLL out the pasta into long flat sheets of the width you want and dust them with semolina to help prevent the cut noodles sticking together.

ROLL up each sheet loosely and cut into slices of whatever width you want. Bear in mind that thicker widths are easier to handle when they are unrolled.

TOSS the strips in more semolina to keep them separate or hang them up to dry, as above.

cutting fresh pasta dough for filling

METHOD 1. Roll out a sheet of pasta, brush with egg wash (1 egg beaten with 2 teaspoons milk) and spoon filling at intervals along its length. Press another sheet of pasta on top. Use a wheel, knife or cutter to cut around the mounds.

METHOD 2. Roll out a sheet of pasta, cut out shapes with a knife or cutter and then put a mound of filling in the centre. Brush the edge with egg wash. Cover with another piece of pasta the same shape or fold the piece of pasta in half.

METHOD 3. Lay a sheet of pasta over a ravioli mould. Press the pasta into the indents, then add a spoonful of filling to each one. Brush the edges with egg wash, lay another sheet over the top and seal by rolling over with a rolling pin.

colours

Fresh pasta is increasingly made with any number of ingredients, as well as the original egg and flour mixture. Different flours, such as buckwheat, are used and pasta can be flavoured and coloured by the addition of other ingredients. Black pasta (nero) is coloured with cuttlefish or squid ink and vegetables such as beetroot, tomato or spinach can colour pasta pink, red or green. Buy good-quality fresh pasta that is not cut too thickly.

quantities

For dried pasta 75 g provides a small portion, 125 g a main course and 150 g a large portion. If you are using fresh pasta the weights will be slightly less (the moisture content of fresh pasta means that it weighs more per portion). Pasta in the recipes in this book is dried unless stated.

cooking

Pasta has to be cooked in lots of rapidly boiling salted water—about 1 litre of water and 1 teaspoon salt per 100 g of pasta. The pan must be large enough for the pasta to move freely. It is not necessary to add oil to the cooking water or the draining pasta; all this does is coat the pasta and encourage the sauce to slide off. When you drain pasta, don't do it too thoroughly—a little water left clinging to the pasta will help the sauce spread through it.

sauces

Pasta sauces vary from thin butter or oil dressings flavoured with garlic, chilli or herbs to robust stew-like sauces of meat or vegetables. Sauces in Italy are applied sparingly: the pasta is the main ingredient and the sauce an addition. Parmesan is often served alongside, but in Italy it would not be offered with sauces containing fish, shellfish or chilli.

Spaghettini aglio e olio

Meaning garlic *(aglio)* and oil *(olio)*, this pasta sauce is best teamed with spaghettini, a thin spaghetti that takes well to the light oily coating. Don't allow the garlic to brown when cooking or it will become bitter.

COOK the pasta in a large saucepan of boiling salted water until *al dente*.

MEANWHILE, heat the oil in a large frying pan over very low heat. Add the garlic and chilli flakes and fry gently for about 2 minutes, or until the garlic has softened but not browned. Remove from the heat.

DRAIN the pasta briefly, leaving some of the water clinging to the pasta. Add the hot pasta and parsley to the frying pan and toss to coat. Taste for seasoning and serve at once with the grated pecorino.

Tomato sauce with penne

In Italy this sauce is generally made with tinned tomatoes, but ripe fresh peeled tomatoes can be used if they have a good flavour. Toss the sauce through pasta (either spaghetti or a ridged tube pasta such as penne or rigatoni), use in lasagnes and baked dishes or serve with polenta.

HEAT the olive oil and add the garlic and herbs, except the basil which must be added at the end or it will become bitter. Cook until the garlic just browns, then add the tomatoes. Season and break up the tomatoes with the edge of a spoon.

SIMMER for 20–30 minutes or until the sauce thickens. Stir occasionally to stop it sticking to the pan.

COOK the pasta in a large pan of boiling salted water until *al dente*. Drain. Stir the basil into the sauce, taste for seasoning and serve over the pasta with the grated Parmesan.

pesto

Ligurian pesto has a reputation for being the best in Italy and is made with pine nuts or walnuts, both of which are local to the area. Store pesto in a jar sealed with a thin film of olive oil to prevent the surface oxidising and turning brown.

Genovese pesto sauce

Traditionally, pesto sauce is served with trenette pasta, green beans and potatoes but you can leave out the vegetables if you prefer or use spaghetti. Pesto is traditionally made in a mortar and pestle but a food processor also works well.

PUT the garlic and pine nuts in a mortar and pestle or food processor and pound or process until finely ground. Add the basil and then drizzle in the olive oil a little at a time while pounding or processing. When you have a thick purée stop adding the oil. Season and mix in the Parmesan.

BRING a large saucepan of salted water to the boil. Add the pasta, green beans and potatoes, stirring well to prevent the pasta from sticking together. Cook until the pasta is *al dente* (the vegetables should be cooked by this time), then drain, reserving a little of the water.

RETURN the pasta and vegetables to the saucepan, add the pesto, and mix well. If necessary, add some of the reserved water to loosen the pasta. Season and serve immediately with the extra Parmesan.

SERVES 4

INGREDIENTS

PESTO

2 garlic cloves

50 g pine nuts

120 g basil, stems removed

150–180 ml extra virgin olive oil

50 g Parmesan, finely grated, plus
   extra to serve

500 g trenette

175 g green beans, trimmed

175 g small potatoes, very thinly
   sliced

Tagliatelle with ragù

The citizens of Bologna call their slow-cooked meat sauce ragù, but it is better known worldwide as bolognese. And, unlike the rest of the world, the Italians would never serve their ragù with spaghetti—in the north, in particular, it is traditionally served with tagliatelle.

SERVES 4

INGREDIENTS

60 g butter

90 g pancetta, finely chopped

1 onion, finely chopped

1 celery stalk, finely chopped

1 carrot, finely chopped

220 g minced beef

220 g minced pork

2 oregano sprigs, chopped, or
  ¼ teaspoon dried oregano

pinch of ground nutmeg

120 g chicken livers, trimmed and
  finely chopped

125 ml milk

125 ml dry white wine

400 g tin chopped tomatoes

250 ml beef stock

350 g fresh tagliatelle

3 tablespoons single cream

grated Parmesan, to serve

HEAT the butter in a saucepan and add the pancetta. Cook until lightly browned and then add the onion, celery and carrot. Cook over moderate heat for 6–8 minutes, stirring from time to time.

ADD the minced beef, pork and oregano to the saucepan. Season with the nutmeg and salt and pepper.

COOK for about 5 minutes, or until the mince has changed colour but not yet browned. Add the liver and cook until it changes colour.

STIR in the milk and simmer for 2 minutes. Pour in the wine, increase the heat and boil over high heat for 2–3 minutes, or until the wine has been absorbed, then reduce the heat and simmer for 10 minutes.

ADD the tomatoes and half the stock, partially cover the pan and leave to simmer gently over very low heat for 3 hours. Add more of the stock as it is needed to keep the sauce moist.

COOK the tagliatelle in a large saucepan of boiling salted water until *al dente*. Stir the cream into the sauce 5 minutes before serving. Check for seasoning, then drain the tagliatelle briefly, toss with the sauce and serve with grated Parmesan.

cooking

Milk and cream are added to meat dishes such as ragù to add richness. If milk is used, it is always added before wine to neutralise any acidity.

Emilia-Romagna

The prosperous and fertile Emilia-Romagna is often said to be the culinary centre of Italy and it certainly produces some of the country's hallmark foods. Parma ham, Parmesan cheese, balsamic vinegar, fresh egg pasta and the meat ragù that is known worldwide as Bolognese sauce all hail from this region. This is pig-farming country and the antipasti of Emilia-Romagna are heavily meat orientated: *culatello, mortadella, prosciutto di parma, prosciutto cotto* and other *salumi* being great favourites that are often served with *torta fritta*, a simple fried bread. Pork is eaten in many forms and the festive speciality is *zampone*, pig's trotters filled with minced pork and spices. The fat used for cooking was traditionally lard or butter rather than the olive oil that is more commonly used now.

This area is a wonderful example of how good food breeds. The whey from the milk used to make the famous Parmigiano Reggiano is fed to the pigs that produce *prosciutto di Parma*. The production processes of both are rigorously controlled to uphold traditional standards: Parmigiano Reggiano is recognisable by the seal stamped on each wheel and Parma ham must conform to stringent regulations on pig-rearing, diet, curing and air-drying.

There is a huge range of pasta available in Emilia-Romagna, usually made with egg and golden in colour. Tortellini is a particular favourite, as are sheets of pasta, baked with meat and vegetables. Sauces are rich and often meat-based, cooked for hours until they melt in the mouth. But vegetables, too, are abundant and are sliced or cut into pieces and baked with olive oil and breadcrumbs.

Balsamic vinegar

This exquisitely rich and fragrant vinegar is made from white *Trebbiano di Spagna* grapes in the city of Modena. The best balsamic vinegars, *aceto balsamico tradizionale di Modena*, are made by blending very aged vinegars (up to 100 years old) with progressively younger ones (but no younger than 12 years) from barrels of different woods. Each different wood adds flavour to the vinegar and old brandy barrels are often favoured. The barrels are housed in attics and get progressively smaller as the vinegar ages. Balsamic vinegar is tasted over time to keep an eye on its aging process and each 100 ml bottle of this rare and precious liquid is certified by the consortium that was set up to approve its quality.

guanciale

Guanciale is the name given to a cured meat made from the salted, air-dried cheeks of pigs. A speciality of Lazio, it is traditional in amatriciana pasta sauce. Guanciale is made in the same way as pancetta, which can generally be used as a substitute.

SERVES 6

INGREDIENTS

1 tablespoon olive oil

250 g pancetta, smoked pancetta or guanciale, cut into small dice

4 tablespoons double cream

6 egg yolks

500 g spaghetti

50 g Parmesan, grated, plus extra to serve

Spaghetti carbonara

This rich Roman pasta dish is classically made with guanciale so, if you can find it, use it as your first choice. The raw eggs are cooked by the heat of the pasta, which is stirred into the sauce just before serving. Carbonara is usually served with spaghetti or bucatini.

PUT the olive oil in a saucepan and cook the pancetta over medium heat, stirring frequently, until it is light brown and crisp. Tip the pancetta into a metal colander to strain off the fat. Mix together the cream and egg yolks and, when the pancetta has cooled, add it to the egg mixture.

COOK the pasta in a large saucepan of boiling salted water until *al dente*. Drain, reserving a little of the cooking water.

RETURN the pasta to the saucepan to retain as much heat as possible, add the egg mixture and Parmesan, season and mix together. Add a little of the reserved water if the sauce is too thick and the pasta is stuck together. The spaghetti should look as if it has a fine coating of egg and cream. Serve immediately with a little extra Parmesan sprinkled over the top.

serving

The egg is cooked by the residual heat of the pasta and the pan, so it is a good idea to serve this dish in warm bowls. Pour some of the boiling pasta water into the bowls, leave for a few minutes and dry them just before serving.

Bucatini all'amatriciana

Named after the town of Amatrice and a speciality of the Lazio region, this dish is traditionally made with guanciale, but pancetta is an acceptable substitute. It is usually eaten with bucatini, a thick hollow spaghetti.

SERVES 4

INGREDIENTS

100 ml extra virgin olive oil

1 red onion, finely chopped

75 g pancetta, smoked pancetta or guanciale

1 tablespoon chopped rosemary leaves

2 garlic cloves, chopped

1 large dried chilli (optional)

200 ml red wine

2 x 400 g tins chopped tomatoes

500 g bucatini

grated Parmesan, to serve

HEAT the olive oil in a saucepan and cook the onion and pancetta over low heat until they are soft and caramelised, being careful they don't burn. Add the rosemary, garlic and chilli and cook the garlic until light brown.

ADD the red wine and bring to the boil, scraping the bottom of the saucepan for anything that may be stuck to it, as this will give flavour to the sauce. When the wine has reduced, add the tomatoes and simmer gently for about 10 minutes, or until the sauce has reduced and thickened. Remove the chilli.

COOK the pasta in a large saucepan of boiling salted water until it is *al dente*. Drain briefly, allowing some of the water to remain clinging to the pasta, then mix with the sauce. Serve with the Parmesan sprinkled over the top.

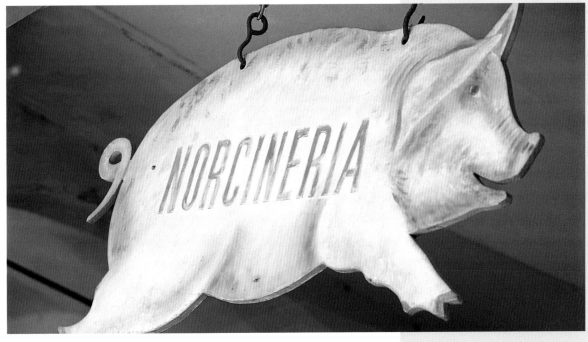

Spaghetti alla puttanesca

SERVES 4

INGREDIENTS

1 small red chilli

1 tablespoon capers

4 tablespoons olive oil

1 small onion, finely chopped

2 garlic cloves, finely sliced

6 anchovy fillets, finely chopped

400 g tin chopped tomatoes

1 tablespoon finely chopped oregano
  or ¼ teaspoon dried oregano

100 g black olives, pitted and halved

400 g spaghetti

1 tablespoon finely chopped parsley

Although versions of this robust, piquant sauce are now made all over Italy, puttanesca is usually associated with Naples and Calabria. Its name means in the manner of a *puttana* (prostitute). This dish is never served with cheese but often sprinkled with fresh parsley just before serving.

buying

You can buy capers preserved both in salt and brine. The salted ones need to be rinsed thoroughly and the brined ones briefly. Baby or small capers are better for this dish as they can be left whole.

CUT the chilli in half, remove the seeds and then chop it finely. Rinse the capers, squeeze them dry and, if they are large, chop them roughly.

HEAT the olive oil in a large saucepan and add the onion, garlic and chilli. Fry gently for about 6 minutes, or until the onion is soft. Add the anchovies and cook, stirring and mashing, until they break down to a smooth paste.

ADD the tomatoes, oregano, olives and capers and bring to the boil. Reduce the heat, season and leave to simmer for about 10 minutes, or until the sauce has reduced and thickened.

MEANWHILE, cook the pasta in a large saucepan of boiling salted water until *al dente*. Drain briefly, leaving some of the water still clinging to the pasta, then add to the sauce with the parsley. Toss well before serving.

RAGNANO (NAPOLI)
FARINA 00 S
PASTA DI SEMOLA
DI GRANO DURO
Peso netto Kg. 1
Umidità 12,50%

Pasta alla Norma

This classic Sicilian pasta sauce combines the creaminess of aubergines with the sweet acidity of tomatoes and the fresh tang of ricotta cheese. The dish is named after the heroine of Vincenzo Bellini's opera of the same name. There are many versions of the recipe, but all contain aubergines.

PUT the aubergine slices in a bowl of salted water for 10 minutes. Drain and dry on a tea towel.

IF using fresh tomatoes, remove the stems and score a cross in the bottom of each one. Blanch in boiling water for 30 seconds. Transfer to cold water, peel the skin away from the cross (it should slip off easily) and chop the tomatoes.

PUT a generous amount of the olive oil in a frying pan and cook the aubergines in batches over medium high heat until golden brown and soft inside, adding more of the oil as you need it. Drain in a colander or on paper towels. Cut the aubergines into 2 cm thick sticks and set aside.

REMOVE all but 2 tablespoons of the oil from the frying pan, add the garlic and cook until light golden brown. Add the tomatoes and season. Cook until the sauce has reduced and thickened. Add the aubergines and the basil leaves, mix well and set aside.

COOK the pasta in a large saucepan of boiling salted water until *al dente*. Drain briefly, leaving some of the water clinging to the pasta, then return the pasta to the saucepan with the aubergine mixture and 100 g of the ricotta.

MIX briefly, check for seasoning and serve immediately with the remaining ricotta crumbled over the top.

SOAKING the aubergines in salted water helps draw out any bitterness and also stops them from soaking up so much oil when they cook. Don't be surprised how much oil you use as aubergines seem to 'drink' the oil they are cooked in.

DRAINING the pasta briefly, leaving some water clinging to the pasta, loosens the sauce a little and helps it spread through the pasta. As the pasta sits, it will continue to soak up the sauce so a little extra liquid always helps.

SERVES 4

INGREDIENTS

1 large aubergine, cut into 2 cm
 thick slices
350 g fresh tomatoes or 400 g tin
 chopped tomatoes
160 ml olive oil
2 garlic cloves, thinly sliced
handful of torn basil leaves
400 g conchiglie
150 g fresh ricotta

Pasta primavera

This favourite pasta dish, with its fresh young vegetables, heralds the arrival of springtime.
If you can't find all the green vegetables suggested here, you can use any tender young varieties:
courgettes and broccoli both work well.

SERVES 4

INGREDIENTS

120 g broad beans (500 g with pods
   still on), fresh or frozen

150 g asparagus, cut into
   short lengths

100 g green beans, cut into short
   lengths

120 g peas, fresh or frozen

30 g butter

1 small fennel bulb, thinly sliced

375 ml double cream

350 g fresh tagliatelle

2 tablespoons grated Parmesan, plus
   extra to serve

broad beans

Broad beans *(fava)* are one of man's
oldest foodstuffs and were once the
only type of bean available. They are
first podded and sometimes their inner
leathery coating is removed to reveal
the bright green bean inside. Frozen
broad beans are a good alternative.

BRING a large saucepan of water to
the boil. Add 1 teaspoon salt, the
broad beans and asparagus and
simmer for 3 minutes. Remove the
vegetables with a slotted spoon and
put them in a sieve. Run under cold
water briefly—this stops them
cooking and preserves their bright
green colour—then set aside.

ADD the green beans and peas to
the pan (if using frozen peas add
them a few minutes later). Cook for
about 4 minutes, then remove with
a slotted spoon and put in a sieve.
Run under cold water briefly to stop
them cooking, then set aside.

PEEL the tough grey outer skins off
the broad beans.

MEANWHILE, heat the butter in a
large frying pan. Add the fennel and
cook over moderately low heat for
5 minutes without letting it brown
at all. Add the cream, season with
salt and pepper and cook at a low
simmer for 2 minutes.

BRING the large saucepan of water
back to the boil, add the pasta and
cook until *al dente*. Drain the pasta
briefly, leaving some water clinging
to the pasta.

ADD the green beans, peas,
Parmesan, broad beans and
asparagus to the frying pan and
lightly toss together. Add the pasta
and lightly toss to coat with the
sauce. Serve immediately with extra
Parmesan sprinkled over the top.

Rigatoni with sausage, fennel seed and tomato

SERVES 4

Good-quality Italian sausages are perfect for this pasta dish as they are firm and don't disintegrate, creating a chunky meat sauce. It is, however, a good idea to reserve a cup of pasta water and add it to the sauce if it proves too thick to coat the pasta properly.

INGREDIENTS

2 garlic cloves, chopped

2 teaspoons fennel seeds

3 tablespoons olive oil

1 onion, finely chopped

4 Italian sausages, skin removed

1 tablespoon chopped thyme leaves

100 ml red wine

400 g tin chopped tomatoes

400 g rigatoni

grated Parmesan, to serve

storing

This pasta sauce can be made in advance and left covered in the fridge for two or three days. It can also be frozen in portions and defrosted as needed.

USING a mortar and pestle, crush the garlic and fennel seeds with a pinch of salt. Alternatively, grind the seeds in a spice grinder and crush the garlic.

HEAT the oil in a saucepan and cook the onion for a few minutes over low heat to soften it. Break up the sausage meat with your hands and add it to the pan. Increase the heat and cook until the meat is lightly browned. Season with salt and pepper. Add the garlic, fennel and thyme, mix briefly, then add the wine. Stir the sauce, scraping up any sausage meat that may be stuck to the bottom of the pan—this will add flavour to the sauce.

COOK the sauce for about 5 minutes or until the wine is reduced, then add the tomatoes and simmer for 10 minutes, or until the sauce has thickened.

COOK the pasta in a large saucepan of boiling salted water until *al dente*. Drain briefly, leaving some water clinging to the pasta. Add to the sauce, toss well and serve sprinkled with the Parmesan.

sausages

Italian sausages are available in several different styles. Fresh cotechino has to be cooked for several hours before use—it contains pork rind that needs to be rendered gelatinous. Luganega are fresh pork sausages, which are very long and sold by weight or length. They can be cooked in a variety of ways or the meat taken out of the skin and used in pasta sauces. Other Italian-style sausages may be flavoured with fennel *(finocchio)*, garlic *(aglio)* or chilli *(peperoncino)*.

Orecchiette with broccoli and chilli sauce

INGREDIENTS

250 g broccoli

400 g orecchiette

75 ml extra virgin olive oil

2 garlic cloves, finely chopped

½ large red chilli, finely chopped

1 tablespoon chopped rosemary

25 g Parmesan, grated, plus extra
   to serve

extra virgin olive oil, to serve

This pasta dish is one of the easiest to make and has the advantage of requiring the use of just one saucepan. The broccoli is cooked with the pasta and breaks up to create its own sauce. Orecchiette, meaning 'little ears', is the most widely eaten pasta of Puglia.

chillies

Chillies (peperoncini) are commonly used in southern Italian cooking. They came to Italy from the New World and were adopted by the poor as a means to add extra flavour to plain dishes such as pasta. In some areas, chillies are also used with salt and pepper as a condiment. Chillies are grown in the south and are used both fresh and dried. They come in various sizes, with the smallest and hottest being known as diavolilli, meaning 'little devils'.

BRING a large saucepan of salted water to the boil. Cut the broccoli into small florets and add them to the water with the pasta. Cook until the pasta is al dente (the broccoli will be very tender and may have broken up) then drain briefly, reserving a small cup of the water.

HEAT the olive oil in the saucepan and add the garlic, chilli and rosemary. Cook gently for a couple of minutes until the garlic is light golden brown. Remove from the heat, add the broccoli and pasta and mix well—the broccoli should break up and create the sauce.

ADD a little of the cooking water to loosen the pasta if necessary, then season well and stir in the Parmesan. Serve immediately with a drizzle of olive oil and the extra Parmesan.

cooking

Because the broccoli is cooked in the same water as the pasta, for longer than you would usually cook it, it will not retain its bright green colouring. For this recipe the broccoli needs to be cooked until it is tender enough to break up and form a sauce.

Tagliatelle with walnut sauce

SERVES 4

Walnuts grow throughout Italy, with the best coming from Campania and Liguria. They are used widely in both sweet and savoury dishes but perhaps one of the best-known recipes is this Ligurian walnut pasta sauce, traditionally served with tagliatelle.

INGREDIENTS

200 g shelled walnuts

20 g roughly chopped flat–leaf parsley

1 garlic clove, crushed

50 g butter, softened

200 ml extra virgin olive oil

30 g Parmesan, grated

100 ml double cream

400 g tagliatelle, pappardelle or pansôti

LIGHTLY toast the walnuts in a dry frying pan over moderately high heat for about 2 minutes, or until they brown and smell nutty. Set them aside until they are completely cold.

PUT the walnuts in a food processor with the parsley and garlic and mix until they are finely chopped. If you do not have a processor, use a knife to finely chop the nuts, parsley and garlic. Add the butter and mix together well.

WITH the motor of the processor running, gradually pour in the olive oil in a steady stream. Again, if you do not have a processor, put the nut mixture in a large bowl and add the oil, mixing well. Add the Parmesan and the cream. Season with salt.

COOK the pasta in a large saucepan of boiling salted water until *al dente*. Drain briefly, then toss with the walnut sauce to serve.

storing

Keep nuts, especially those that are quite oily such as walnuts, in the fridge or freezer to stop them turning rancid.

NUTS such as walnuts are best toasted before use to bring out their sweetness and flavour. Toasting also gives the nuts a better colour. Leave them until they are completely cold before chopping or grinding or they will become oily.

00 flour

In Italy, flours *(farina)* are graded from the finest and whitest (00) to those that are made using the whole grain. Soft wheat 00 *(doppio zero)* flour is the type most often used for baking and to make fresh pasta, rather than the harder durum wheat semolina used in dried pasta.

Lasagne al forno

Lasagne al forno is often made with lasagne verde, fresh pasta coloured with spinach. You can use sheets of either fresh egg pasta or store-bought dried lasagne. Lasagne refers to the actual sheets of pasta and *al forno* simply means baked in the oven.

TO make the meat sauce, heat the butter in a frying pan and add the onion, carrot, celery, garlic and pancetta. Cook over low heat for 5–6 minutes, or until softened. Add the beef, increase the heat a little and cook for 8 minutes, or until coloured but not browned, stirring to break up any lumps of mince. Add the oregano and nutmeg and season well.

STIR in the chicken livers and cook until they change colour. Pour in the vermouth, increase the heat and cook until it has evaporated. Add the beef stock and tomato purée and simmer for 2 hours. Add a little hot water, if necessary, during this time to keep the mixture moist, but towards the end of cooking allow all the liquid to be absorbed. Stir in the cream, remove from the heat and leave to cool for 15 minutes.

TO make the béchamel sauce, put the milk in a saucepan with the bay leaf and the onion studded with the cloves. Bring to the boil, remove from the heat and leave to stand for at least 20 minutes. Melt the butter in another saucepan and mix in the flour to make a roux. Cook over low heat, stirring, for 2 minutes. Remove from the heat, strain the milk and add it to the roux, stirring to prevent lumps. Simmer gently for 10 minutes until the sauce is creamy. Add the cream, season with salt, pepper and nutmeg and pour into a bowl. Cover the surface with clingfilm to prevent a skin forming. Preheat the oven to 180°C (350°F/Gas 4) and grease a large ovenproof dish.

IF you are using fresh pasta, roll out the dough very thinly with a pasta machine or large rolling pin and cut it into nine manageable sheets, each about one-third of the size of your dish. Cook the pasta in batches in a large saucepan of boiling salted water until *al dente*. Scoop out each batch with a slotted spoon when cooked and drop it into a bowl of cold water. Spread out the sheets in a single layer on a tea towel, turning them over once to blot dry. Trim away any torn edges. If you are using dried pasta, boil the sheets briefly and blot dry, to prevent them soaking up too much liquid.

SPREAD a third of the meat sauce in the dish. Scatter with a third of the mozzarella, then cover with a slightly overlapping layer of pasta sheets. Spread a third of the béchamel over this and sprinkle with Parmesan. Repeat the layers, finishing with a layer of béchamel and Parmesan.

PLACE the dish on a tray to catch any drips. Bake the lasagne for about 40 minutes or until it is golden brown and bubbling, then leave to rest for 10 minutes before serving.

ROLL out the dough with a pasta machine or large rolling pin. Then, using the dish as a guide, cut out the sheets to roughly one third the size of the dish. You can make the sheets bigger but at this size they are easier to handle. Generally, oil is not added to pasta cooking water but in this case it may help to prevent the sheets sticking together.

SERVES 6

INGREDIENTS

MEAT SAUCE

30 g butter

1 onion, finely chopped

1 small carrot, finely chopped

½ celery stalk, finely chopped

1 garlic clove, crushed

120 g pancetta, chopped

500 g minced beef

¼ teaspoon dried oregano

pinch of ground nutmeg

90 g chicken livers, trimmed and finely chopped

75 ml dry vermouth or dry white wine

350 ml beef stock

1 tablespoon tomato purée

2 tablespoons double cream

BÉCHAMEL SAUCE

850 ml milk

1 bay leaf

1 small onion

6 cloves

50 g butter

40 g plain flour

125 ml double cream

½ nutmeg, freshly grated

½ quantity fresh pasta dough (see page 36) or 9 fresh or dried lasagne sheets

150 g mozzarella, grated

60 g Parmesan, grated

Vincisgrassi

A classic lasagne from The Marches, vincisgrassi was supposedly created for General Windischgratz of the Austrian Army during the Napoleonic Wars. The title of the dish is thought to be a corruption of his name. Vincisgrassi is best made a day in advance to let the flavours develop.

SERVES 6

INGREDIENTS

MEAT SAUCE

1 kg cotechino sausages, casings removed, chopped

40 g butter

800 g chicken thigh fillets, cut into thin strips

300 g chicken livers, trimmed and chopped

75 ml dry Marsala

200 ml chicken stock

MUSHROOM SAUCE

1 onion, finely chopped

40 g butter

10 g dried porcini mushrooms, soaked in hot water for 30 minutes, drained and chopped

100 g button mushrooms, finely sliced

pinch of ground nutmeg

1 tablespoon chicken stock

BECHAMEL SAUCE

850 ml milk

1 bay leaf

1 small onion

6 cloves

50 g unsalted butter

40 g plain flour

125 ml double cream

1/2 nutmeg, freshly grated

1/2 quantity fresh lasagne dough (see page 36), rolled out thinly, or 6 dried lasagne sheets

75 g Parmesan, grated

TO make the meat sauce, fry the sausage in the butter until browned. Add the chicken and chicken liver and fry quickly until browned. Season, add the Marsala and cook until evaporated. Add the stock, cover and cook for 25 minutes. To make the mushroom sauce, cook the onion in the butter until soft. Add the porcini and mushrooms and cook for 2–3 minutes. Season, add the nutmeg and stock and simmer until the liquid evaporates.

TO make the béchamel sauce, put the milk in a saucepan with the bay leaf and the onion studded with the cloves. Bring to the boil, remove from the heat and leave to stand for at least 20 minutes. Melt the butter in another saucepan and mix in the flour to make a roux. Cook over low heat, stirring, for 2 minutes. Remove from the heat, strain the milk and add it to the roux, stirring to prevent lumps. Simmer gently for 10 minutes until the sauce is creamy. Add the cream, season with salt, pepper and nutmeg and pour half into a bowl. Add the mushroom sauce to the other half and mix well.

IF you are using fresh pasta, roll out the dough very thinly and cut into six sheets. Cook in batches in boiling salted water until *al dente*. Refresh in cold water and blot dry on a tea towel. Trim any torn edges. If you are using dried pasta, boil the sheets briefly and blot dry before use.

PREHEAT the oven to 200°C (400°F/Gas 6). Put a layer of pasta in a greased ovenproof dish. Top with half the meat sauce, then half the mushroom sauce. Sprinkle with a third of the Parmesan. Repeat the layers, ending with a layer of béchamel and Parmesan. Bake for 30 minutes until golden brown.

cooking

Boiling the dried lasagne sheets briefly before use and blotting them dry will prevent them soaking up too much of the liquid from the sauce.

Le Marche

The Marches is one of Italy's least known regions despite the fact that it borders Tuscany, Umbria and Emilia-Romagna. It has a flat coastal strip of land along the Adriatic but is mainly a hilly area with a mountain range, the Apennines, that isolates it from the rest of its central Italian neighbours. Because of this, The Marches has always had to be self-sufficient. The hills are more verdant than those of neighbouring Tuscany and Umbria and both black and white truffles, porcini and fennel grow here. In fact, Acqualagna, a small town in the foothills of the Apennines, is the source of the rarest and most prized white truffle of all, the *tuber magnatum pico*.

As in Umbria, pork products and game are common here: *lonza*, cured loin of pork, is particularly popular and a spreadable salami called *ciauscolo* is served as antipasto. The isolation of the inland farming areas is reflected in the use of wild foods, such as hare, rabbit and boar, that are still commonly served. Cheeses include casciotta from Urbino, pecorino and an unusual local variety called *formaggio di fossa* that is aged in straw-filled trenches in a cave.

Olives grow well in The Marches and are among Italy's best. One of the region's most well-known products is *ascolane*—large olives that have been stuffed, then breadcrumbed and deep-fried. Vincisgrassi is the local version of lasagne: it is extremely rich and traditionally contained chicken giblets, truffles and veal ragù. Along the coast seafood is plentiful and the area is renowned for its local versions of *brodetto*, Italian fish stew, which vary from town to town but always contain at least eight varieties of fish or shellfish.

Porchetta

This whole milk-fed suckling pig, boned and then roasted on a spit, is well known in many areas of central Italy where it is prepared for any great meal or festivity. It is a true speciality in The Marches, where it is stuffed with the local wild fennel, rosemary and garlic and flavoured with white wine. Traditionally, porchetta was cooked in wood-fired ovens but now the spits are often mounted in vans which set up in market places. The meat is then carved and served in a split roll, to be eaten standing up as a snack.

truffles

Truffles *(tartufo)* are one of the world's most expensive ingredients and are surrounded by a certain mystique. They are difficult to cultivate commercially and still mainly only found in the wild. The harvest is not an exact science and the find is considered to be a prize. Both black and white truffles are found in Italy, the most famous being the white Alba truffle and the black truffle from Umbria. If fresh truffles are not available, preserved ones in jars can be used instead. Truffle paste and truffle oil are also available.

Truffle and porcini lasagne

SERVES 8

Truffles and porcini are the delights of an Italian autumn and, although they are best eaten fresh in season, they are available preserved or dried all year round. If you prefer, omit the truffle and porcini paste and just use the truffle oil.

TO make the béchamel sauce, put the milk in a saucepan with the bay leaf and the onion studded with the cloves. Bring to the boil, remove from the heat and leave to stand for at least 20 minutes. Melt the butter in another saucepan and mix in the flour to make a roux. Cook over low heat, stirring, for 2 minutes. Remove from the heat, strain the milk and add it to the roux, stirring to prevent lumps. Simmer gently for 10 minutes until the sauce is creamy. Add the cream, season with salt, pepper and nutmeg and pour into a bowl. Cover the surface with clingfilm to prevent a skin forming.

TO make the filling, put the porcini in enough hot water to just cover them and leave to soak for about 15 minutes. Remove the porcini, reserving the soaking liquid, and coarsely chop them. Heat the oil in a frying pan and cook the porcini for a few minutes, season with salt and pepper and then add the soaking liquid. Bring to the boil and simmer gently until all the liquid has been absorbed back into the mushrooms.

IF you are using fresh pasta, roll out the dough very thinly with a pasta machine or large rolling pin and cut it into 15 manageable sheets, each about one-third of the size of your dish. Cook the pasta in batches in a large saucepan of boiling salted water until *al dente*. Scoop out each batch with a slotted spoon when cooked and drop it into a bowl of cold water. Spread out the sheets in a single layer on a tea towel, turning them over once to blot dry. Trim away any torn edges. If you are using dried pasta, boil the sheets briefly and blot dry, to prevent them soaking up too much liquid.

PREHEAT the oven to 180°C (350°F/Gas 4). Butter a large ovenproof dish and put a layer of pasta sheets on the bottom. Smear about a teaspoon of truffle and porcini paste over the pasta. Don't be tempted to use too much as the paste has a strong flavour. Sprinkle with a little pecorino, a few cooked porcini, a ladle of béchamel, salt and pepper and a few drops of truffle oil. The oil has a very strong flavour, so use sparingly. Repeat the layers four times, ending with the béchamel, pecorino and truffle oil.

PLACE the dish on a tray to catch any drips and bake for 20–30 minutes. To check if the lasagne is cooked, poke a knife into the middle and then remove it: if the blade feels hot, the lasagne is ready.

IT is very important to cook a béchamel sauce for a reasonable amount of time. You can make a béchamel quickly but it will not have the same smooth velvety texture and you may even be able to taste the uncooked flour. There may seem to be a lot of béchamel but it does give a good creamy texture to the dish. Use the porcini and truffle paste sparingly, or the flavour will overpower the lasagne.

INGREDIENTS

BECHAMEL SAUCE

850 ml milk

1 bay leaf

1 small onion

6 cloves

50 g unsalted butter

40 g plain flour

125 ml double cream

½ nutmeg, freshly grated

30 g dried porcini mushrooms

½ tablespoon olive oil

1 quantity fresh pasta dough (see page 36) or 250 g dried lasagne sheets

6 teaspoons truffle and porcini paste

75 g pecorino or Parmesan, grated

50 ml truffle oil

Artichoke and spinach cannelloni

This recipe is made using lasagne sheets to wrap up the artichoke and spinach filling. If you prefer, you can use store-bought cannelloni tubes instead. Some pancetta or prosciutto can also be cooked with the artichokes to elaborate the recipe.

SERVES 6

INGREDIENTS

FILLING

3 tablespoons olive oil

2 large artichoke hearts, peeled, quartered and thinly sliced or 375 g cleaned hearts

1 onion, thinly sliced

2 garlic cloves, thinly sliced

1 teaspoon finely chopped rosemary

100 ml dry white vermouth or wine

250 g spinach, washed and drained

425 ml double cream

75 g Parmesan, grated

½ teaspoon freshly grated nutmeg

1 quantity fresh pasta dough (see page 36) or 250 g dried lasagne sheets

butter, for greasing

WHEN cutting the pasta sheets, make sure that the grain runs across the width and not the length, or the pasta might split when rolled. This is especially applicable to store-bought fresh pasta, which tends to be thicker and stiffer than home-made. Roll the cannelloni carefully, but don't worry if some of the filling escapes.

TO make the filling, pour the olive oil into a large saucepan or frying pan and cook the artichokes and onion over medium-high heat for 5 minutes, seasoning with salt and pepper. Stir occasionally to prevent burning. Add the garlic and rosemary and cook for another few minutes. Add the vermouth or wine and 100 ml water and reduce the liquid into the artichokes until they are softened. Add the spinach, stirring until it is wilted. (If the spinach is large leafed, remove from the heat and use a pair of scissors to coarsely cut it up in the pan.) Add 300 ml of the double cream and bring to the boil. Boil briefly, then remove from the heat, add half the Parmesan and the nutmeg and check the seasoning.

IF using fresh pasta, roll it out very thinly with a pasta machine or large rolling pin and cut it into eight 17 x 12 cm sheets (the grain of the pasta should run with the width and not the length of the sheet, or the pasta will split when rolled up).

TO cook the pasta, bring a saucepan of salted water to the boil and add a dash of oil. This prevents the pasta sheets from sticking to each other but will not affect the filling later. Blanch the pasta for 10 seconds if fresh or 5 minutes if dried, then drop it into a bowl of cold water. Spread the sheets out in a single layer on a tea towel, turning them over once to blot dry each side. Trim away any torn edges.

TO assemble the cannelloni, preheat the oven to 180°C (350°F/Gas 4). Butter a rectangular or square 2.5 litre capacity dish (use one about 20 x 26 cm). Lay out the sheets of pasta on the work surface (work quickly so they don't stick) and divide the filling among them. Spread out the filling and roll each sheet into a fat tube. Put the tubes side by side in the dish, seam side down. Pour over the remaining cream, sprinkle Parmesan on top and season.

PLACE the dish on a tray to catch any drips if the cream bubbles over. Bake for 30 minutes or until the top is golden brown. Remove from the oven and leave to cool for 10 minutes before serving.

Sardegna

Bottarga

A speciality of Cabras, bottarga is made by pressing and curing the roe of grey mullet or tuna. It is bought as a block and as much shaved off as is needed. Bottarga has a very strong flavour and is often used sparingly as a condiment or flavouring. But it can also be thinly sliced and sprinkled with oil and lemon juice for serving as antipasto, or grated over pasta to make *spaghetti alla buttariga*.

Situated off the eastern coast of Italy, Sardinia has always felt itself quite separate to the mainland, which the locals refer to as *il continente*. Despite being surrounded by sea, the Sardinians only became coastal dwellers in the mid-twentieth century—the land around the coast of their island is marshy and was prone to malaria-carrying mosquitoes. Instead, the population went inland and developed a dairy culture based on sheep. The inhospitable mountainous interior, covered with Mediterranean scrub bush, forced the Sardinians to be resourceful with their foodstuffs. As well as sheep's milk and cheese, shepherds ate a type of flat dry bread called *pane carasau* or *carta di musica* ('music paper' bread) which would keep for weeks on end. This diet would be supplemented with local fruit and vegetables, with olives, vines and fennel all growing well in the hot dry climate. Sardinian honey is excellent and the local cheeses are very good, especially the ricotta and pecorino sardo, which is now exported. The ricotta is often served up simply with a drizzle of honey as a snack.

Although the natives went inland, most invaders only occupied the coast, with the Spanish leaving the largest mark and some areas still speaking Catalan. Today there are many Sardinian fish stews using local fish or baccala and Alghero is famous for its spiny lobsters *(aragosta)*.

Sardinia's best-known foods include *porceddu*, a roast suckling pig basted with lard that is the national dish; *culingiones*, pasta filled with potato and wild mint; tiny saffron-flavoured gnocchi called *malloreddus* (little bulls); and bottarga, the pressed and aged roe of grey mullet.

Sardinian ravioli

Culingiones, Sardinian ravioli, are traditionally half-moon shaped, although in some recipes they appear as squares or rectangles. Often heavy and filled with potato and wild mint, these are a lighter version stuffed with ricotta, herbs and Sardinian pecorino cheese.

TO make the filling, mix the herbs with the ricotta, pecorino, egg and nutmeg. Season.

TO make the ravioli, roll out the pasta dough to the thinnest setting of the machine or with a rolling pin. Don't roll out more than you can handle at a time.

CUT circles out of the dough with a 9 cm round cutter or an upturned wine glass. Mix together the egg and milk and brush over each circle just before filling.

PLACE 2 teaspoons of the filling in the centre of each circle. Fold over the top of the circle to make a half-moon shape. Use your finger to press down around the filling to remove any air pockets. Run your finger firmly around the edge to seal well.

PUT the ravioli, well spaced out, on a tray dusted with semolina and leave to dry for a few minutes before cooking. The ravioli can be cooked immediately or left for up to 1 hour.

COOK the ravioli in batches in a large saucepan of boiling salted water until *al dente*. Remove with a slotted spoon and rest the spoon on a tea towel to drain away any remaining water.

SERVE with melted unsalted butter or a tomato sauce (see page 38) and grated pecorino.

MAKE sure you don't overfill the ravioli or they may burst when cooked. Cook until just al dente: *if you let them get too soft they will become soggy.*

SERVES 4

INGREDIENTS

FILLING

4 tablespoons mixed fresh herbs
    such as flat-leaf parsley, basil,
    mint, marjoram, oregano and
    thyme, chopped
250 g ricotta (preferably sheep's
    milk)
250 g pecorino (preferably
    Sardinian), grated
1 egg
pinch of freshly grated nutmeg

1 quantity fresh pasta dough
    (see page 36)
1 egg
2 teaspoons milk

pecorino

Pecorino is one of the most popular cheeses in Italy. Versions of it are produced in many areas but the one from Sardinia is particularly famous. Pecorino is made from sheep's milk and always by the same method, although varieties may be aged in different ways. *Pecorino sardo* is a highly-flavoured salty cheese, softer than the hard *pecorino romano*.

Pizzoccheri

SERVES 6

INGREDIENTS

PIZZOCCHERI

200 g buckwheat flour

100 g plain bread flour

1 egg

120 ml milk, warmed

CABBAGE, POTATO AND CHEESE SAUCE

350 g savoy cabbage, roughly chopped

180 g potatoes, cut into 2 cm cubes

4 tablespoons extra virgin olive oil

1 small bunch sage, finely chopped

2 garlic cloves, finely chopped

350 g mixed cheeses (mascarpone, fontina, Taleggio and Gorgonzola), cubed

grated Parmesan, to serve

Pizzoccheri is a buckwheat pasta from Valtellina near the Swiss border that is traditionally served with potatoes, cabbage and cheese. This recipe uses four different cheeses—you don't have to use equal quantities of each, but can vary the amounts depending on which type you prefer.

TO make the pizzoccheri, sift the two flours into a bowl and add a pinch of salt. Make a well in the centre and add the egg. Mix the egg into the flour and then gradually add the milk, mixing continuously until you have a soft dough. You may find that you need more or less milk than specified, as quantities will vary depending on the dryness of the flour.

KNEAD the dough for a few minutes, or until it is elastic, and then cover and leave to rest for an hour. Using a pasta machine or rolling pin, roll out the dough very thinly and cut into ribbons about 1 cm wide.

TO make the sauce, bring a large saucepan of salted water to the boil. Add the cabbage and potato and cook for about 3–5 minutes, or until cooked through, and then add the pasta for the last 2 minutes of cooking. (If you are using ready-made dried pasta, cook the pasta, cabbage and potatoes together for about 5–8 minutes, or until they are all cooked.)

DRAIN the pasta, cabbage and potatoes, reserving a cup of the cooking water. Dry the saucepan, then add the olive oil and gently cook the sage and garlic for 1 minute. Add the mixed cheeses to the pan. Mix briefly, then add the pasta, cabbage and potatoes and season with salt and pepper.

REMOVE the saucepan from the heat and gently stir the mixture together, adding some pasta water to loosen it up a little if necessary. Serve with Parmesan sprinkled over the top.

buying

If you can find an Italian cheese called *bitto*, include it in the cheese mix for the pizzoccheri instead of the fontina. Bitto is the cheese traditionally used for this recipe, but it is very hard to come by. If you don't want to make your own fresh pizzoccheri, you will be able to find it in specialist pasta shops.

KNEAD the pasta dough until it is smooth and elastic—this will take several minutes. Don't rush this part of the pasta making or the texture will not be as good.

BUCKWHEAT pasta is a little harder to handle than ordinary egg pasta so take care when you are rolling or it may split.

THE pasta for this dish is usually cut into ribbons about 1 cm wide. Do this by loosely rolling up the sheet of pasta and cutting it into slices. If preferred, cut it into thinner, or even thicker, ribbons.

buckwheat

Buckwheat *(grana saraceno)* is one of the earliest grains used to make bread in Italy. The Saracens or Moors brought it via the spice route in the Middle Ages. Today, buckwheat is grown in the Valtellina valley where it is made into pizzoccheri, and in the Veneto where it is used to make polenta. Buckwheat is available in health food shops if you can't find it in your local supermarket.

Potato gnocchi with pancetta and basil

SERVES 4

Potatoes make a deliciously light and fluffy gnocchi that can be eaten with the sauce suggested here, served with any of the pasta sauces in this chapter or used as an accompaniment to a rich meat dish such as venison casserole.

INGREDIENTS

POTATO GNOCCHI

1 kg floury potatoes, unpeeled

2 egg yolks

2 tablespoons grated Parmesan

125–185 g plain flour

SAUCE

75 g pancetta

50 g butter

handful of basil leaves, torn

TAKE each piece of dough and press your finger into it to form a concave shape. Then, holding the piece at each end, roll the outer surface over the tines of a fork to make deep ridges.

AT this point the gnocchi will look like little blocks. Fold the outer edges in towards each other to make a hollow in the middle. These will open as the gnocchi cook.

PRICK the potatoes all over and bake for 1 hour, or until tender. Cool for 15 minutes, then peel and mash (do not use a food processor or the potatoes will become gluey).

MIX in the yolks and Parmesan, then gradually stir in the flour. When the mixture gets too dry to use a spoon, use your hands. Once a loose dough forms, transfer to a lightly floured surface and knead gently. Work in enough extra flour to give a very soft, light, pliable dough.

DIVIDE the dough into six portions. Dust your hands lightly in flour, then, working with one portion at a time, roll out on a floured surface to make a rope about 1.5 cm thick. Cut into 1.5 cm lengths. Take each piece of dough and press your finger into it to form a concave shape, then roll the outer surface over the tines of a fork to make deep ridges. Fold the outer lips in towards each other to make a hollow in the middle. Place on a lightly floured tray and leave to rest, ideally for 10 minutes or more.

TO make the sauce, fry the pancetta in the butter until crisp and set aside.

BRING a large saucepan of salted water to the boil, then reduce the heat a little. Add the gnocchi in batches, stir gently and return to the boil. Cook until they rise to the surface. Remove with a slotted spoon and drain. Add the basil to the pancetta and toss together, season well and sprinkle over the gnocchi.

potatoes

Potatoes *(patata)* have never been a widely used carbohydrate in the Italian diet in comparison to pasta, polenta or rice. They do, however, appear in salads, as a vegetable side dish and as potato gnocchi. Generally, waxy potatoes such as Pink Fir Apple and Kipfler are used in salads—boiled and then dressed with oil and vinegar. Large all-purpose potatoes such as King Edward, Idaho and Desirée are good for chips and fried potatoes, with floury winter potatoes such as Tonda di Napoli being best for gnocchi. Some all-purpose potatoes such as Bintje can be used for all three types of cooking.

Spinach and ricotta gnocchi with sage butter

Gnocchi verdi are best made with fresh spinach. If you do have to use frozen spinach, make sure it is leaf spinach—you will find the chopped variety has often lost all density and does not make successful gnocchi.

SERVES 4

INGREDIENTS

GNOCCHI

1.5 kg fresh spinach, stalks removed,
  or 400 g thawed frozen spinach

50 g butter

1 onion, finely chopped

1 garlic clove, finely chopped

1 tablespoon chopped marjoram
  leaves

1 small nutmeg, grated

250 g ricotta

2 eggs

75 g plain flour, plus extra
  for dusting

50 g fresh breadcrumbs

100 g Parmesan, grated

SAGE BUTTER

75 g butter

15 g sage, stems removed

grated Parmesan, to serve

TO make the gnocchi, cook the spinach in a large saucepan with a generous amount of salt and a little water until it just begins to wilt. Drain, then rinse in cold water and squeeze as dry as possible. Finely chop.

MELT the butter and cook the onion and garlic until soft and translucent. Add the marjoram, spinach and nutmeg and season. Remove from the heat, put the spinach in a large bowl and spread it out to cool completely.

STIR in the ricotta, eggs, flour, breadcrumbs and Parmesan. Taste for seasoning and add more salt, pepper or Parmesan, if needed. The gnocchi should be well seasoned as they will be dusted with flour and then cooked in water, which tends to dilute their flavour a little. Put the mixture in the fridge and allow it to chill and stiffen up.

ROLL the gnocchi into walnut-sized balls, dusting your hands regularly with flour as the mixture will be sticky, and put them on a lightly floured tray. This might be a little messy, so occasionally rinse your hands in warm water.

TO make the sage butter, melt the butter and stir in the sage.

BRING a large saucepan of salted water to the boil, then reduce the heat a little. Add the gnocchi in batches, stir gently and return to the boil. Don't overcrowd the saucepan with the gnocchi or they might break up. Cook until they rise to the surface. Remove with a slotted spoon and drain. Once they are cooked, pour on the sage butter and sprinkle with Parmesan.

DUST your hands well with flour before rolling the gnocchi because the mixture can be very sticky. Roll the gnocchi into walnut-sized balls. (These may seem larger than gnocchi you usually see, but traditional sizes vary all over Italy. If you try to make them smaller, they will not hold together very well.)

Roman gnocchi

SERVES 4

INGREDIENTS

45 g unsalted butter, melted

30 g Parmesan, grated

3 egg yolks

1 litre milk

pinch of freshly grated nutmeg

200 g semolina

TOPPING

40 g butter, melted

90 ml double cream (optional)

30 g Parmesan, grated

Sometimes referred to as semolina gnocchi, these baked discs are made with eggs, Parmesan and semolina and are quite different from the potato gnocchi that is more commonly eaten in the north. Roman gnocchi is a very traditional dish from Rome and the Lazio.

WHEN you lift out the semolina slab, keep it on its piece of baking paper. Peel this off when the slab is safely out. If you are going to use a glass instead of a cutter, make sure it has a nice thin edge.

LINE a 30 x 25 cm shallow baking tin with baking paper, leaving some overhang on each side. Beat together the butter, Parmesan and egg yolks and season lightly. Set aside.

HEAT the milk in a large saucepan and season with salt, pepper and the nutmeg. When the milk is just boiling, pour in the semolina in a steady stream, stirring constantly. Reduce the heat and continue to cook, stirring, for about 10–12 minutes, or until all the milk has been absorbed and the mixture pulls away from the side of the pan in one lump.

REMOVE the saucepan from the heat and beat in the egg yolk mixture with a wooden spoon until smooth. Spoon quickly into the tin (if you take too long, the mixture will begin to stiffen). Smooth the surface with a knife dipped in cold water. Set aside to cool completely.

PREHEAT the oven to 180°C (350°F/Gas 4) and grease a 25 x 18 cm shallow casserole or baking tray. Lift the semolina slab out of the tin and peel off the baking paper. Cut the semolina into circles, using a 4 cm biscuit cutter dipped in cold water. If you don't have a cutter, use an upturned glass instead. Arrange the circles, slightly overlapping, in the greased casserole.

TO make the topping, blend together the butter and cream (if using). Pour this over the gnocchi and sprinkle the Parmesan on top. If you are using just butter, simply dot it over the top. Bake for about 25–30 minutes, or until golden. Serve at once.

semolina

Semolina *(semolino)* is made from ground durum wheat, the same wheat that is used to make dried pasta. Its most famous use, other than for pasta, is to make Roman gnocchi *(gnocchi alla Romana)* or a form of couscous that is eaten in Sicily.

riso e polenta

risotto rice

There are three well-known varieties of risotto rice that are widely available today.

ARBORIO RICE: a large plump grain rich in amylopectin, the starch that dissolves in cooking to produce a stickier risotto.

VIALONE NANO: a stubby small grain with more of another starch, amylose, that does not soften easily in cooking. Contains enough amylopectin to give a looser consistency but keeps more of a bite in the middle.

CARNAROLI: a new variety developed in 1945 by a Milanese rice grower, carnaroli is a cross between Vialone and a Japanese strain. Small production makes this grain more expensive. The outer skin has enough of the soft starch to dissolve and make the risotto creamy but it also contains more of the tough starch than any of the other risotto rices and so keeps a firm consistency.

texture

The texture of risotto varies through-out northern Italy. Milanese risottos are much stiffer than those of Venice, which are served *all'onda*, meaning 'like waves'. You can make a risotto to any consistency you like. For a wetter risotto, add a tablespoon or two of hot stock right at the end, just before you serve.

pans

You can use almost any kind of pan for cooking risotto provided it has a wide base that will provide an even heat. Deep frying pans and shallow saucepans work well. Remember that what looks like a small amount of rice at the start will grow in volume by about three times, so make sure the pan is big enough.

making risotto

USE a large deep frying pan or shallow saucepan with a heavy base that will distribute the heat evenly. Make sure the stock or liquid you are going to add is hot—keep it at a low simmer on the stove.

COOK the rice in the butter first. This creates a seal around the grains, trapping the starch. Stir frequently, not only to prevent the rice from sticking to the bottom of the pan but to ensure all the grains are cooked evenly.

ADD the liquid a ladleful at a time. Stir constantly so that the rice cooks evenly and releases some of the starch, giving the risotto a creamy consistency. If you cook the rice too slowly, it will become gluey; too fast and the liquid will evaporate—keep it at a fast simmer.

SEASON the rice early on while it is absorbing flavour. Once it is cooked and the grains saturated, it won't soak up the seasoning as well. Taste the liquid around the rice to check the seasoning after the first couple of ladles of stock.

DON'T swamp the rice with too much liquid, but add just enough to cover it so it cooks evenly. Once you have used nearly all the stock, start tasting the rice to prevent overcooking. The rice should be al dente.

IT is impossible to gauge the exact amount of stock you might require. Stop cooking the rice as soon as it is creamy but still has a little texture in the middle of the grain. The risotto should be rich and thick like porridge, not too wet or dry.

shaping suppli and arancini

ROLL a small amount (about 50 g) of cooked, cooled risotto into a ball about the size of a walnut.

PRESS a hole in the middle of the ball with your thumb. Place a small amount of filling (often a cube of cheese) into the middle and press the risotto rice back around it to reform the ball.

PRESS the risotto rice firmly so it is compact. Roll each ball in flour, egg and breadcrumbs, pressing so the crumbs attach themselves to the rice.

making polenta

PUT the specified amount of cold water and salt in a deep heavy-based saucepan and bring to the boil. Add the polenta in a steady stream, using a wooden spoon to stir the water vigorously as you pour the polenta in.

AS soon as you have added all the polenta, reduce the heat so the water is just simmering and keep stirring for the first 30 seconds to prevent lumps.

THE finished texture of the polenta will improve the more you stir it. Leave it to bubble away for about 40 minutes, stirring every few minutes to prevent it sticking. When cooked, it should be thick enough to fall from the spoon in lumps.

grilling polenta

POUR the cooked polenta onto a flat plate or serving dish and leave to cool. Do not store the polenta in the fridge or condensation will form and make it stick when grilled.

CUT the polenta into triangles or strips.

LIGHTLY brush the pieces of polenta with olive oil and grill or chargrill for about 3 minutes on each side. You can use grilled polenta for canapé bases as well as as an accompaniment to stews and sauces.

shaping polenta

POLENTA can easily be moulded into shapes for layering with sauce. Pour the polenta into a deep serving dish, bearing in mind you want it to be no more than 2.5 cm thick or it will be too stodgy.

THE polenta will mould itself into the shape of the dish. Allow to cool completely. Once cooled, the polenta is wonderfully pliable and easy to handle.

TO slice, carefully turn the polenta upside down out of the dish and onto a board. Use a long sharp knife to slice it. The polenta slices can then be layered with sauce and reformed in the dish.

'wet' and grilled polenta

Wet polenta is served in northern Italy as an accompaniment to sauces and rich stews in much the same way that mashed potatoes are served in England. Never throw away leftover cooked polenta: it can be poured into a dish and left to set firm, then grilled or chargrilled as an accompaniment.

buying

Polenta is the name of the dish—the raw ingredient is actually cornmeal. It is important to buy cornmeal that is meant for making polenta rather than corn bread or anything else. Cornmeal for polenta is called polenta on the packet and generally comes from Italy. Stone-ground Italian polenta is the best you can get.

flavouring

Polenta can be flavoured with a variety of other ingredients if you want to give it a lift. Dried herbs or chillies can be added at the beginning, grated cheese and grilled or fried vegetables can be stirred in at the end. You can also use stock or milk to cook the polenta rather than water.

Lombardia

Gastronomia Peck

Not a speciality in itself but a famous shop in Milan that is world-renowned for its food. The Milanese take their eating seriously and Peck is the kind of emporium that supplies every edible you can possibly imagine. As well as fresh produce like cheese and truffles and dried products such as pasta, Peck sells ready-cooked food. Its rosticceria turns out porchetta, roast meats, baked pasta dishes and prepared vegetables every day. Whole meals can be bought here with no extra preparation needed before serving—the ultimate 'take-away'.

Lombardy is a northern landlocked region, bordering Switzerland, with a rich agricultural tradition and an abundance of fine produce. Rice is grown for risotto in the Po valley and corn for polenta, both regional staples, although in the mountain regions of the Valtellina the hearty buckwheat pasta pizzoccheri is renowned—one of the few pastas to be made in northern Italy. Soups are a staple, but the local minestrone is made with rice rather than pasta. Cheeses include Gorgonzola, Grana Pedano, mascarpone and Taleggio that was traditionally matured in mountain caves—all well known outside Italy.

The mountain region is not as prosperous as the rich cities of Milan and Mantova, where wealthy families in the fifteenth century introduced a strong French influence into the food with their love of meat stews and cream. Lombardy enjoys meat antipasti: *bresaola* from Valtellina is an air-dried beef; *Violin di carne seca* a ham made from goat meat; and *salame Milanese* a smooth spiced salami.

Cakes and sweets are also a speciality of the region, Panettone comes from Milan and the nougat *torrone* from Cremona. Lombardy is rich in specialities: bollito misto is served with *mostarda di frutta* from Cremona and osso buco is a favourite, traditionally served with risotto alla Milanese. Agnoli are the filled pasta preferred in Mantova, and tortelli in Cremona.

The wines of Lombardy include some of Italy's greatest: Barolo, Barbaresco, Barbera d'Alba and Asti Spumante.

Risotto Milanese

Risotto Milanese takes its brilliant yellow colouring from saffron and its rich flavour from beef marrow. It is the classic accompaniment to osso buco but is also perfect as a first course. If beef marrow is hard to find, leave it out or use a fatty piece of finely chopped prosciutto or pancetta.

PUT the vermouth or wine in a bowl, add the saffron and leave to soak for 10 minutes. Heat the chicken stock in a saucepan and maintain at a low simmer.

MELT the butter and beef marrow in a deep heavy-based frying pan and gently cook the onion and garlic until soft but not browned. Add the rice and reduce the heat to low. Season and stir to coat the grains of rice in the butter and marrow.

ADD the vermouth and saffron to the rice and increase the heat to medium. Cook, stirring, until all the liquid has been absorbed.

STIR in a ladleful of the stock and cook at a fast simmer, stirring constantly. When the stock has been absorbed, stir in another ladleful. Continue like this for about 20 minutes, or until the rice is *al dente*. Add a little more stock or water if you need to—every risotto will use a different amount.

STIR in 100 g of the Parmesan and sprinkle the rest over the top to serve.

SERVES 4

INGREDIENTS

200 ml dry white vermouth or
    white wine

1 large pinch of saffron strands

1.5 litres chicken stock

100 g butter

75 g beef marrow

1 large onion, finely chopped

1 garlic clove, crushed

350 g risotto rice

150 g Parmesan, grated

cooking

When cooking risotto, make sure that the heat is neither too high nor too low. The rice must absorb the stock at a fast simmer. If it cooks too fast, the liquid will evaporate rather than be absorbed; too slow and the rice will become soggy.

75

Porcini risotto

This is a delicious classic risotto made with dried porcini, which have a wonderful earthy flavour. The porcini are soaked in water to soften them and then the soaking water is added to the stock so that none of the flavour is wasted.

SERVES 4

INGREDIENTS

30 g dried porcini mushrooms

1 litre chicken or vegetable stock

100 g butter

1 onion, finely chopped

250 g mushrooms, sliced

2 garlic cloves, crushed

375 g risotto rice

pinch of ground nutmeg

1 tablespoon finely chopped parsley

45 g Parmesan, grated

PUT the porcini in a bowl, cover with 500 ml hot water and leave to soak for 15 minutes. Squeeze them dry, reserving the soaking liquid. If the porcini are large, roughly chop them. Strain the soaking liquid into a saucepan and add enough stock to make up to 1 litre. Heat up and maintain at a low simmer.

MELT the butter in a deep heavy-based frying pan and gently cook the onion until soft but not browned. Add the mushrooms and porcini and fry for a few minutes. Add the garlic, stir briefly, then add the rice and reduce the heat to low. Season and stir to coat the grains of rice in the butter.

INCREASE the heat to medium and add a ladleful of the stock. Cook at a fast simmer, stirring constantly. When the stock has been absorbed, stir in another ladleful. Continue like this for about 20 minutes, or until the rice is *al dente*. Add a little more stock or water if you need to—every risotto will use a different amount.

STIR in the nutmeg, parsley and half the Parmesan, then serve with the rest of the Parmesan sprinkled over the top.

porcini

Porcini are considered the kings of mushrooms. They can be picked wild when in season or bought in markets and vegetable shops. If they are not available—or are simply too expensive—then dried porcini can be used. Dried porcini are sold in small packets and are widely available.

cooking

You can use a variety of pans to cook a risotto but a large deep frying pan gives the best surface area. Make sure the pan has a heavy base as this will help the risotto cook more evenly and prevent it sticking.

Asparagus risotto

This risotto is given an intensity of flavour by cooking and blending the asparagus stems to use as stock. You could try the same method with other vegetables such as broccoli and peas. Obviously, the recipe is best made when asparagus is in season and has a good flavour.

TO make the asparagus stock, wash the asparagus and snap off the woody ends but don't throw them away. Cut the delicate tips off the asparagus and set aside. Finely chop the asparagus stems.

POUR 750 ml water into a small saucepan, add a pinch of salt and bring to the boil. Cook the woody asparagus ends in the water for about 10 minutes, pressing them with the back of a slotted spoon to release their flavour. Remove the ends with the spoon and throw them away. In the same water, cook the asparagus tips for 2 minutes, then remove, drain and set aside. Finally, cook the chopped asparagus stems for 3 minutes.

POUR the water and asparagus stems into a blender and mix until smooth. Pour into a measuring jug—you should have 750 ml of liquid. If you don't, top up with water. Pour the stock back into the saucepan and maintain at a low simmer.

HEAT 75 g of the butter in deep heavy-based frying pan and gently cook the onion until soft but not browned. Add the garlic and thyme and stir briefly. Add the rice and reduce the heat to low. Season and stir to coat the grains of rice in the butter.

ADD the vermouth to the rice and increase the heat to medium. Cook, stirring, until all the liquid has been absorbed.

STIR in a ladleful of the stock and cook at a fast simmer, stirring constantly. When the stock has been absorbed, stir in another ladleful. Continue like this for about 20 minutes, or until the rice is *al dente*. When you have one ladleful of stock left, add the asparagus tips and the remaining stock and cook until the liquid is absorbed. Adding the delicate asparagus tips at the end of cooking prevents them breaking up and helps them maintain their bright green colour.

STIR in the remaining butter and the Parmesan. Leave the risotto in the pan for 1–2 minutes to allow the flavours to infuse. Sprinkle with the remaining Parmesan to serve.

REMOVING the tough woody ends of the asparagus is very easy: simply hold the spear firmly and bend the end gently. It will snap at its natural breaking point.

SERVES 4

INGREDIENTS

450 g asparagus

100 g butter

1 onion, finely chopped

1 large garlic clove, finely chopped

1 tablespoon chopped thyme

225 g risotto rice

150 ml dry white vermouth or white wine

25 g Parmesan, grated, plus shavings to serve

Red wine risotto

SERVES 4

INGREDIENTS

500 ml chicken stock

1 thyme sprig

100 g butter

1 onion, finely chopped

1 large garlic clove, finely chopped

225 g risotto rice

500 ml good-quality dry red wine

25 g Parmesan, grated, plus extra
  to serve

The secret to making this risotto spectacular is to use only the best ingredients. A good-quality wine is essential—the traditional variety used in Italy is the dry Amarone of Valpolicella but you can use any dry but rich red.

HEAT the chicken stock in a saucepan and maintain at a low simmer. Strip the leaves from the thyme sprig.

MELT the butter in a deep heavy-based frying pan and gently cook the onion and garlic until soft but not browned. Add the thyme and rice and reduce the heat to low. Season and stir to coat the grains of rice in the butter.

ADD half the red wine to the rice and increase the heat to medium. Cook, stirring, until all the liquid has been absorbed. Stir in half the stock and cook at a fast simmer, stirring constantly. When the stock has been absorbed, stir in the rest of the wine.

STIR in nearly all the rest of the stock and cook until the rice is *al dente*. Add a little more stock or water if you need to—every risotto will use a different amount.

STIR in the Parmesan and sprinkle a little extra over the top to serve.

cooking

Add salt and pepper while you are still cooking the risotto so the rice absorbs the seasoning: if you season at the end of cooking, it will remain in the liquid rather than be absorbed by the grains of rice. Check for seasoning by tasting the liquid around the rice once it has started to become creamy.

Piemonte e Valle d'Aosta

These two northern areas both have borders with France, which gives them some culinary overlap. Piedmont is a highly agricultural region: wheat, corn and rice are grown, cows are farmed for beef and veal and the highland regions produce game. Unusually, the fields of the higher plains are irrigated by a network of canals. Wild porcini feature in many of the gutsy meat stews. The land is fertile and rich with vegetables as well as being Italy's most important risotto rice-growing region. The town of Alba is famous for its white truffles that are sprinkled over melted fontina in the local fondue-like *fonduta* and the local ricotta is among the best in Italy. Turin is the home of nougat and chocolate, and the dessert *zabaione*. Favourite dishes are bagna caôda, bollito misto, *brasto* (beef braised in wine) and fritto misto.

The Valle d'Aosta is a mountainous Alpine region once used as a hunting ground for the House of Savoy, which governed this area, Piedmont and Burgundy in France. It is the smallest region of Italy, but has Europe's highest mountains. As in the rest of Italy, it is possible to divine the cuisine simply by looking at a map: cheeses such as *fontina robbiola* are produced by the dairy herds in the high fields; game is caught in the forests; apples, pears and chestnuts grow in the hills; and fish is caught in the rivers and lakes. Breads are flavoured with rye and fontina and favourite dishes include *zuppa di castagne* (chestnut soup), *carbonada* and polenta with fontina. Cream is used in many dishes, particularly in the local baked desserts. Gnocchi is eaten in the Valle d'Aosta, risotto in Piedmont, and pasta is now enjoyed in both areas.

La grolla

A speciality of the Valle d'Aosta, *la grolla* is the name given to a ritual of hospitality and friendship. A wooden vessel with up to eight spouts is filled with *caffè valdostano*, a mixture of coffee, grappa and sugar. This is then passed around the group, with each person drinking from one of the spouts.

INGREDIENTS

1.5 litres chicken or vegetable stock

100 g butter

1 large onion, finely chopped

2 garlic cloves, finely chopped

350 g fresh or frozen peas

350 g risotto rice

200 ml dry white vermouth or
   white wine

50 g Parmesan, grated, plus extra
   to serve

Risi e bisi

Risi e bisi is served much wetter than most other risotti. The consistency should be more like thick soup than a risotto. This is the simplest version of a risi e bisi, although sometimes pancetta may be added. You can use fresh peas when in season, but frozen are fine the rest of the time.

HEAT the stock in a saucepan and maintain at a low simmer.

MELT 75 g of the butter in a deep heavy-based frying pan and gently cook the onion and garlic until soft but not browned. If you are using frozen peas, blanch them in the chicken stock for 1 minute, then drain them over a bowl and set aside. Pour this stock back into the saucepan.

ADD the rice to the frying pan and reduce the heat to low. Season and stir to coat the grains of rice in the butter. Add the vermouth and increase the heat to medium. Cook, stirring, until all the liquid has been absorbed.

STIR in a ladleful of the stock and cook at a fast simmer, stirring constantly. When the stock has been absorbed, stir in another ladleful. If you are using fresh peas, add them after the first couple of ladles of stock. If using frozen blanched peas, add them after half the stock has been used. Continue adding a ladleful of stock at a time for about 20 minutes, or until the rice is *al dente*. Add a little more stock or water if you need to—every risotto will use a different amount. The consistency of this dish should be like a thick soup or wet risotto.

REMOVE the risotto from the heat and leave to rest for 5 minutes, then stir in the remaining butter and the Parmesan. Serve with extra Parmesan.

preparing

You can subtly alter the flavour of your risotto by changing the stock. Vegetable stock will give a milder result than chicken stock. You can increase the flavour of both home-made and store-bought stocks yourself. For example, for risi e bisi, if you are using fresh peas, you could simmer the pods in the stock for 5 minutes. Remove them before using the liquid.

spinach

Spinach *(spinaci)* grows in the north and centre of Italy and was brought to the country by the Arabs. It is a popular vegetable accompaniment but also features in many recipes. You can buy ordinary large-leaved spinach or small baby spinach.

Spinach risotto cake

This moulded risotto is made with spinach, but it can also be prepared using risotto Milanese (see page 75). Arborio rice is specified as it is the most glutinous, helping the cake to stick together. Serve with a rich slow-cooked meat dish such as osso buco or venison casserole.

SERVES 6

INGREDIENTS

250 g baby spinach

750 ml chicken stock

100 g butter

1 onion, finely chopped

1 garlic clove, finely chopped

225 g arborio rice

150 ml dry white vermouth or white wine

¼ teaspoon freshly grated nutmeg

25 g Parmesan, grated, plus extra to serve

CHOP the spinach finely so that it mixes easily into the risotto. Make sure that all the stock has been absorbed before you remove the risotto from the heat. The consistency is important for this cake—if you have a wet risotto, it won't hold its shape when unmoulded.

COOK the spinach in a small amount of salted water until just wilted. Refresh in cold water and squeeze dry. Finely chop and set aside.

HEAT the chicken stock in a saucepan and maintain at a low simmer.

MELT 75 g of the butter in a deep heavy-based frying pan and gently cook the onion and garlic until soft but not browned. Add the rice and reduce the heat to low. Season and stir to coat the grains of rice in the butter.

ADD the vermouth to the rice and increase the heat to medium. Cook, stirring, until all the liquid has been absorbed.

STIR in a ladleful of the stock and cook at a fast simmer, stirring constantly. When the stock has been absorbed, stir in another ladleful. Continue like this until a quarter of the stock is left, then mix in the chopped spinach. Continue to add the last of the stock. When making risotto cake, it is not so essential to keep the rice *al dente*—if it is a little more glutinous, it will stick together better. Make sure all the liquid is absorbed or the cake may break up when unmoulded. Remove from the heat and stir in the nutmeg, Parmesan and the remaining butter.

SMEAR a little butter into a mould such as a 1.25-litre cake tin. Spoon the risotto into the mould, pressing it down firmly. Leave to rest for 5 minutes, then unmould and place on a warm serving plate with some Parmesan sprinkled over the top.

MAKES 20

INGREDIENTS

large pinch of saffron strands

250 ml white wine

750 ml chicken stock

2 thyme sprigs

100 g butter

1 onion, finely chopped

1 garlic clove, finely chopped

225 g risotto rice

50 g Parmesan, grated

100 g mozzarella or fontina, diced

75 g plain flour

2 eggs, beaten

75 g dried breadcrumbs

500 ml oil, for deep-frying

Arancini

Meaning 'little oranges', arancini are a classic Sicilian meal or antipasto. They are made with saffron risotto and stuffed with fillings such as mozzarella, ham or chicken livers. Use arborio rice rather than carnaroli as this is more glutinous and helps the balls stick together.

WHEN making arancini you need the risotto to be fairly stiff. Keep your hands as cool as possible or the warmth from them will heat the mixture and soften it. Give the balls a good coating of breadcrumbs—it is the crumbs that fry golden brown and any patches you miss will show up when they are cooked.

PUT the saffron in a bowl with the white wine and soak for 10 minutes. Heat the chicken stock in a saucepan and maintain at a low simmer. Strip the leaves from the thyme sprigs.

MELT the butter in a deep heavy-based frying pan and gently cook the onion and garlic until soft but not browned. Add the thyme and rice and reduce the heat to low. Season and stir to coat the grains of rice in the butter.

ADD the wine and saffron to the rice and increase the heat to medium. Cook, stirring, until all the liquid has been absorbed. Stir in a ladleful of the stock and cook at a fast simmer, stirring constantly. When the stock has been absorbed, stir in another ladleful. Continue like this for about 20 minutes. Add a little more stock or water if you need to—every risotto will use a different amount. When making arancini, it is not so essential to keep the rice *al dente*—if it is a little more glutinous, the balls will stick together better. Make sure the risotto is thick or the arancini may break up.

REMOVE from the heat, stir in the Parmesan, then spread out on a tray lined with greaseproof paper. Leave in the fridge for a couple of hours or overnight to allow the butter and the starch in the rice to solidify.

ROLL a small amount of risotto into a walnut-sized ball. Press a hollow in the middle with your thumb, insert a small cube of cheese in the hole and firmly press the rice back into place around the cheese. Roll in the flour, then the egg and then in the breadcrumbs, pressing down to coat well.

HEAT the oil in a deep frying pan to 180°C (350°F), or until a piece of bread fries golden brown in 15 seconds. If the oil starts to smoke, it is too hot. Deep-fry the arancini in batches for about 3–4 minutes, making sure they cook evenly on all sides. Drain on paper towels and serve hot or at room temperature.

saffron

It is often pointed out that saffron *(zafferano)* is one of the most expensive commodities in the world, and is literally worth more than its own weight in gold. However, it is so light and so little is usually needed that it is not an expensive item to buy. Saffron strands are the stigmas of a particular type of crocus and have to be harvested by hand. They can be bought in small packets or as a ground powder (the whole stigmas are preferable). The best-quality saffron comes from Spain and a tiny amount is also grown in Abruzzi in Italy. Cheaper saffron is inferior in aroma and flavour. The most important thing to remember when using saffron is that it is very strong and can be overpowering, so don't be tempted to use more than the recipe specifies.

Wet polenta with mushrooms

Wet polenta is often served in Italy to accompany a main course just as mashed potato is served in England. Polenta with wild mushrooms is one of the easiest dishes to prepare and is often served as a first course *(prima piatti)* instead of pasta.

SERVES 6

INGREDIENTS

1 tablespoon salt

300 g fine polenta

60 ml olive oil

400 g wild mushrooms, such as fresh
  porcini, sliced if large

2 garlic cloves, crushed

1 tablespoon chopped thyme

150 g mascarpone

50 g butter

50 g Parmesan, grated, plus extra
  to serve

wild mushrooms

Picking, cooking and eating wild mushrooms *(fungi)* is something of a national pastime in Italy. Luckily, fungi grow all over Italy, especially in areas that have high mountain valleys. Porcini are the most famous, with their wonderful meaty texture and unique aroma and flavour. But there are numerous other types of wild mushroom to be found in Italy, such as saffron milkcaps, shaggy inkcaps, chanterelles and morels. All are equally delicious and can be used in dishes that call for wild mushrooms, or tossed in butter and garlic and eaten on their own.

BRING 1.5 litres of water to the boil in a deep heavy-based saucepan and add the salt. Add the polenta in a gentle stream, whisking or stirring vigorously as you pour. Reduce the heat immediately so the water is simmering and keep stirring for the first 30 seconds to prevent lumps appearing—the more you stir, the better the finished texture of the polenta. Leave the polenta to gently bubble away for about 40 minutes, stirring it every few minutes to stop it sticking to the pan. The finished polenta should drop from the spoon in thick lumps.

WHILE the polenta is cooking, heat the olive oil in a large frying pan, then add enough mushrooms to cover the base of the pan. Cook over high heat, stirring frequently, until any liquid given off by the mushrooms has evaporated.

ADD the garlic and thyme and cook briefly. Remove the mushrooms from the pan and cook the next batch. Return all mushrooms to the pan and season well.

WHEN the polenta is almost cooked, reheat the mushrooms, add the mascarpone and let it melt.

ADD the butter and Parmesan to the cooked polenta and season with pepper. Spoon the polenta onto plates and top with the mushroom mixture. Sprinkle with extra Parmesan to serve.

cooking

You need a deep saucepan for cooking polenta because it bubbles and can spit. A deep saucepan will prevent you getting splattered and burnt. You'll need a long wooden spoon too.

Grilled polenta with sausage and tomato sauce

Grilling or chargrilling polenta gives it a crisp exterior while it keeps its soft centre. The cooked wet polenta is left to cool in a dish, then cut into triangles and cooked on a griddle or grill. The sausage and tomato accompaniment is also good with wet polenta.

BRING 1.5 litres of water to the boil in a deep heavy-based saucepan and add the salt. Add the polenta in a gentle stream, whisking or stirring vigorously as you pour. Reduce the heat immediately so the water is simmering and keep stirring for the first 30 seconds to prevent lumps appearing—the more you stir, the better the finished texture of the polenta. Leave the polenta to gently bubble away for about 40 minutes, stirring it every few minutes to stop it sticking to the pan. The finished polenta should drop from the spoon in thick lumps. Stir in the butter and Parmesan.

INGREDIENTS

POLENTA

1 tablespoon salt

300 g coarse-grain polenta

50 g butter

50 g Parmesan, grated, plus extra
  to serve

SAUSAGE AND TOMATO SAUCE

3 tablespoons olive oil

8 firm Italian pork sausages

1 onion, halved and sliced

2 garlic cloves, chopped,

200 ml red wine

400 g tin tomatoes

POUR the polenta onto a flat plate or serving dish and leave to cool at room temperature. Don't refrigerate—this will create condensation and make the polenta stick when it is grilled.

cooking

When using a griddle, make sure that it is really hot before you start or the polenta will stick and you won't be able to pull it off in one piece.

TO make the sauce, heat the olive oil in a deep frying pan and cook the sausages over medium-high heat, lightly browning on all sides. Try to avoid burning the base of the pan. Remove the sausages and set aside. If the pan is burnt, rinse it first, otherwise add the onion and cook gently until softened, scraping the dark brown sausage fat from the bottom of the pan. This will help darken the sauce and improve its flavour.

ADD the garlic, cook for a few more minutes, then pour in the red wine. Cook for about 5 minutes, or until the liquid has reduced and the sauce thickened. Add the tomatoes and, when the sauce starts to thicken, add the sausages, stirring frequently to prevent the base of the pan from burning. Season with salt and pepper.

WHEN the sauce is nearly ready, preheat a griddle or grill. Cut the polenta into triangles or strips, brush with olive oil and grill for about 3 minutes on each side. Spoon tomato sauce over the sausage and sprinkle the polenta with grated Parmesan to serve.

polenta

The word 'polenta' actually refers to the title of the dish, but over time the ground cornmeal has become known by the same name. It is traditionally eaten in the north of Italy, especially in the mountainous areas where corn grew more easily than wheat. Cornmeal for polenta comes in different grades and is best chosen depending on what it is to accompany: coarser cornmeal is best with robust flavours while the finer grade is more suited to delicate sauces. A fine, white cornmeal (polenta bianca) is found in some areas such as Veneto and is usually served with fish.

Baked polenta with four cheeses

This recipe uses a combination of cheeses: Gorgonzola for strength, Taleggio for texture, mascarpone for creaminess and Parmesan for flavour. The dish can be prepared in advance and then cooked at the last minute. It is incredibly rich so try serving it with a simple rocket salad.

BRING 1.5 litres of water to the boil in a deep heavy-based saucepan and add the salt. Add the polenta in a gentle stream, whisking or stirring vigorously as you pour. Reduce the heat immediately so the water is simmering and keep stirring for the first 30 seconds to prevent lumps appearing—the more you stir, the better the finished texture of the polenta. Leave the polenta to gently bubble away for about 40 minutes, stirring it every few minutes to stop it sticking to the pan. The finished polenta should drop from the spoon in thick lumps. Stir in the butter.

POUR the polenta into a large 2.25-litre oiled gratin or casserole dish that is about 5.5 cm deep. The polenta should reach no further than halfway up the side of the dish or the filling will overflow. Leave to cool completely.

TO make the tomato sauce, first strip the leaves off the rosemary or thyme. Heat the olive oil in a saucepan over low heat and cook the garlic gently until light brown. Add half the rosemary or thyme and then the tomatoes. Season with salt and pepper and cook gently, stirring occasionally, until reduced to a thick sauce.

PREHEAT the oven to 175°C (350°F/Gas 4). Carefully turn the polenta out of the dish onto a board, then slice it horizontally in two. Pour half of the tomato sauce into the bottom of the dish, place the bottom slice of the polenta on top of the sauce and season with salt and pepper. Scatter the Gorgonzola and Taleggio over the top. Using a teaspoon, dot the mascarpone over the polenta and then sprinkle with half of the Parmesan and the remaining rosemary or thyme. Put the other slice of polenta on top and pour over the last of the tomato sauce. Sprinkle with the remaining Parmesan and bake for 40 minutes. Leave to rest for at least 10 minutes before serving.

YOU may feel that the polenta will be delicate and hard to handle but it is, in fact, very easy. The set polenta cuts beautifully and is quite elastic. However, you will need a long serrated knife to slice it.

SERVES 6

INGREDIENTS

POLENTA

1 tablespoon salt

300 g polenta

75 g butter

TOMATO SAUCE

2 rosemary or thyme sprigs

3 tablespoons extra virgin olive oil

2 garlic cloves, thinly sliced

2 x 400 g tins tomatoes or
    350 g ripe tomatoes, peeled and
    chopped (see page 172)

200 g Gorgonzola, cubed

250 g Taleggio, cubed

250 g mascarpone

100 g Parmesan, grated

pesci e frutti di mare

fish

sardines

Small oily fleshed fish, sardines *(sarde)* can vary quite considerably in size. Different varieties of sardine are caught all over the world but some of the best are found in the Mediterranean. Sardines are best eaten very fresh as their flesh deteriorates quite quickly.

red mullet

One of the more recognisable fish from the Mediterranean, red mullet *(triglia)* has a lovely red skin that retains its colour when cooked, making it attractive for grilling. The white flesh is quite firm and sweet. Mullet are sometimes called goatfish because of their barbel beards.

swordfish

Swordfish *(pesce spada)* are large fish, usually cut into steaks or sold as pieces of fillet. They are caught off the coast of Sicily and southern Italy, which is where they are eaten most. The flesh is paler than that of tuna and not quite so strongly flavoured.

sea bream

A large family of fish, varieties of sea bream *(dentice)* are found in the Mediterranean, Atlantic, Caribbean and Pacific. They are quite large fish and good for serving whole, but they also can be cooked as steaks and fillets. The flesh is firm and white.

tuna

Tuna *(tonno)* is a large fish with oily flesh that can be used as steaks, pieces of fillet or cut into cubes. It grills well as it is fairly robust and holds its own with strong flavours like lemon and tomato. There are many varieties of tuna, all of which are interchangeable in recipes though the colour of the flesh may vary. There was a large tuna fishing industry in Sicily and the south of Italy, but now, despite the tuna markets at Palermo and Catania, this is somewhat in decline. Tuna is caught off the coast of Sicily in huge tunnels of nets: a practice peculiar to the region.

whitebait

These small fish come from a variety of families, depending on where they are fished. Usually they are from the herring family and have oily flesh. Larger whitebait can be used instead of sardines in recipes, while the smaller ones are best used whole in dishes like fritto misto.

sole

This flat fish is found in the Mediterranean and North Sea. There are several varieties of sole *(sogliola)* including the much prized Dover sole. Other flat fish, such as lemon sole, may also be called sole although they are not actually the same species. Sole has a delicate white flesh that grills well.

sea bass

A reasonably large fish that is very good for cooking whole, sea bass *(branzino)* has silvery black scales and firm white flesh that holds together well. They are large enough to feed several people and make a good centrepiece for a meal, especially as they contain relatively few bones.

shellfish

prawns

There many different types of prawn *(gambero)*. Rather than judging by size, buy any that are fresh and in season— these will taste sweeter than frozen prawns, which are often woolly. Varieties of prawn are interchangeable in recipes: just ensure you have enough per person.

mussels

There are two main types of mussel *(cozze)* available: black or European mussels with their blueish black shells; and the green-lipped mussels of Southeast Asia, also called New Zealand mussels. Black mussels are smaller and generally have a better flavour; they are farmed and are usually sold cleaned and ready to cook. Mussels can vary in quality according to the time of year and may be less plump during the spawning season. When mussels are in season they are usually abundantly available. You can keep them wrapped in a wet cloth in a cool, dark place such as the vegetable crisper of your fridge for up to two days.

scallops

Scallops *(capasanta* or *conchiglia)* have smooth white muscles and orange roes and are often sold without their shells. There are many varieties but without the shells they can all look similar. Buy scallops that are not too plump and white—these may be waterlogged.

squid

Available both whole and as cleaned tubes, squid *(calamari)* come in varying sizes. Different species are available worldwide and are all interchangeable. Whole squid may contain an ink sac that can be used for risotto nero.

clams

Known as *vongole* in Italy, there are many species of clam (interchangeable in most recipes), but some are only sold locally to where they are fished. The two main types are hard-shelled (pictured) and soft-shelled clams, which never close their shells completely.

crab

Crabs *(granchio* or *granceola)* vary in size and shape. Some, like the blue crab (pictured), have thin front claws, while mud, European edible and Dungeness crabs have large, meat-filled front claws. The meat will weigh about one-third of the crab's total body weight.

rock lobster

There are several varieties of lobster *(aragosta)* available: some are brown or red, others blue and some patterned in green or blue and white. Always buy live lobsters to be absolutely guaranteed of their freshness. Spiny or rock lobsters (pictured) are found in warmer waters and differ from other varieties in that they have no large front claws. They are, however, interchangeable in recipes.

octopus

Octopus *(polpo)* is very popular in Italy and can usually be bought cleaned from the fishmonger, although it is not hard to prepare at home. Baby octopus do not need to be tenderised but large octopus may have to be beaten with a mallet. Long boiling also tenderises octopus.

buying fish

Fish should look and smell fresh when you buy it. The eyes should be clear and shiny, not sunken, and the skin should be slippery and shiny. Fresh fish does not smell fishy.

storing

Fish can be kept for about 24 hours in the fridge (it will keep for longer but will not be in as good condition). Whole fish needs to be gutted before it is stored—fish with their guts deteriorate at a much faster rate. The gutted fish should be patted dry, put on a clean plate, covered with clingfilm and stored in the coldest part of the fridge.

gutting and trimming

After gutting the fish, rinse it well—leaving blood in the fish may taint the flesh and leave a bitter taste. For the same reason, snip out the gills. If the fins are looking ragged, trim them with scissors. For fish such as salmon, the tail is often mitred (cut into a 'V' shape) to neaten it.

filleting

You can ask the fishmonger to fillet the fish or do it yourself (you'll need a knife suitable for filleting with a sharp flexible blade). Round fish yield two fillets, one from each side of the fish. Flat fish give either two large or four fillets (two from each side). Depending on the size of the fish, you will need one or more fillets per person, or a piece of fillet if the fish is very large.

scaling and gutting

THE best way to remove scales is with a fish scaler. Hold the fish's tail and, lifting it slightly, scape against the direction of the scales. Alternatively, run the back of a knife firmly over the skin against the direction of the scales to scrape them off.

USING a pair of scissors, snip from the vent along to the gills, along the soft belly and remove the guts. Snip the gills out by pulling back the flap that covers them—this is easiest with a pair of scissors.

TRIM the end of the tail and trim off any side fins. Leave the dorsal fin (the fin at the top) as this is a useful gauge during cooking—it pulls out easily once the fish is cooked through.

filleting round fish

FIRST trim off all the fins then, using a filleting knife, cut through the flesh along the backbone and down the side of the head, hugging the knife close to the bone to avoid removing too much flesh.

LIFT the fillet by running your knife blade between the flesh and the bones, starting at the head and working along to the tail end. The fillet should lift off in one neat piece.

TURN the fish over and remove the other fillet in the same way. Reserve the bones and head for making stock. If you don't want to make stock that day, freeze them until needed.

filleting flat fish

LAY the fish dark skin side up. Trim around the outside of the fish, cutting off any fins. Cut around the base of the head, then down the centre of the spine.

SLIDE the knife under the flesh at the head end and, keeping the knife flat against the bone, slide it down towards the tail until the fillet comes off in one piece.

TURN the fish over and remove the other two fillets in the same way.

skinning

LAY the fillet skin side down on a chopping board with its tail towards you. Make a small cut through the flesh to the skin.

PUT the knife blade through the cut against the skin and slide or push the blade away from you. Hold onto the skin firmly.

CARRY on sliding the blade up to the head. You may need to move the blade from side to side as the fillet gets thicker.

butterflying

GUT small fish such as sardines through the belly and remove the head by snapping and pulling it off.

PULL the stomach apart gently and place the fish down on its opened stomach. Press your finger down on either side of the backbone to help loosen it.

TURN the fish the other way up and gently pull the backbone out through the belly. You may need to pinch it off at the tail end. Leaving the tail attached to the fillets make them look more attractive.

filleting small fish

FILLET the fish by running your thumbnail or a sharp knife along each side of the backbone through the skin.

PULL the head upwards. The head, bones and guts should all come away together.

YOU should now be left with the fillets loosely joined at the stomach.

skinning

Depending on the recipe, you may or may not need to skin your fish. If the fish will be covered with a sauce, it is easier to eat with its skin removed. Remove the skin before cooking, unless you are cooking the fish whole, in which case you can carefully peel it off afterwards. Dover sole can have their skins removed whole. To do this, make a small cut at the tail end and loosen a piece of skin, then hold the fish down with one hand and the skin in the other and firmly pull the skin towards the head—it should peel off in one piece.

is this fish cooked?

There are several ways to tell if a fish is cooked. You can pull gently on the dorsal fin—if the fish is cooked it will come out easily. You can press the flesh through the skin with your fingers—it will feel flaky under the surface when it is ready. Or you can look inside the belly of the fish to see if the flesh right next to the backbone is cooked.

fish stock

This can be made easily with the bones and heads of non-oily fish. Put the bones in a large pan with some onion, carrot, celery, peppercorns, parsley, a bay leaf and a sprig of thyme and cover with water. Bring to the boil and simmer for 20 minutes only. Strain and cool.

buying shellfish

Shellfish, particularly crabs, lobsters, oysters, clams and mussels, should be bought live whenever possible to guarantee freshness. Prawns are generally bought dead and many of them have previously been frozen. Choose fresh smelling shellfish that looks healthy.

storing

Shellfish, like fish, should be eaten quickly after buying. If, however, you need to store live shellfish, put it in a container, cover with a damp cloth and store in the vegetable crisper. Prawns should be patted dry and stored in a covered container. Squid should be cleaned and then frozen in portions (it is as good used frozen as from the fridge).

cleaning

Though shellfish bought from a reputable source will be clean, it is always best to remove any dark intestinal tracts from prawns, lobsters and scallops and the mouths from crabs and lobsters. Scrub any shells clean.

peeling and deveining prawns

PULL off the head and peel the shell from the body of the prawn, leaving it on the tail (this makes the prawn look more attractive).

DEVEIN the prawn by removing the dark digestive tract that runs along its back. Either pull it out from one end...

OR make a very shallow cut down the back of the prawn and lift it out. If you cut too deeply your prawns will 'butterfly' out as they cook.

cleaning squid

CLEAN the squid by first pulling off the skin and wings. Pull out the transparent vertebrae and tentacles and scoop out the insides.

YOU can use a spoon to scrape out any remaining innards to make sure the inside of the squid is clean, but take care when you do this that the body remains whole.

CUT the tentacles away from the rest of the innards at the front of the beak and eyes. Wash the inside of the squid and the tentacles, making sure any sand is removed, then leave to drain in a colander for a few minutes.

cleaning scallops

OPEN a scallop by holding it firmly in one hand in a thick cloth (to protect your hand) and sliding a knife between the shells. Slide the blade against the flatter shell to release the muscle on one side.

REMOVE the scallop from its shell by running a sharp knife between the scallop and shell. Pull off all the frilly bits around the scallop. Wash and reserve the shells.

PULL away the white muscle and digestive tract around the scallop, leaving the roe intact (or you can remove the roe if you prefer).

cleaning clams

CHECK to make sure all the clams are alive by tapping any open ones on the side of the sink. If they do not close, throw them away.

LEAVE them in cold salted (100 g salt per 4 litres water) water for 2-3 hours to expel any grit. Change the water if it starts to get dirty.

RINSE the clams and scrub any barnacles off the shells. Check again to see if any open ones are dead and need to be discarded before cooking.

cleaning mussels

CLEAN the mussels by first scrubbing the shells to remove any dirt. Pull the beards from between the shells.

IF any mussels are open after they have been cleaned, tap them on the side of the sink to see if they will close.

DISCARD any mussels that stay open— they are already dead and shouldn't be cooked.

soaking salt cod

SOAK the salt cod in cold water for 24-48 hours. The stiffer the salt cod, the longer you will need to soak it.

AFTER every 3 hours, drain the salt cod and add fresh water. Soaking is best done at room temperature but if it is hot you can put the cod in the fridge.

THE salt cod is ready when the fish has plumped up and the water is no longer very salty (test the water by dipping your finger in and tasting it).

is this shellfish cooked?

Generally the flesh of shellfish will turn opaque and firm up when it is cooked. Any double shells will open and prawns may curl up. Crab, lobster and prawn shells will turn red or pink.

crabs

Crabs are popular in Italy, especially in Venice where *moleca* or soft-shelled crabs have a season. Just after they shed their old hard shell they can be eaten whole, shell and all, usually dipped in flour and then deep-fried.

serving

Most shellfish, especially lobster and crabs, are best served at room temperature or warm. Chilled seafood has very little flavour as the cold masks it.

salted or dried fish

Salted or dried cod has a long history of use in Italy. It became a popular item for Catholics to eat on Fridays when meat was forbidden. While coastal communities had access to fresh fish, those inland made use of the preserved varieties. Now, salt cod and stockfish are part of the traditional culinary repertoire of Italy.

Marinated anchovies

SERVES 4 as a starter

INGREDIENTS

400 g fresh anchovies, filleted
 (see page 95)

4 tablespoons extra virgin olive oil

3 tablespoons lemon juice

2 garlic cloves, crushed

2 tablespoons finely chopped parsley

2 tablespoons finely chopped basil

1 small red chilli, seeded and
 chopped

Fresh anchovies are fished all around the Mediterranean, but Italy's best are considered to be those caught off the Gulf of Naples and in Salerno and Cefalu in Sicily. You will need very fresh anchovies for this dish. Serve with plenty of bread to mop up the juices.

buying

Buy the freshest anchovies you can find and use them immediately. Because anchovies are oily fish their flesh will deteriorate fairly rapidly, making it much harder to clean them without tearing.

CAREFULLY wash the fish under cold water and pat dry with paper towels. Place the fillets, skin side down, in a single layer in a shallow serving dish.

MIX the remaining ingredients together with some salt and pepper and pour evenly over the anchovies.

COVER the dish with clingfilm and leave the anchovies to marinate in the fridge for at least 3 hours.

BEFORE serving, bring the anchovies back to room temperature so they regain their full flavour. Serve with bread as a starter or part of an antipasto platter.

parsley

There are two main types of parsley (*prezzemolo*) used in Italian cooking. Flat-leaf, or Italian, parsley is used to add flavour to dishes, while curly parsley, with its tightly furled leaves, is relegated mainly to use as a garnish.

Sicilian-style stuffed sardines

The fish for this recipe need to be really fresh as sardines, like mackerel, do not last long out of the water. The sardines are butterflied and the fresher the fish, the harder this is to do, so you may want to ask your fishmonger to do it for you.

SERVES 4 as a starter

INGREDIENTS

8 sardines or large whitebait, butterflied (see page 95)

2 tablespoons extra virgin olive oil

1 small onion, thinly sliced

1 fennel bulb (about 300 g), thinly sliced

25 g pine nuts

2 tablespoons flat-leaf parsley, roughly chopped

10 g fresh breadcrumbs

1 garlic clove, chopped

2 tablespoons lemon juice

extra virgin olive oil

lemon wedges, to serve

RINSE the sardines in cold water, drain on paper towels and place in the fridge until needed. Preheat the oven to 200°C (400°F/Gas 6).

TO prepare the stuffing, pour the olive oil into a saucepan and add the onion, fennel and pine nuts. Cook over medium heat until soft and light brown, stirring frequently. Mix 1 tablespoon of the parsley with 1 tablespoon of the breadcrumbs and set aside.

ADD the garlic and remaining breadcrumbs to the fennel mixture and cook for a few minutes to lightly crisp the breadcrumbs. Add the remaining parsley, season and set aside. This mixture can be prepared in advance and left in the fridge, but bring back to room temperature before cooking.

DRIZZLE some olive oil in an ovenproof dish, large enough to fit four butterflied sardines in a single layer. Put four sardines in the dish, skin side down, season, then spread the stuffing over the sardines. Put the remaining four sardines on top, skin side up, positioning them tail to tail like a sandwich. Season again and sprinkle with the mixture of parsley and breadcrumbs. Drizzle with the lemon juice and a little olive oil.

PUT in the oven and cook for about 10 minutes, depending on the size of the sardines (if the filling is still warm, the sardines will take less time to cook). Serve either hot from the oven or at room temperature, with a wedge of lemon. Serve as a starter or part of an antipasto platter.

THIS dish looks best when the sardines are fitted neatly together, sandwiching the filling. Lay the bottom fillets in a dish that will fit them easily—don't try to squash them in. Spread the filling neatly over the sardines, then arrange the other sardines on top. Tidy up any loose bits of filling.

INGREDIENTS

650 g baby octopus, cleaned

1 garlic clove

2 tablespoons lemon juice

100 ml extra virgin olive oil

1 tablespoon chopped mint

1 tablespoon chopped parsley

1 teaspoon Dijon mustard

pinch of cayenne pepper

120 g misticanza (mixed salad leaves)

lemon wedges, to serve

Octopus salad

Baby octopus are a common sight in coastal southern Italy and can be either barbecued on skewers or made into salads, as here. They are small enough to have tender flesh and are delicious with a fresh tasting dressing.

IF the octopus seem seem particularly big (they should be in bite-sized portions) cut them into halves or quarters.

BRING a large saucepan of water to the boil and add the octopus. Simmer for about 8–10 minutes, or until tender.

LIGHTLY smash the garlic clove with the flat side of a knife. Make a dressing by mixing together the lemon juice, olive oil, mint, parsley, mustard and cayenne with some salt and pepper. Add the garlic and leave to infuse.

DRAIN the octopus well and put in a bowl. Pour the dressing over the top and allow to cool for a few minutes before transferring to the fridge. Chill for at least 3 hours, then arrange the octopus on a bed of misticanza. Bring to room temperature, remove the smashed garlic clove and drizzle a little of the dressing over the top. Serve with lemon wedges to squeeze over.

cooking

Octopus are only at their best when they are completely tender. If you have larger octopus, make sure you cut them into small pieces and cook until they are tender enough to be pierced with a fork.

Garlic prawns

Prawns in Italy vary in size from the tiny *gamberetti*, which can be eaten whole, to freshwater *gamberi di aqua dolce*. For this recipe, it is best to use the larger *gamberoni* with their good sweet flavour.

PUT the olive oil in a large frying pan and add the butter, chilli and garlic. Cook, stirring over low heat for about 3 minutes until the garlic and chilli are fragrant. Do not allow the garlic to brown or it will taste bitter. Add the prawns.

COOK the prawns for 3 minutes on one side. By this time they should have turned pink and started to brown a little. Turn the prawns, add the wine and cook for another 4 minutes or until the prawns are completely cooked through.

ADD the parsley, season well with salt and pepper and toss everything together. Serve with bread to mop up the garlic juices. This recipe can also be served cold as part of an antipasto platter.

SERVES 4

INGREDIENTS

60 ml olive oil

80 g butter

1 red chilli, finely chopped

6 garlic cloves, crushed

20 large prawns, peeled and
  deveined (see page 96)

60 ml white wine

3 tablespoons chopped parsley

Prawn, cannellini bean and mint salad

SERVES 4

This dish is best made with fresh cannellini or borlotti beans, but will also work with dried or tinned beans. The recipe can be served warm or cold, as a salad or part of an antipasto platter.

INGREDIENTS

250 g fresh cannellini beans, 200 g
   dried beans or 410 g tinned beans

4 garlic cloves

1 bay leaf

6 tablespoons extra virgin olive oil

1 small tomato

juice and zest of 1 large lemon

450 g prawns, peeled and deveined
   (see page 96)

½ large mild red chilli, finely
   chopped

4 tablespoons chopped mint

175 g rocket, or other salad leaf

DRIED beans contain hard-to-digest enzymes that have given them a reputation for being 'windy'. If you're worried about this, changing the soaking and precooking water several times and skimming off any foam will remove more of the enzymes.

IF using fresh beans, there is no need to soak and precook them. If using dried beans, soak them in cold water for at least 6 hours or overnight. Drain the beans, put them in a saucepan, cover with water and bring to the boil. Drain again, rinsing away any foam that has appeared on the surface of the water. If using tinned beans, simply rinse well and drain before mixing with the olive oil and lemon juice below.

TO cook the fresh or dried beans, cover with water and bring to the boil, then add 2 unpeeled garlic cloves, the bay leaf and 1 tablespoon of the olive oil (the oil softens the skin of the beans). Reduce the heat and simmer gently for about 20–30 minutes for fresh beans and about 40 minutes for dried, or until tender. Do not salt the beans during cooking as this will toughen the skins. Drain the beans, keeping the garlic.

REMOVE the skin from the tomato by removing the stem and scoring a cross in the bottom. Blanch in boiling water for 30 seconds. Transfer to cold water and peel the skin away from the cross (it should slip off easily).

REMOVE the skin from the two boiled garlic cloves and smash these and the tomatoes with the back of a fork (they will be soft enough to break up). While the beans are still hot, mix them with 3 tablespoons of the olive oil, half the lemon juice, the zest, the garlic and tomato and some salt and pepper. This can be prepared in advance and left in the fridge to infuse for a couple of hours.

FINELY chop the remaining 2 garlic cloves. Heat a large frying pan until very hot, then add the remaining olive oil and the prawns. Season with salt and pepper and cook until the prawns turn pink. Add the garlic, chilli, half the mint and the remaining lemon juice at the last moment of the cooking. Toss together briefly and remove from the heat.

JUST before serving, arrange the rocket leaves on a large platter or four individual plates. Gently warm up the beans (if they were prepared beforehand or if you are using tinned beans) and mix in the rest of the mint. Scatter the beans over the rocket and then arrange the prawns on top. Drizzle over any juices that may have collected.

Salt cod fritters

Cod from northern Europe was traditionally preserved in salt for consumption inland. Its popularity in Mediterranean countries is a legacy of meatless days observed by the Catholic church. In some parts of Italy where it is very popular, salt cod is often sold presoaked, ready for use.

MAKES 16

INGREDIENTS

400 g potatoes, cut into pieces

1 onion, sliced

4 garlic cloves, sliced

1 bay leaf

800 ml milk

200 ml dry white vermouth or
   white wine

450 g salt cod, soaked

4 tablespoons flat-leaf parsley,
   roughly chopped

pinch of ground nutmeg

2 egg yolks

2 tablespoons plain flour, plus a
   little extra for dusting

oil, for frying

lemon wedges, to serve

COOK the potatoes in simmering water for 15-20 minutes or until tender. Drain and mash them, then set aside to cool.

PUT the onion, garlic, bay leaf, milk and vermouth in a saucepan, season with pepper and bring to the boil. Add the salt cod, reduce the heat and simmer, covered, for about 10–15 minutes or until the fish is cooked and flakes away from the skin. Leave in the liquid until cool enough to handle.

PLACE the fish on a board and separate the meat from the skin and bones (you should have about 300 g). Put the flaked fish in a bowl and add the potatoes, parsley, nutmeg, egg yolks, flour and a little pepper. Mix all the ingredients together and taste for seasoning—you should not need to add any salt. Put the mixture in the fridge for 15 minutes and then roll into 16 small balls and flatten each one slightly.

HEAT the oil in a frying pan. Dust the fritters with a little flour and fry them in batches for about 2 minutes on each side. Drain on paper towels and serve warm with lemon wedges.

cooking

Some salt cod can be very salty and hard and might need more changes of water. Taste the soaking water if you want to know if salt is still coming out of the fish.

salt cod

Salt cod *(baccalà)* originally came from Norway. It is thought to have entered the Italian diet as an alternative to fresh fish on Fridays— particularly useful if you lived in the middle of the country, far from the coast. For best results, buy thick steaks of salted cod that are creamy white in colour and not too blanched or yellow. Avoid the tail ends as these have little meat.

Veneto

Best known for its capital, Venice, the Veneto is also home to the well-known cities of Padua and Verona. Venice itself has a special food history: for a long time it was the centre of the world spice trade with produce from the East such as nuts, dried fruit and exotic flavourings passing through the port and traders bringing a multitude of different culinary styles to the city. Sweet-and-sour fish, pasta sauces spiked with nutmeg and cinnamon, and pastries perfumed with rosewater all have their roots in the cooking of the Orient. Outside the capital, the food of the Veneto is fairly simple. The area around Venice provides radicchio and chicory from Treviso, asparagus from Bassano and cherries and peaches from Verona. While pasta and rice are both enjoyed, pale yellow polenta is the traditional staple, often served with seafood rather than meat.

Regional specialities include risi e bisi, a Venetian version of risotto that is usually liquid enough to eat with a spoon, pasta e fagioli and *bigoli*, thick noodles from Venice. Tiramisu originated in Treviso. *Baccalà* is popular and meat and offal are eaten in greater quantity than many other regions, with Venetian liver another popular dish. Cheeses include two varieties of Asiago from Vicenza and local toma from the mountain regions in the North. Antipasto in the Veneto means fish and seafood, cooked and simply dressed with lemon or dipped in batter and deep-fried. The coast yields the Venetian speciality *moleche*, a soft-shelled crab—this is marinated in egg and Parmesan, breadcrumbed and fried to be eaten whole. For those with a sweet tooth, Venice is also a city of ice cream with hundreds of different flavours to choose from.

Wines of the Veneto

The Veneto is an intensive wine-producing region and bottles some of the best in Italy. It has seventeen wines that have been awarded the stringent and prestigious DOC *(Denominazione di Origine Controllata)* rating, which guarantees authenticity and certain minimum standards of quality. Bardolino, Valpolicella and Soave all come from here as does the sparkling wine Prosecco.

Amarone, a very strong red, is produced in Verona by the passito method—the grapes are dried slightly and allowed to turn mouldy before being crushed to produce a rich juice with concentrated sugars and tannin. Amarone uses three grape varieties and each one is said to be affected in a different way by the 'noble rot'.

Sfogie in saor

This 'sweet and sour' sole is traditionally eaten during Venice's Feast of the Holy Redeemer. Sole is most commonly used but the recipe also works well with a mixture of red fish fillets. If you can, prepare it a day in advance to give the flavours time to infuse.

cooking

Choose the vinegar and wine according to which fish you're using. If you're making the recipe with sole, try white wine and white wine vinegar. If you're using red fish such as mullet, you could use red wine and vinegar.

PUT the saffron in a bowl with the vinegar and leave to soak. Meanwhile, put half the olive oil in a saucepan and gently cook the onion and garlic until softened, being careful that the garlic does not burn.

PUT the coriander and peppercorns in a mortar and pestle and lightly crush them. If you don't have a mortar and pestle, use the base of a rolling pin. Alternatively, the spices can be added whole, but crushing does help to release their flavour and aroma.

ADD the crushed spices to the saucepan with the cinnamon and allspice (if using). Mix briefly to lightly toast the spices, then add the saffron, vinegar, wine and sugar. Bring to the boil and gently simmer for a couple of minutes. Set aside and add the oregano.

SCATTER the flour over a large plate, season with salt and pepper and mix briefly. Make sure the fish fillets are dry by pressing them between two sheets of paper towel, then dust the fish in the flour and pat lightly to remove any large clumps of flour.

HEAT a large frying pan with the remaining olive oil, then fry the fish on both sides until golden brown and cooked through.

USE a gratin dish large enough to snugly fit the fish in a single layer and pour half the vinegar mixture into the dish. Add the fish and then the remaining liquid. Leave to marinate for at least 1 hour before serving.

SERVE as a starter, for lunch or as part of an antipasto platter.

SERVES 4 as a starter

INGREDIENTS

pinch of saffron strands

90 ml white or red wine vinegar

200 ml extra virgin olive oil

1 red onion, thinly sliced

2 garlic cloves, sliced

1 teaspoon coriander seeds

1 teaspoon black peppercorns

1 small cinnamon stick, roughly broken

1 small teaspoon ground allspice (optional)

90 ml white or red wine

3 teaspoons sugar

2 tablespoons oregano leaves

2 tablespoons plain flour

4 x 100 g sole fillets

Baked whole fish with fennel

SERVES 4

INGREDIENTS

2 heads of fennel

4 tablespoons extra virgin olive oil

1 onion, chopped

1 garlic clove, crushed

1 whole fish, such as sea bass or
  sea bream, gutted and scaled
  (see page 94)

1 lemon, quartered

2 teaspoons chopped oregano, or
  ½ teaspoon dried oregano

lemon wedges, to serve

This is a good recipe to make for a dinner or lunch party. It is fairly easy to prepare and looks very impressive when served. The combination of fennel and oregano works well with most fish, so you could try something like salmon instead of the bass or bream.

PREHEAT the oven to 190°C (375°F/Gas 5) and grease a large shallow ovenproof dish. Finely slice the fennel, keeping the green fronds to use later.

HEAT the olive oil in a large frying pan and gently cook the fennel, onion and garlic for 12–15 minutes until softened but not browned. Season with salt and pepper.

STUFF the fish with a heaped tablespoon of the fennel mixture and a quarter of the fennel fronds. Brush the skin with a little more extra virgin olive oil, squeeze the lemon over and season well.

SPOON the remainder of the cooked fennel into the dish and sprinkle with half of the oregano. Arrange the fish on top. Sprinkle the remaining oregano over the fish and cover the dish loosely with foil (if you cover it tightly, the fish will steam). Bake for 25 minutes, or until just cooked through—the flesh should feel flaky and the dorsal fin will pull out easily. Serve with lemon wedges.

TO test whether fish is cooked, you can use one of three methods. Press the skin to see if the flesh feels flaky underneath (you may find it helpful to press the skin beforehand so you know what it feels like uncooked). Or, pull the dorsal fin—it should pull out easily when the fish is cooked. Or, check if the flesh next to the backbone is cooked.

Tuna involtini

Involtini are thin sheets of fish or meat, stuffed with vegetables and herbs and then either roasted or pan-fried. In northern Italy veal is generally used but, in Sicily, they use the meaty tuna or swordfish and make a more sweet and sour filling, an influence of the Arabs.

PREHEAT the oven to 200°C (400°F/Gas 6) and heat up the baking dish you are going to use.

USING a mallet or rolling pin, beat out the tuna steaks between two sheets of greaseproof paper until about 0.5 cm thick. Try to keep the tuna shape as even as possible. Place in the fridge until ready to use.

HEAT 4 tablespoons of the olive oil in a frying pan and cook the onion until soft and translucent. Add the spinach and stir until it is just wilted. (If using large-leaf spinach, remove the large stems and roughly chop before adding.) Stir in the olives, pine nuts and basil. Season.

PLACE the tuna steaks on a work surface. Remove the top layer of greaseproof paper. Divide the filling among the tuna steaks and roll them up, tucking the stuffing inside. Peel off the bottom sheet of greaseproof as you roll. Roll the tuna in the breadcrumbs.

DRIZZLE 1 tablespoon of olive oil into the hot baking dish and put the tuna seam side down in the dish. Drizzle the rest of the olive oil on top and bake in the oven for about 5 minutes, or until the centres of the rolls are hot (test with a skewer). Remove from the oven and serve either hot or cold with a squeeze of lemon juice on top.

SERVES 4

INGREDIENTS

4 x 150 g tuna steaks

6 tablespoons extra virgin olive oil

1 large onion, quartered and finely sliced

200 g small leaf spinach

100 g olives, pitted and chopped

50 g pine nuts, lightly browned

1 small bunch basil, torn

4 tablespoons dried breadcrumbs

lemon wedges, to serve

THIN out the tuna steaks by putting them between two sheets of greaseproof paper and beating them evenly all over with the side of a rolling pin or a mallet (do not use a studded meat mallet or you will tear the flesh).

THE bottom piece of greaseproof paper will help you to roll the involtini—just make sure that you don't roll the paper into the roll. The paper also helps to keep the shape neater.

Stuffed squid

Calamari ripieni can be served either hot or at room temperature. Very small tender squid are best for this recipe—you can use larger squid, but you may need to increase the cooking time and take care that the liquid does not evaporate.

INGREDIENTS

TOMATO SAUCE

2 tablespoons extra virgin olive oil

1 garlic clove, thinly sliced

800 g tin chopped tomatoes

100 ml red wine

2 tablespoons chopped flat-leaf parsley

8 squid (about 600 g), cleaned (see page 96)

STUFFING

100 ml olive oil

1 small onion, finely chopped

1 small head of fennel, finely chopped

2 garlic cloves, chopped

75 g arborio rice

large pinch of saffron strands

1/2 large red chilli, chopped

150 ml white wine

3 tablespoons chopped flat-leaf parsley

STUFF the squid carefully and gently. If you force the filling in, the tubes may tear or burst. Don't fill right up to the tops—you need to be able to seal them easily with cocktail sticks. It is also important to leave a little room for the filling to expand or it may burst out of the tube when cooking.

TO make the sauce, put the olive oil and garlic in a saucepan and fry gently for 1 minute. Add the tomatoes and simmer until some of the liquid has evaporated and the sauce is quite thick. Add the wine and parsley and cook the sauce until it has reduced and thickened. Set aside.

FINELY chop the squid tentacles and set aside with the bodies (put them in the fridge if the kitchen is hot).

TO make the stuffing, heat the oil in a large saucepan and gently cook the onion, fennel and garlic for about 10 minutes or until soft. Add the rice, saffron, chilli and chopped squid tentacles and cook for a few minutes, stirring frequently until the tentacles are opaque. Season, then add the wine and 6 tablespoons of the tomato sauce.

COOK, stirring frequently, until the tomato and wine has reduced into the rice. Cook for about 5 minutes or until the liquid has reduced, then add 125 ml water and continue cooking until the rice is tender and all the liquid has been absorbed. You may need to add a little more water if the rice absorbs all the liquid and is not quite tender. Add 2 tablespoons parsley and set aside to cool for a few minutes.

STUFF the squid with the filling, using a teaspoon to push it down into the bottom of the tubes. Do not overfill the tubes—you need to be able to close them easily without any filling squeezing out. Seal the tops with cocktail sticks.

PUT the remaining tomato sauce in a saucepan with 200 ml water. Cook for 2 minutes, then add the stuffed squid. Cover the saucepan and simmer gently for about 30–45 minutes or until the squid are soft and tender—the cooking time will depend on the size of the squid so test it and give it a little more time if you need to. Don't stir the squid too much when cooking or the filling will fall out (if a little does fall out it will just add flavour to the sauce). Shake the pan a little if you are worried about the squid sticking to the bottom.

REMOVE the cocktail sticks and sprinkle with the remaining parsley just before serving.

Whole fish cooked in salt water

SERVES 4

INGREDIENTS

1 small bunch of seaweed (or dried
   seaweed, soaked until pliable)

4–8 tablespoons sea salt

1 kg whole fish such as sea bass
   or sea bream, scaled, gutted and
   trimmed (see page 94)

1 small onion, roughly chopped

1 small carrot, roughly chopped

6 black peppercorns

1 small bunch herbs, such as parsley,
   oregano and basil, or a mixture of
   all three

1 lemon or 4 tablespoons white wine
   or vinegar

rocket leaves and lemon wedges,
   to serve

SAFFRON AIOLI

pinch of saffron strands

4 egg yolks

2 garlic cloves, crushed

1 tablespoon lemon juice

400 ml extra virgin olive oil

In Italy, this dish is often cooked with sea bass, a fish with delicate but firm white flesh. The smaller fish are usually grilled, with the larger ones being baked or poached. Seaweed is usually available fresh from fishmongers, or dried from the Japanese section of the supermarket.

PUT the seaweed on the base of a fish poacher or large saucepan. (If using dried seaweed, soak it first to reconstitute it.) Taste a bit of your seaweed to see how salty it is—if it is very salty then use the lesser amount of salt specified.

PLACE the fish on top. Add enough water to cover the fish entirely and add the salt, onion, carrot, peppercorns and herbs. Squeeze the juice from the lemon and add to the pan, then cut the lemon into quarters and add that, or the wine or vinegar.

BRING the water to a gentle simmer, cover and poach the fish for 10–15 minutes until just cooked (press the flesh to see if it feels flaky or pull the dorsal fin, which will come out easily when the fish is ready). Leave in the water for 10 minutes or cool completely and serve at room temperature.

TO make the aïoli, soak the saffron in 1 tablespoon hot water. Put the egg yolks, garlic and lemon juice in a mortar and pestle or food processor and pound or mix them together. Add the oil, drop by drop, mixing until thick and creamy. Add the saffron and taste for salt.

REMOVE the fish from the water, briefly drain on a tea towel and serve on the rocket with the aïoli and lemon wedges.

DRIED seaweed needs to be reconstituted in cold water until it is pliable. If you are using fresh seaweed, make sure you rinse it well.

MAKE sure that the poaching water is at a very gentle simmer. Don't overcook the fish or it will be dry and fibrous. The best way to check if it is cooked is to pull gently on the dorsal fin: if it comes out easily the fish is ready.

salt

Salt *(sale)* as an ingredient is not as simple as it seems. Sea salt is produced by evaporating sea water to form large, often flaky, crystals. Sea salts are often expensive and considered a gourmet food. Maldon salt (from England), Guérande and Ile de Ré (from France) and salt from Trapani in Sicily are all well known. Sea salt has a better flavour than table salt and will enhance a recipe. Rock salt that is mined from natural deposits is unrefined with large crystals and is used for grinding. Table salt is usually produced by evaporating salt water under vacuum pressure to produce a fine grain. Iodised salt is table salt with added iodine.

vermouth

Vermouth, either Martini or Cinzano, is widely used in Italian cooking. Like wine, it adds depth of flavour. Make sure you use dry vermouths for cooking—the sweet ones will be too sugary.

Ligurian fish stew

The fish suggestions given are intended only as a guideline—better to choose something fresh and seasonal, rather than worrying about following the recipe exactly. You can ask your fishmonger to prepare the fish for you but ask to keep the bones to make the stock.

CUT all the fish fillets into chunks. To make the fish stock, rinse the fish bones in lots of cold water, removing any blood or intestines. Put the prawn shells and fish bones in a large saucepan, cover with water and slowly bring to a simmer. Skim the top of the stock with a spoon or ladle to remove any froth that forms. Add the onion, carrot and parsley stalks, then simmer gently for about 30 minutes. Fish stock does not need to be boiled any longer than this or it can become a little bitter.

STRAIN the stock through a fine colander and measure out 1 litre. If there is more stock than this, strain it back into the saucepan and simmer until reduced to 1 litre. Set aside. If preferred, the stock can be prepared in advance and frozen or stored in the fridge for a couple of days until needed.

PUT the saffron in a bowl with 200 ml of the vermouth or wine and leave to soak. Cook the red onion and fennel in the olive oil for about 5 minutes to soften the onion. Add the garlic and the tomatoes. Bring to the boil and simmer gently until the sauce has reduced and thickened. Season with salt and pepper and add the saffron, vermouth and potatoes. Increase the heat and boil for 5 minutes, then add the fish stock, reduce the heat and simmer for 10 minutes, or until the potatoes are cooked. The base of the soup can be prepared in advance up to this point.

BRING the remaining 100 ml vermouth to the boil in another saucepan and add the mussels. Cover and cook quickly for about 1 minute, or until the shells have just opened. Pick through the mussels, discarding any that haven't opened. Remove the mussels from their shells and put in a bowl. Pour over the cooking liquid, discarding any sediment left in the bottom of the saucepan.

BRING the soup base to the boil and add the prawns and fish. Stir briefly, season with salt and pepper and simmer for about 5 minutes, keeping the heat low so the fish does not fall apart. Stir in the mussels with their cooking liquid towards the end to reheat them. Remove from the heat and rest for 10 minutes to allow the flavours to develop. Add the parsley and serve in hot bowls topped with crostini.

COOK the fish stock at a bare simmer—boiling will make it cloudy. Skim off any froth that forms on the surface and don't cook the stock for longer than 30 minutes or it can become bitter.

SERVES 8

INGREDIENTS

250 g red mullet or red snapper fillet, bones reserved (see page 94)

250 g cod, halibut or turbot fillet, bones reserved (see page 94)

250 g monkfish fillet or any other firm-fleshed white fish, bones reserved (see page 94)

6 large prawns, peeled, shells reserved

1 small onion, chopped

1 carrot, chopped

15 g flat-leaf parsley, roughly chopped, stalks reserved

large pinch of saffron strands

300 ml dry white vermouth or wine

1 red onion, halved and thinly sliced

1 large head of fennel, thinly sliced

6 tablespoons extra virgin olive oil

3 garlic cloves, thinly sliced

800 g tin chopped tomatoes

450 g waxy potatoes, quartered lengthways

450 g mussels, cleaned (see page 97)

crostini, to serve (see page 18)

Grilled swordfish with anchovy and caper sauce

SERVES 4

Swordfish is found in abundance off the coastlines of Calabria and Sicily. Catania, on Sicily's east coast, has a wonderful fish market where swordfish and tuna are sold regularly. Either can be used for this versatile recipe, and any other firm-fleshed fish would be a good substitute.

INGREDIENTS

SAUCE

1 large garlic clove

1 tablespoon capers, rinsed and
  finely chopped

50 g anchovy fillets, finely chopped

1 tablespoon finely chopped
  rosemary or dried oregano

finely grated zest and juice of
  ½ lemon

4 tablespoons extra virgin olive oil

1 large tomato, finely chopped

4 swordfish steaks

1 tablespoon extra virgin olive oil

bruschetta, to serve (see page 19)

PUT the garlic in a mortar and pestle with a little salt and crush it, or crush it with some salt on a chopping board using the flat of your knife blade. To make the sauce, mix together the garlic, capers, anchovies, rosemary or oregano, lemon zest and juice, oil and tomato. Leave for 10 minutes.

PREHEAT a griddle or grill to very hot. Using paper towels, pat the swordfish dry and lightly brush with the olive oil. Season with salt and pepper. Sear the swordfish over high heat for about 2 minutes on each side (depending on the thickness of the steaks) or until just cooked. The best way to check if the fish is cooked is to pull apart the centre of one steak—the flesh should be opaque. (Serve with the cut side underneath.)

IF the cooked swordfish is a little oily, drain it on paper towels, then place on serving plates and drizzle with the sauce. Serve with bruschetta to mop up the sauce.

MAKE sure the griddle or grill is really hot or your fish will take too long to cook. The griddle will also make much better sear marks if it is very hot. Check the fish is cooked by gently pulling apart the centre of one steak.

Calabria

Calabria is set in the toe of Italy's boot shape. It has a relatively recently developed coastline as historically its people preferred to live inland, in the hills away from the marshes, mosquitoes and invaders of the coast. The grapes and olives that grow in the hills give way to groves of fruit trees, particularly citrons, lemons and oranges, and then figs and almonds on the flatter coastal plains. Southern Italian cuisine is still heavily influenced by the Arabs and Greeks who once occupied the region and Calabria, with its long coastline, has a history of invasion. The Romans, Greeks, Goths, Byzantines, Saracens, Jewish traders, French, Spanish and Austrians all passed this way, adding their own ideas to Calabrian cuisine but also producing a necessary local repertoire of dishes created under siege.

Dried pasta is the staple here, made with durum wheat and water rather than egg and usually dressed with vegetable sauces. Vegetables are also stuffed and baked and this is the home of the aubergine, so recipes abound. Meat is eaten inland and fish by the coast, with swordfish, tuna, anchovies and sardines all plentiful. Cheeses include mozzarella, scamorza, provolone and caciocavallo and the locally made goats cheeses are also popular. Chilli peppers (peperoncini) are a favourite flavouring and used to spike everything from salami to pasta sauces, so it is no surprise that dishes described as Calabrese are usually hot.

Wines from Calabria include Cirò, the oldest wine in Italy, which is available in both red and white. The white variety is Calabria's best and most reliable wine.

Citron

A very large citrus fruit, citron is grown mainly for its thick warty peel which is candied. In the seventeenth and eighteenth centuries, the juice was made into a soft drink called *acquacedrata* which is no longer produced. Citron peel has a stronger, more resinous flavour than lemon peel and is widely used in the desserts and baking of southern Italy.

pollame

chicken

In Italy chickens *(pollo)* are usually maize fed and so have yellow skin. They are also often free range and therefore tend to be quite lean. Chickens are versatile birds and can be roasted whole, boned and stuffed, jointed or spatchcocked. They can be grilled, roasted, poached or stewed. The bones are also essential for making stock for soups or risottos.

duck

Duck *(anastra)* is a rich and very fatty bird that was, and sometimes still is, seen as a delicacy. This makes it less common in traditional Italian cuisine, though its popularity is increasing. The bird can be roasted whole, but is often jointed as the breasts need short cooking times and can be served pink, whereas the legs contain a lot of sinew and are best slow cooked. Duck is often combined in recipes with fruit such as cherries or spices like juniper.

turkey

Turkey *(tacchino)* was first introduced to Italy from the Americas along with corn. The bird's size and capacity to feed large groups cheaply was its main attraction. Turkeys are usually roasted whole or the breast is served as scaloppine. As the Italians do not tend to rear their birds quite as large as the Americans and English, they can be cooked in similar ways to chicken.

goose

The largest birds eaten whole, geese *(oca)* are raised on farms. They have fatty flesh and need to be cooked through to render this to fat. Geese are often roasted whole at Christmas like turkeys, but the stuffing should be cooked outside the bird because of the high fat content running into the stuffing. Goose is often combined with acidic flavours such as orange or cherry to cut through the fat.

jointing poultry

LAY the bird on a board with the cavity end facing you. Pull both legs away from the carcass and twist the thigh bones out of their body sockets.

USING a knife, cut through the flesh to remove the leg. Keep the small piece of meat, known as an oyster, that is found at the back of the body attached to the leg meat.

CUT between the drumstick and the thigh along the natural fat line, which is visible on the underside of the thigh. Your knife should slide easily through the joint.

CUT down either side of the backbone and lift it out. This is easier to do with a pair of poultry shears.

TURN the bird over, remove the wishbone and cut down the centre of the breastbone. Using poultry shears makes it easier to cut through the cartilage.

CUT through each piece of breast at an angle so it makes two equal pieces. Leave the wing attached to one piece and trim off the wing tips and any straggly pieces of skin.

spatchcocking poultry

SPLIT the bird by cutting down each side of the backbone with a sharp knife or pair of poultry shears. Discard the backbone.

PUT the bird cut side down on your chopping board and press firmly down on the rib cage, squashing it out flat.

YOU should end up with a bird that is flattened out. Trim off the wing tips and any excess fat or skin.

boning poultry

PULL the flap of skin from the neck down around the shoulder to expose the wishbone and the joint where the wing bone joins the shoulder. Carefully cut around the wishbone and snap it out.

TURN the bird over. Cut through the joints between the wings and backbone but leave the wing bones in.

REMOVE the shoulder bones by scraping away any flesh and cutting through the cartilage that joins them to the breastbone. Pull on the shoulder bones: they are attached together but both ends should now be loose.

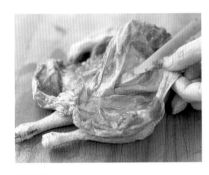

ONCE the shoulder bones are out, use your knife to scrape down the bones of the carcass, making sure the flesh comes away in one piece. Angle the blade of the knife towards the bones so it doesn't slip and cut through the flesh.

WHEN you reach the legs, pull the thigh bones out of their sockets. Leave the bones in the legs to give them more definition when they are cooked.

CARRY on scraping down the carcass until you reach the bottom. Now sever the cartilage at the bottom of the breastbone on one side and cut through the bottom vertebrae on the other. You should now be able to lift out the carcass.

making stock

PUT 2 kg chicken bones, trimmings, wings and necks in a large saucepan with 2 chopped carrots, 1 halved onion, 1 chopped leek, 1 chopped celery stalk, a bouquet garni and 6 peppercorns. Add 4 litres of cold water.

BRING to the boil and skim off any froth. Simmer the stock for 2 hours, skimming at regular intervals (adding a splash of cold water will precipitate any scum).

STRAIN the stock and leave to cool in the fridge. When it's completely cold, you can lift off the layer of fat from the top.

pigeon

Pigeons *(pigeone)* are one of the many game birds found in Italy, particularly in forest areas in the autumn when the shooting season is at its peak. These small birds need a brief cooking time to keep them succulent. The simplest method is to roast them whole, but they also work well in casseroles and stews with autumn flavours such as mushrooms, new season's wine or autumn fruit to flatter their rather gamey flavour.

quail

Quail *(quaglia)* are small game birds that are both hunted and farmed in Italy. They have a more delicate flavour than pigeon and can be grilled, roasted or cooked in stews and casseroles. Serve one per person.

guinea fowl

Guinea fowl *(faraona)* have a flavour somewhere between that of chicken and pheasant. They are usually farmed and are widely available. Like other game birds, they roast well and are good in casseroles or stews that keep the flesh moist. They can be used instead of chicken in most dishes.

pheasant

Pheasant *(fagiano)* was introduced to Italy as a game bird from Asia in the Middle Ages and has become firmly established in areas like Tuscany and Umbria. Pheasants are now both hunted and farmed and are usually either roasted whole or used in stews and casseroles. The birds are usually only hung for a short while, so the meat is only slightly gamey. If you use wild birds that have been hunted, make sure all the lead shot has been removed before cooking.

Pollo alla diavola

Meaning 'devil's-style chicken', this classic Tuscan dish was traditionally cooked on a grill over an open fire—the flames licking up from below were thought to be reminiscent of the fires of hell.

INGREDIENTS

- 2 x 900 g chickens, spatchcocked (see page 120)
- 150 ml olive oil
- juice of 1 large lemon
- 2 sage leaves
- 3–4 very small red chillies, finely minced, or 1 teaspoon dried chilli flakes
- ½ white onion
- 2 garlic cloves
- 4 tablespoons chopped flat-leaf parsley
- 2½ tablespoons softened butter
- lemon slices, to serve

PLACE the chickens side by side in a shallow dish.

MIX together the olive oil, lemon juice, sage and chilli and season well with salt and pepper. Pour over the chicken, cover and leave to marinate in the fridge for 1 hour, turning once.

WHILE the chicken is marinating, chop the onion, garlic, parsley and butter in a blender or food processor until the ingredients are fine and paste-like. (If you want to do this by hand, chop the vegetables and herbs finely and then mix them into the softened butter.) Season with salt and pepper. Preheat the grill to its highest setting.

PLACE the chickens skin side down on a grill tray. Position the tray about 10 cm below the heat and grill the chickens for 10 minutes, basting with the marinade once or twice. Turn the chickens and grill, basting occasionally, for another 10–12 minutes, or until the juices run clear when a thigh is pierced to the bone with a skewer.

SPREAD the butter paste over the skin of the chickens. Reduce the heat and grill for about 3 minutes until the coating is lightly browned. Serve hot with the butter from the grill pan poured over the chickens, or cold without the extra butter, accompanied by lemon slices.

COOKING chicken thoroughly can be particularly difficult when grilling, as the parts closest to the grill can start to blacken before the rest is cooked. Check the bird is cooked through by piercing the thickest part of the thigh with a skewer—the juices should run clear.

butter

Butter *(burro)* is not as widely used in Italian cooking as oil. It is more common in the north of the country, in the dairy-producing areas, and is used in baked goods. Generally it is unsalted and often has a very pale colour and a taste more similar to lard than conventional butter.

Quails wrapped in vine leaves

In Italy, quails are often covered with a slice of pancetta and roasted over a spit. The fat in the pancetta keeps the meat from drying out as it cooks. In this recipe, the quails are wrapped in vine leaves and roasted in the oven—the vine leaves give flavour as well as keep the meat moist.

SERVES 4

INGREDIENTS

4 rosemary sprigs

4 quails

2 tablespoons olive oil

4 teaspoons balsamic vinegar

2 teaspoons brown sugar

4 large vine leaves, fresh
  or preserved

PREHEAT the oven to 180°C (350°F/Gas 4). Stuff a sprig of rosemary into each quail and then tie its legs together. Tuck the wings behind its back.

HEAT the olive oil in a frying pan and add the quails. Brown them all over and then add the balsamic vinegar and brown sugar and bubble everything together, coating the quail well. Remove from the heat.

BLANCH the vine leaves in boiling water for 15 seconds and then drain and pat dry with kitchen towels. Wrap one vine leaf around each quail, making sure the seam is at the back of the quail. Put the quail in a roasting tin, seam side down, and cook for 15 minutes.

CHECK the quails are cooked by piercing the thickest part of the thigh with a skewer—the juices should run clear.

IF you are using fresh vine leaves, you will have to blanch them in boiling water in order to make them supple enough to wrap around the quail.

WRAP the quails carefully—you want them to look as neat as possible after they have been cooked. Keep the seam, where the sides of the vine leaves meet, at the back of the quail.

vine leaves

The leaves from grape vines can be used as a wrapping for food while it cooks. Fresh vine leaves need to be blanched in boiling water first but preserved vine leaves (bought in jars or pouches in brine) can be used without preparation.

Basilicata

Basilicata (or Lucania) is one of Italy's poorest regions, a largely inland state with short stretches of coastline on the Ionian and Tyrrhenian Seas. It is a mountainous region, whose winters rival those of the Alto Adige for chill, and has relatively few inhabitants. Much of the land is parched and inhospitable but, like the rest of the south, it has a rich and varied *cucina povera* based on local ingredients.

Vegetables are widely grown with tomatoes, peppers, beans and artichokes being favourites. A local wild onion is used in stews or to make onion marmalade. Mushrooms grow in the hills and are added to stews. Cheeses are soft, for example mozzarella and burrata, and made with cow's milk. Historically, chicken or rabbit would be eaten for Christmas, Easter, at weddings and on feast days.

Basilicata's most famous food is *lucanica*, a type of spiced sausage that is served as an antipasto as well as being used as an ingredient. As in other poor areas, the locals are adept in using the pig in all its guises, from salami to sausages, and eking out the meat for as long as possible. However it is served though, the pig would always be flavoured with *diavlicchio*, the region's red hot chillies, even down to the lard which would be flavoured and stored in jars to spread on bread. Pasta, which is dry, takes the form of *lagne*, a type of broad flat noodle tossed with tomato sauce, or pasta squares flavoured with chilli.

The local wine, Aglianico del Vulture, is made from vines derived from those planted by the Greeks in the sixth century BC and is considered one of Italy's best reds.

Tinned peeled tomatoes have been used in Italy since the end of the eighteenth century. The best brand for tinning are San Marzano plum tomatoes and it is these that are sold worldwide as Italian tinned tomatoes. It is perfectly acceptable to use tinned tomatoes for recipes such as sauces— they are of uniform ripeness and are already peeled for ease of preparation. You may need to add a pinch of sugar to counteract their acidity.

Chicken cacciatora

Just like the French *chasseur, alla cacciatora* means 'hunter style'. The dish is originally from central Italy but, like so much Italian fare, every region has put its own twist on the recipe. This version, made with tomatoes, is probably the most well known.

HEAT half the oil in a large casserole. Add the onion, garlic, celery and pancetta and cook, stirring occasionally, over low heat for 6–8 minutes, or until the onion is soft and golden.

ADD the mushrooms, increase the heat and cook, stirring occasionally, for 4–5 minutes. Spoon out onto a plate and set aside.

ADD the remaining olive oil to the casserole and lightly brown the chicken pieces, a few at a time. Season them as they brown. Spoon off any excess fat and return all the pieces to the casserole. Add the vermouth or wine, increase the heat and cook until the liquid has almost evaporated.

STIR in the tomatoes, sugar, oregano, rosemary, bay leaf and 75 ml cold water. Bring everything to the boil, then stir in the reserved pancetta mixture. Cover, turn down the heat and leave to simmer for 30 minutes, or until the chicken is tender but not falling off the bone.

IF the liquid is too thin, remove the chicken from the casserole, increase the heat and boil until the sauce has thickened. Discard the sprigs of herbs and taste for seasoning. Return the chicken to the casserole and add the additional oregano sprigs before serving.

SERVES 4

INGREDIENTS

3 tablespoons olive oil

1 large onion, finely chopped

3 garlic cloves, crushed

1 celery stalk, finely chopped

150 g pancetta, finely chopped

125 g button mushrooms, thickly sliced

4 chicken drumsticks

4 chicken thighs

90 ml dry vermouth or dry white wine

800 g tin chopped tomatoes

1/4 teaspoon sugar

1 oregano sprig, plus 4–5 sprigs, to garnish

1 rosemary sprig

1 bay leaf

Stuffed guinea fowl

The flavour of guinea fowl is similar to that of chicken but slightly stronger. In Tuscany, guinea fowl are often roasted, in Lombardy, they are wrapped in clay and cooked in the oven, while in Veneto they are usually stuffed (as here) and cooked in an earthenware pot.

SERVES 4

INGREDIENTS

100 g dried borlotti beans or 400 g
  tinned

4 garlic cloves

1 bay leaf

4 tablespoons olive oil

25 g dried porcini

75 g green lentils

1 small onion, finely chopped

100 g pancetta or smoked bacon,
  diced

100 g almonds or pistachio nuts,
  chopped

1 sage sprig, chopped

1 x 1.5 kg guinea fowl or 2 x 800 g
  guinea fowl, boned, leaving the
  wings and lower legs intact (see
  page 121)

2 tablespoons red wine

SEW up the cavity to contain the stuffing while the bird cooks. Use a poultry needle or large darning needle threaded with strong cotton or thin string.

cooking

If the stuffing is used when it is still hot (straight from the saucepan) and the bird is cooked immediately, it will only require 1 hour in the oven. If you prepare the stuffing in advance and fill the bird with cold stuffing, allow an extra 20 minutes cooking time at the reduced temperature. If you are not intending to cook the bird immediately, allow the stuffing to cool down completely before using.

SOAK the borlotti beans in cold water for at least 6 hours and then drain (if you are using tinned, you don't need to soak and precook). Put the beans in a saucepan of water, bring to the boil, then drain, rinsing away any foam that has appeared on the surface of the water. Return the beans to the saucepan, cover with water and bring to the boil again, adding 2 garlic cloves, the bay leaf and 1 tablespoon of the oil. Simmer gently for about 40 minutes, or until tender. Do not add salt to the beans or they will toughen. Drain and set aside.

PUT the porcini in a bowl, cover with 150 ml hot water and leave to soak for about 15 minutes. Meanwhile, cook the lentils in a saucepan of water with 1 garlic clove for about 20 minutes, or until the lentils are soft but not mushy. Drain well.

HEAT the remaining olive oil in a pan and cook the onion and pancetta until the onion is soft and the pancetta lightly browned.

PREHEAT the oven to 200°C (400°F/Gas 6). Spread the almonds or pistachios on a tray and roast for 10 minutes until light golden brown, then chop. Drain the porcini, reserving the soaking liquid, roughly chop them, then add to the onion mixture with the sage and the remaining garlic clove and stir to prevent browning. Stir in the drained beans, lentils and nuts. Cook for a few minutes and season to taste.

PUSH the stuffing into the cavity of the bird and sew up the opening with thick cotton or thin string. If you don't have any needles for this, seal the cavity with a couple of cocktail sticks. If you have any extra stuffing, cook it separately in a small covered dish for the last 20 minutes of cooking time. Brush the guinea fowl with oil.

ROAST the guinea fowl for 20 minutes, then reduce the heat to 180°C (350°F/Gas 4) and cook for another 20 minutes. Check the bird is cooked by piercing the thickest part of the thigh with a skewer—the juices should run clear. Alternatively, gently pull away one of the legs from the body to check. Check the stuffing is cooked through by pushing a skewer into the cavity for 3 seconds—the skewer should feel very hot when you pull it out. If it isn't, cover the bird with foil and cook until it is. Leave to rest for about 15 minutes before serving to allow the meat to relax and become tender.

WHILE the guinea fowl is resting, make a thin gravy by bubbling together the juices in the pan, the liquid from the porcini and the red wine. Pour over the guinea fowl to serve.

Marinated duck legs

SERVES 4

INGREDIENTS

1 teaspoon juniper berries

2 garlic cloves, thickly sliced

4 x 20 cm rosemary sprigs, broken
 in half

125 ml balsamic vinegar

4 large or 8 medium duck legs
 (about 875 g in total)

Although we tend to usually eat duck breast, the legs are also delicious. This recipe is slow roasted so the meat is tender enough to fall off the bone. Because the meat tends to shrink once cooked, make sure the legs are from a large bird.

WHEN browning the duck legs, you should be able to use the fat stored under the skin to cook them. Start them cooking gently, fat side down, until the fat melts, then turn up the heat a little to brown the skin.

TO make the marinade, squash the juniper berries with the back of a spoon to release their flavour. Put the berries in a shallow dish large enough to snugly fit the duck legs in one layer. Add the garlic, rosemary and balsamic vinegar, mixing everything together well.

TRIM the duck legs of any excess fat. Put them, flesh side down, in the dish and leave to marinate for at least 1 hour or overnight in the fridge. Remove from the fridge about 15 minutes before roasting so they are not too cold.

PREHEAT the oven to 190°C (375°F/Gas 5). Remove the duck legs from the marinade and dry them on paper towels. Reserve the marinade.

HEAT an ovenproof frying pan or casserole (one that will easily fit all the duck legs) over medium heat. Brown the legs, fat side first, so that the fat is released, creating enough oil to brown the skin. Once the duck is browned on both sides, arrange the legs neatly in one layer, cover and put the pan in the oven. The fat will slowly cook the flesh, keeping it moist while it cooks. Roast the duck for 1-1 1/2 hours, or until the meat is very tender. Remove the lid for the last 30 minutes.

REMOVE from the oven, take out the legs and pour off any excess fat. Put the pan back on the stove, add the marinade, bring to the boil and cook for 5 minutes or until the sauce has reduced and thickened. If the sauce is too thick, dilute it with a dash of water. Put the duck legs back into the sauce. Allow the duck to rest for about 10 minutes before serving. Serve with gnocchi, polenta or lentils.

Pigeon with raisins and pine nuts

If you can buy wild pigeon rather than farmed squab, the flesh will have a much more robust flavour. These pigeons are marinated in balsamic vinegar before cooking, which gives the skin a good brown glaze.

cooking

When grilling the pigeons the heat must be high enough to cook them through and brown the skin, but not so hot that they burn before they are properly cooked. Pigeon can be served a little pink if you prefer—it does not have to be as well cooked as chicken.

PUT the pigeons in a bowl with the balsamic vinegar, making sure each piece is coated, and marinate in the fridge for at least 4 hours. Drain the pigeons, reserving the vinegar.

HEAT the olive oil in a frying pan and cook the onion and pine nuts until the onion is soft and transparent and the pine nuts golden brown. Add the garlic, raisins and rosemary and cook for 2 minutes. Pour in the reserved vinegar and the wine and cook for 10 minutes over medium heat. Season.

GRILL the pigeons for 5–10 minutes on each side until the skin is browned and the flesh cooked through (pull a leg away from the body to check if it is cooked). Place the pigeons on a serving dish.

SCRAPE the juices left in the grill pan into the sauce. Bring the sauce back to the boil and pour it over the pigeons. Delicious served with gnocchi.

SERVES 4

INGREDIENTS

4 pigeons, squabs or poussin, spatchcocked (see page 120)

200 ml balsamic vinegar

2 tablespoons olive oil

1 large red onion, finely sliced

50 g pine nuts

2 garlic cloves, crushed

30 g raisins

2 rosemary sprigs, chopped

100 ml red wine or water

balsamic vinegar

Balsamic vinegar (aceto balsamico) is a very special vinegar. It is made, like sherry, using a solera system. This means that the vinegar is moved into successively smaller barrels each year as it develops from the must of Trebbiano grapes to a dark brown syrupy vinegar. The production of balsamic vinegar is protected by a consorzio made up of the Modena families who make it. High-quality balsamic vinegar is labelled 'tradizionale' while slightly cheaper versions are sold as 'aceto balsamico di Modena'.

lemons

Lemons *(limone)* are grown predominantly in Sicily with some also coming from Calabria, Campania and Sardinia. Lemons are used extensively in Italian cuisine, both as a flavouring and a souring agent. The juice is used as a dressing for salads and drizzled over fish, meat and poultry.

Turkey spiedini

The trick to making skewers is to ensure all the ingredients are cut to the same size so they cook evenly. This recipe uses slices of lemon, but if you want a stronger flavour you can use the lemon zest and pith instead. Pork, veal or chicken mince can be used instead of turkey.

PUT the fennel seeds and garlic in a mortar and pestle and crush with a pinch of salt. If you don't have a mortar and pestle, crush them in a small bowl with the end of a rolling pin or in a spice grinder

MIX the fennel and garlic with the turkey mince and herbs and season with pepper. Test the seasoning by frying a teaspoon of the mixture in a little oil and tasting for flavour.

PEEL the lemon completely, removing the zest and white pith. Cut the lemon into four thick slices, then cut the slices in half, making eight pieces (for a stronger flavour, use the lemon zest instead of the flesh). Roll the turkey mince into 16 small balls, pressing firmly so they won't break up when cooked.

TO assemble a kebab, start with a piece of bread, spear it onto the skewer and push it to the end. Next, push on a ball of turkey and shape it to the thickness of the bread. Next, place a slice of lemon, followed by a turkey ball, a bay leaf, a piece of bread, a turkey ball, lemon slice, turkey ball, bay leaf and finish with a piece of bread. Put the kebabs on a plate and drizzle with olive oil (mostly over the bread so that it soaks up some of the oil).

HEAT a griddle or grill to very hot, then reduce the heat to medium. Season the kebabs and cook for about 15 minutes, turning once. Check that the heat is not too high—the kebabs need to brown and cook through rather than burn on the outside. Squeeze a little lemon juice over the top before serving.

THERE should be four turkey balls per skewer. It doesn't really matter how you order the ingredients on the skewers as long as each person gets the same amount. When you are grilling the skewers don't have the heat too high or thinner ingredients like the bay leaves may burn.

SERVES 4

INGREDIENTS

1 teaspoon fennel seeds

1 garlic clove

400 g turkey mince

2 tablespoons chopped oregano, marjoram or thyme

1 large lemon

1 thick slice of bread, crust removed, cut into 2 cm cubes

8 bay leaves

1 tablespoon olive oil

4 metal or wooden kebab skewers or sticks

Roast goose

A 4.5 kg bird will feed six generously and served with vegetables it makes a filling meal. As goose is so fatty, do not stuff the bird but cook the stuffing separately. Otherwise the juices from the bird will run into the stuffing, making it oily.

SERVES 6

INGREDIENTS

1 x 4.5 kg young goose

2 tablespoons sea salt

2 lemons, halved

bunch of thyme, sage or rosemary

6 dried figs or prunes

6 garlic cloves

500 ml chicken stock

1 heaped teaspoon cornflour,
   optional

100 ml port

STUFFING

50 g butter

1 tablespoon olive oil

350 g parsnips, peeled and finely
   chopped

4 cm piece fresh ginger, finely
   chopped

2 garlic cloves, finely chopped

20 g dried porcini mushrooms,
   soaked in 100 ml hot water
   for 15 minutes

50 g dried apricots, chopped

450 g whole peeled chestnuts,
   roughly chopped

50 g walnut pieces

TRUSS the goose neatly by tying its legs together and tucking its wings behind its back. This will give the bird a much neater shape when cooked. As the goose cooks, remove the fat from the tin with a bulb baster. If you tip the fat out, you often lose the other juices as well.

CLEAN and dry the goose by removing the giblets and rinsing it quickly, then remove the parson's nose and any excess fat from the cavity. If you buy the goose in a plastic bag, remove the plastic and leave uncovered in the fridge overnight to dry out the skin. Prick the skin all over with a fork, so the fat will run out when cooking.

PREHEAT the oven to 220°C (425°F/Gas 7). Rub the skin with the sea salt and a sprinkling of pepper and season the cavity with salt and pepper. Put the lemons in the cavity with the herbs, figs and garlic. Tie the goose legs together with string and tuck the wings behind its body. Place breast side up on a wire rack set into a roasting tin.

PUT the goose in the oven and cook for 10 minutes, then reduce the heat to 180°C (350°F/Gas 4). Allow 15 minutes cooking time per 450 g. Baste the bird with 2-3 tablespoons of boiling water after the first 20 minutes. This helps to render more fat from the bird and makes the skin crisp. Take the goose out of the oven every 20 minutes and remove the fat from the roasting tin (a basting bulb is ideal for this). After 1 hour, turn the bird on its side. Remove the fat from the tin (you can keep it for roasting potatoes). After about 1½ hours, turn the bird over onto the other side. Baste with more water (about 3 tablespoons) and keep removing any fat. Turn the bird back onto its back for the last 30 minutes.

TO check that the bird is cooked through, pull away one of the drumsticks—if it moves easily and the juices run pale yellow, the goose is cooked. Leave the bird to rest for about 30 minutes, loosely covered with foil and a tea towel.

TO make the stuffing, melt the butter and oil and slowly cook the parsnips for about 10 minutes, stirring frequently. Add the ginger and garlic, season and stir briefly. Drain the porcini, reserving the liquid, and coarsely chop them. Add the apricots and porcini to the parsnips, stir for a couple of minutes, then add the soaking liquid, discarding any sediment left at the bottom of the bowl. Simmer until all the liquid has evaporated and the parsnips are soft. Add the chestnuts and walnuts and season.

JUST before serving, remove the goose from the roasting tin and place the tin over medium heat. Add the stock and stir in the cornflour if you like your gravy thick. Add the port and cook, stirring well, for about 5 minutes. Season to taste and serve with the goose and stuffing.

chicken stock

Chicken stock is a useful ingredient to keep around at all times. If you make your own, from the carcass of a roast, freeze it in portions and use straight from the freezer. Ready-made liquid stocks can also be good.

Stuffed pheasant

Pheasant is popular throughout Italy, particularly in Tuscany and Umbria, and both wild and farmed pheasant are eaten. Pheasant has dark flesh and a pleasant gamey flavour. Serve it with wet polenta, risotto or a potato gratin.

TO make the stuffing, heat 50 ml of the oil in a saucepan and cook the pancetta and sausage pieces until golden brown. Add the onion, celery, carrot, garlic and fennel seeds and cook for 10 minutes, stirring frequently, until lightly braised.

DRAIN the porcini, reserving the soaking liquid, and roughly chop them. Add the porcini and sage to the vegetables, season, and cook for another minute. Pour in the mushroom soaking liquid and half the wine and cook, stirring occasionally, for about 10-15 minutes or until reduced.

PREHEAT the oven to 200°C (400°F/Gas 6). Clean the pheasants by removing any excess fat and straggly skin and rinsing and drying them with paper towel. Season the cavities and divide the stuffing between them. If you are not intending to cook them immediately, allow the stuffing to cool down completely before using.

PLACE the pheasants in a roasting tin and season with more salt and pepper. Drizzle with the remaining olive oil and roast for 20–30 minutes, depending on whether the birds were stuffed with hot or cold stuffing—if the stuffing was cold, use the longer cooking time. Check the birds are cooked by piercing the thickest part of the thigh with a skewer—the juices should run clear. Alternatively, gently pull away one of the legs from the body to check. Check the stuffing is cooked through by pushing a skewer into the cavity for 3 seconds—the skewer should feel very hot when you pull it out. If it isn't, cover the bird with foil and cook until it is. Leave to rest for 15 minutes before serving to let the meat relax and become tender.

TO make the sauce, remove the pheasants from the roasting tin. Put the tin over medium heat and stir in the remaining wine, scraping up all the juices and bits to deglaze the pan. Add the stock and simmer until slightly thickened. Pour over the pheasants to serve.

THE simplest way to make a sauce with lots of flavour is to deglaze the pan you have used for cooking. This means adding a liquid such as wine or stock to the hot pan and scraping up any sediment and juices that may be stuck to the bottom. The liquid is then simmered briefly to reduce it.

SERVES 4

INGREDIENTS

170 ml extra virgin olive oil

100 g pancetta or smoked bacon, diced

300 g Italian sausages or cotechino, removed from the skin and torn into small pieces

1 large red onion, chopped

2 large celery stalks, chopped

2 carrots, chopped

5 garlic cloves, chopped

2 heaped teaspoons fennel seeds, crushed

40 g dried porcini mushrooms, soaked in 200 ml hot water for 15 minutes

1 sage sprig, chopped

300 ml red wine

2 x 1.5 kg pheasants

150 ml chicken stock or water

carne

pork

Pork is Italy's most commonly used meat, both fresh and cured into hams, salami, pancetta and sausages. The fat is rendered as lard and used for frying or shaved over salads as a flavouring. Pork is cooked as chops or cutlets cut from the ribs or roasted as loin, leg or shoulder joints. The mince is used for meatballs *(polpette)*. Sucking pigs are stuffed with herbs and roasted whole as *porchetta*. This is sold as slices and often eaten in bread rolls.

lamb

Lamb *(agnello)* is popular all over Italy, although in the north it is eaten a little younger than in the south. Cutlets from the best end of neck are grilled, while breasts, shoulder and legs are roasted, on the bone or stuffed. Cubed lamb is used in stews and ragùs. Milk-fed lambs, roasted whole, were a favourite in Rome in ancient times.

beef

Beef *(manzo)* is reared on the lush grasslands of northern and central Italy and is cooked in many different ways. The brisket (part of the breast and ribs) is rolled up and used for bollito misto or cubed and used in stews. Chuck steak from the shoulder is also good for stews and ragùs as it has plenty of connective tissue that breaks down to give a smooth tender texture. The fillet that lies beneath the backbone can be used raw for carpaccio, or grilled or pan-fried. The sirloin and wing rib (part of the long rib of the beef) can be roasted whole or cut into steaks such as the T-bone used for Florentine steak. The rump (the lowest part of the back) is cut into steaks but also roasted or boned and simply simmered in stews.

chining and trimming pork

PUT the rack of pork ribs on a chopping board, ribs facing downwards. Using a sharp boning knife, cut down the side of the chine bone to the vertebrae. Hold the chine bone in one hand and the joint in the other and snap off the chine bone.

TRIM the layer of fat off the back of the joint leaving just enough to act as a protective layer and to baste the joint.

TRIM the meat away from the very end of each rib bone, exposing the bone. This looks attractive and makes it easier to cut the meat into chops after cooking but is not strictly necessary. Cook the pork bone side down so the ribs act as a rack.

trimming a leg of lamb

  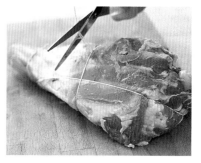

USING a small knife, cut away any excess fat covering the leg of lamb. Cut through the tendon joining the meat to the knuckle and trim off any meat from the bone. Using a saw, cut off the knuckle end of the shank bone to neaten it.

NEXT, turn the leg over and, using a boning knife, cut around the edges of the pelvic bone. Following its contour down to the ball and socket joint, cut through the tendons that join the two bones and then pull out the pelvic bone.

FOLD the flap of flesh back over the lamb and use a piece of string to tie it in place. Wind the string round the shank end and up both sides of the leg. Tie another piece of string across the joint.

trimming beef fillet

TRY to buy a piece of beef fillet of even thickness. Using a small sharp knife, trim off any fat.

TRIM off any membrane by sliding the blade of your knife underneath while pulling the membrane taut. Neaten any straggly pieces.

IF your fillet is uneven along its length it won't cook at the same rate. Fold the thinner end back under the thicker end to make it an even thickness all the way along. If you are roasting it, tie it all the way along with kitchen string.

testing meat for doneness

STEAK can be tested for doneness by pressing it with your finger and then comparing the tenderness with the feel of the flesh at the base of your thumb.

WHEN meat is rare, it still feels very tender, much the same as the flesh at the base of your thumb when it is relaxed. When well cooked, it feels much firmer, like the base of your thumb if you press your thumb and little finger together.

FOR large joints of meat you will have to use a meat thermometer or push a skewer into the meat. Leave the skewer there for 5 seconds, then pull it out and touch it carefully to the inside of your wrist or your lip—it should feel extremely hot when the meat is cooked through.

jointing a rabbit

PUT the gutted and skinned rabbit face down on the chopping board. Using a boning knife, cut through the joints that attach the forelegs to the carcass. Set these aside.

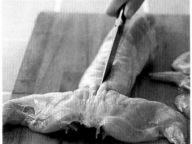

IF the rabbit is large, cut through the saddle just above the hind legs with a large knife. Push down on the knife until you cut all the way through down the side of the backbone.

SEPARATE the hind legs by cutting through the flesh on either side of the backbone. Cut down the other side of the backbone and discard it.

CUT each hind leg in two if they are large by cutting in a straight line through the knee joint. You should be able to slide the knife blade through the socket.

DIVIDE the saddle into four equal pieces by cutting down through the spine. The kidneys should still be on the carcass so avoid cutting into these.

THE top part of the saddle will be mainly rib cage and will not yield very much meat. In some cases, it may also contain the heart and lungs.

veal

One of the most popular meats in Italy, veal *(vitello)* is used in many different ways. The cutlets, cut from the ribs, are dusted in flour or coated in crumbs and then fried. *Scaloppine* and *picata* (thin slices cut from the rump or silverside) are used for dishes like saltimbocca. The shoulders and legs can be roasted whole or cubed for stew and ragùs and the loin used for vitello tonnato. Veal shanks *(ossibuchi)* are from the veal shins and cut into thick pieces. The bone has marrow in the centre and is surrounded by a thick piece of meat. Veal mince is also used for *polpette*.

wild boar

Wild boar *(cinghiale)* are both hunted and farmed in Italy and are a particular speciality of Tuscany and Umbria. The meat is sought after as it has a stronger flavour than pork, making it ideal for cooking with wine and robust ingredients like juniper in stews and ragùs. Though it can be roasted, wild boar is best cooked in liquid so the meat does not dry out.

venison

Venison or deer meat *(cervo* or *capriolo)* is used mainly for casseroles or ragùs as its meat is low in fat and can be quite dry. Joints can be roasted but they fare better if pot roasted in liquid. Most venison available now is farmed rather than wild.

rabbit

Rabbit *(coniglio)* is a popular meat in Italy: it can be used much like chicken in many recipes and is relatively cheap. Rabbit can be roasted, either whole or as joints, but is more often used in ragùs, to dress pasta or in stews. Wild hare *(lepre)* is also popular when available. This can be cooked by the same methods but has a stronger flavour.

Pork cooked in milk

SERVES 6

INGREDIENTS

2.25 kg pork loin, chined and
skinned (see page 140)

50 ml olive oil

4 garlic cloves, cut in half
lengthways

4 sage or rosemary sprigs

1 litre milk

peeled zest of 2 lemons

juice of 1 lemon

The sauce for this dish will look lumpy and curdled but don't be alarmed; it will taste delicious. Chining the pork (removing the backbone from the ribs) makes it much easier to carve between the ribs, but if you don't want to go to the trouble it's completely optional.

PREHEAT the oven to 200°C (400°F/Gas 6). Heat the olive oil in a roasting tin. Add the pork and brown the meat on all sides. Remove the pork and pour away the fat in the roasting pan. Add the garlic and sage to the roasting tin and place the pork on top, bone side down. Season with salt and pepper and pour the milk over the pork. Return to the heat and bring just to the boil. Remove from the heat, add the lemon zest and drizzle with the lemon juice. The milk will start to curdle and might look alarming, but this is how the sauce is supposed to look.

TRANSFER the roasting tin to the oven and cook for about 20 minutes. Reduce the heat to 150°C (300°F/Gas 2) and cook for another 1–1¼ hours, depending on the thickness of the meat. If the milk evaporates before the end of cooking time, add a little more to keep the meat roasting in liquid. Baste the meat with the juices every 30 minutes. Do not cover, so that the juices reduce and the fat on the pork becomes crisp.

TO test if the pork is cooked, poke a skewer into the middle of the meat, count to ten and pull it out. Touch it on the inside of your wrist: if it feels very hot, the meat is cooked through. Remove the pork from the oven and leave it to rest for at least 10 minutes. Remove the herbs and garlic.

SERVE with wet polenta or roasted potatoes with a little of the sauce spooned over the top.

cooking

If the sauce is still very watery by the time the pork has finished cooking, remove the meat from the roasting tin and simmer the sauce on the stovetop until it thickens.

THE ribs act as a rack to rest the meat on as it cooks.

WHEN you pour the lemon juice into the pan, the milk will start to curdle—it is supposed to do this, so don't worry.

THE sauce should be a rich dark creamy colour with wonderful tasty lumps. Don't be tempted to strain it or you'll ruin its unique texture.

Osso buco alla milanese

You will find versions of this recipe that are made with tomatoes, but osso buco is a Milanese dish and traditionally tomatoes are not used in the cooking of northern Italy. The absence of the tomato allows the more delicate flavours of the gremolata to come through.

DUST each piece of veal shank with seasoned flour. Heat the oil, butter, garlic, onion and celery in a heavy-based frying pan or saucepan that is big enough to hold the shanks in a single layer (but don't add the shanks yet). Cook for about 5 minutes over low heat until soft but not browned. Add the shanks to the pan and cook for 12–15 minutes, or until well browned all over. Arrange the shanks in the pan, standing them up in a single layer. Pour in the wine and add the bay leaf, allspice and cinnamon. Bring to the boil and cover the pan. Turn the heat down to low.

COOK at a low simmer for 15 minutes, then add 125 ml warm water. Continue cooking, covered, for about 45–60 minutes (the timing will depend on the age of the veal) or until the meat is tender and you can cut it with a fork. Check the volume of liquid once or twice during cooking time and add more warm water as needed.

TO make the gremolata, mix together the lemon zest, parsley and garlic.

TRANSFER the veal shanks to a plate and keep warm. Discard the bay leaf. Increase the heat under the pan and stir for 1–2 minutes until the sauce has thickened, scraping up any bits off the bottom of the pan as you stir. Season with salt and pepper if necessary and return the veal shanks to the sauce. Heat everything through, then stir through half the gremolata. Serve sprinkled with the remaining gremolata. Usually accompanied by risotto alla milanese.

preparing

IF your veal shanks do not look as if they will hold together neatly while they cook, tie a piece of butcher's string around the girth of each one. Remember to take the string off before serving.

SERVES 4

INGREDIENTS

12 pieces veal shank, about 4 cm thick

plain flour, seasoned with salt and pepper

60 ml olive oil

60 g butter

1 garlic clove, finely chopped

1 onion, finely chopped

1 celery stalk, finely chopped

250 ml dry white wine

1 bay leaf or lemon leaf

pinch of allspice

pinch of ground cinnamon

GREMOLATA

2 teaspoons grated lemon zest

2 tablespoons finely chopped flat-leaf parsley

1 garlic clove, finely chopped

Beef braised in red wine

SERVES 4

INGREDIENTS

750 g trimmed thick beef fillet (see
    page 140)

3 garlic cloves, thinly sliced

2 tablespoons chopped rosemary

10–20 thin slices pancetta (about
    120 g) or speck

20 g dried wild mushrooms

2 tablespoons extra virgin olive oil

1 onion, halved and sliced

150 ml red wine

400 g tin chopped tomatoes

This dish is perfect for entertaining—you can cook it in advance and it will sit in the casserole for up to an hour. Just before serving, bring the sauce back to the boil very briefly to warm it up. If you are using a whole fillet of beef, fold the thin end under so the meat is an even thickness.

PUSHING the slices of garlic into the beef helps the flavour to infuse, but make sure the garlic is sliced very thinly so that it cooks through. Coating the beef in a layer of pancetta adds flavour and keeps the meat moist while it is cooking. Make sure you don't burn the pancetta or beef while you are browning it. If the base of the casserole starts to burn before the beef is sealed, remove the beef and finish sealing it in a frying pan, then return it to the cleaned casserole. If you leave the bits in the casserole, the finished sauce will taste burnt.

WITH the point of a sharp knife, make several small incisions around the beef. Using one of the sliced garlic cloves, push a slice into each incision. Scatter 1 tablespoon of the rosemary over the beef and season with salt and pepper.

LAY the rashers of pancetta in a line on a board, positioning them so they touch each other, to create a sheet of pancetta to wrap the beef in. Put the beef fillet across them and fold over the pancetta to enclose the fillet. Tie the beef up with string (use six ties down the length of the beef to keep the beef and pancetta together). Wrapping the beef in pancetta not only gives it flavour, but helps prevent the meat drying out in the oven. Leave in the fridge to rest for at least 15 minutes. Put the dried mushrooms in a bowl and cover with 200 ml hot water. Leave to soak for 10 minutes.

PREHEAT the oven to 190°C (375°F/Gas 5). Heat the olive oil in a casserole or ovenproof saucepan on the stovetop. Add the beef and sear on all sides until the pancetta is golden brown. When sealing the beef, it is important to keep the temperature at medium-high heat so it doesn't brown too quickly and burn (this will affect the flavour of the sauce). Sometimes a little of the pancetta might fall off—don't worry, it will just add flavour to the sauce. Remove the beef from the casserole and set aside.

ADD the onion to the casserole, reduce the heat and cook gently until soft. Add the remaining garlic and rosemary and cook for a few minutes more.

REMOVE the mushrooms from the water, squeeze dry and add them to the onion, reserving the soaking water. Cook the mushrooms for a couple of minutes, then add the mushroom water, discarding any sediment at the bottom of the bowl, and boil until nearly all the liquid has evaporated. Add the red wine and cook for a few minutes, then add the tomatoes and cook for a further 5–10 minutes to reduce the liquid to a thick sauce. Season.

RETURN the beef to the casserole, turning it over in the sauce to coat all sides. Bring the sauce to the boil, cover with a lid and place in the oven. Cook the beef for about 15 minutes for rare or 20 minutes for medium rare. Remove from the oven and leave to rest, covered, for at least 15 minutes. Remove the string. Serve with wet polenta, saffron risotto or mashed potato.

pancetta

Like bacon, pancetta is made from the belly of the pig. *Pancetta stesa*, which comes in a lump like bacon, is cured and cut into chunks, slices or cubes to be sold. Pancetta is also available smoked *(pancetta affumicata)*. *Pancetta arrotolata* is a leaner piece of meat, which is rolled before being cured. Pancetta is usually cooked but *arrotolata* can also be served raw as part of an antipasto platter.

Lazio

All roads in this region do lead to Rome and Lazio is certainly dominated by its capital city. However, the rural areas do have a somewhat different cuisine to the city. Rome itself has a style of eating derived from *cucina povera*, the peasant cooking of the south that is based on what the majority poor could make palatable to eat, with a few richer papal dishes thrown in. In rural areas a lot of lamb is eaten and where the region borders Tuscany and Campania the dishes are heavily influenced by the cooking of these areas.

The *cucina povera* of Rome is the Italian cuisine most heavily based on offal, including tripe, hearts and dishes such as *pajata*: veal intestines still filled with milk which are eaten roasted. Several other dishes, such as spaghetti carbonara, eke out the bare minimum of meat to make a meal. The cuisine which emerged from the Vatican used the better, more expensive, parts of the same animals, such as whole roasted milk-fed baby lamb *(abbacchio al forno)*. Cheeses include pecorino Romano and ricotta Romana. The markets are rich with an abundance of vegetables from the fertile volcanic soil, while Lazio's coastline provides fish and seafood and Lago di Bolsena is famous for its eels.

Other dishes associated with Rome are the small discs of semolina known as gnocchi alla Romana and the balls of deep-fried risotto filled with mozzarella called suppli al forno. Dried pasta is widely eaten, both long and short shapes, and flavoured with sauces such as amatriciana and arrabbiata.

Salt

Roman food is also characterised by its use of salt, with food being more heavily salted here than elsewhere in Italy. Rome lies on the old Via Salaria, the salt trading route that runs from the Adriatic to Rome. When salt was an expensive commodity it was a sign of generosity and extravagance to add plenty of it to food. The English word 'salary' is derived from *salario*: the wages paid to Roman soldiers in this precious flavouring.

Roast lamb

SERVES 4

Lamb is a popular meat in Italy, particularly in the central and southern areas. Very young milk-fed lamb, usually under six months old, is often roasted whole on the spit, while lamb that is a little older is used for ragùs or stews. The leg or shoulder can be roasted whole, often with a little wine.

INGREDIENTS

2 rosemary sprigs

3 garlic cloves

75 g pancetta

2 kg leg of lamb, shank bone cut off just above the joint, trimmed of excess fat and tied (see page 140)

1 large onion

125 ml olive oil

375 ml dry white wine

RUBBING the flavouring paste into cuts in the lamb's flesh makes the flavour penetrate further into the meat. Resting the meat on slices of onion helps prevent the meat catching and adds extra flavour to the sauce. If the onion isn't burnt after cooking, serve it as an accompaniment.

PREHEAT the oven to 230°C (450°F/Gas 8). Strip the leaves off the rosemary sprigs and chop them with the garlic and pancetta until fine and paste-like (a food processor works well for this). Season with a little salt and plenty of pepper.

WITH the point of a sharp knife, make incisions about 1 cm deep all over the lamb. Rub the rosemary filling over the surface of the lamb, pushing it into the incisions.

CUT the onion into four thick slices and put them in the centre of a roasting tin. Place the lamb on top and gently pour the olive oil over it. Roast for 15 minutes. Reduce the temperature to 180°C (350°F/Gas 4) and pour in 250 ml of the wine. Roast for 1 1/2 hours for medium-rare, or longer if you prefer. Baste a couple of times and add a little water if the juices start to burn in the tin. Transfer the lamb to a carving platter and leave to rest for 10 minutes.

REMOVE the onion (if it isn't burnt, serve it with the meat) and spoon off the excess fat from the tin. Place over high heat on the stovetop, pour in the remaining wine and cook for 3–4 minutes, or until the sauce reduces and slightly thickens. Taste for seasoning. Slice the lamb and serve with the sauce spooned over the top.

buying

You can roast kid (young goat) in the same way and, in fact, that is probably what was originally used. The same recipe can also be used for veal: roasting time is 25 minutes for every 450 grams, plus 10 minutes for the pot.

pine nuts

Pine nuts *(pinoli)* are the seeds of the umbrella pine. They grow in many areas in Italy and are predominantly used in stuffings, biscuits and cakes and to make pesto. Buy the freshest you can find and don't store them for too long or they'll turn rancid. However, they do freeze well.

Veal polpette

Every Italian home has its own recipe for polpette—meatballs made with either minced veal, beef or pork. These are dressed in a tomato sauce and are traditionally served simply with bread, but you can also use pasta or wet polenta.

HEAT 60 ml of the olive oil in a saucepan and cook the onion and pine nuts until the onion is soft and the pine nuts are light golden brown. Add the garlic and cook for a few more minutes, then set aside to cool.

PUT the herbs, fennel seeds, breadcrumbs, ricotta, Parmesan and lemon zest in a bowl and add the mince. Add the cooled onion and pine nuts, season with salt and pepper and mix briefly until all ingredients are combined. Leave to rest in the fridge for at least 30 minutes or overnight.

FOR best results and to check for correct seasoning, cook one small meatball in a little of the oil while the rest of the mixture is resting in the fridge. Taste for flavour and adjust the mixture accordingly.

TO make the polpette, roll the mixture into balls about the size of walnuts. Flatten them slightly to make it easier to cook them on both sides and push any pine nuts that are protruding back in or they will burn.

HEAT the remaining oil in a large frying pan and cook the polpette over medium-high heat until golden brown. You might need to cook them in two batches but remove any sediment left in the pan after the first batch to prevent it burning. The polpette are quite fragile so handle them carefully. Make sure there is enough oil to prevent them from sticking to the pan. Remove the polpette and set aside.

TO make the sauce, drain all but 1 tablespoon of the olive oil from the pan, add the wine and cook for a few minutes to reduce the liquid. Add the tomatoes, season with salt and pepper and simmer for 15 minutes, breaking up any large chunks of tomato. Add the meatballs to the tomato sauce and reduce the heat to a gentle simmer.

COVER the pan and cook for a further 10 minutes, carefully turning the meatballs over in the sauce. Leave to rest for 10 minutes. Scatter with the extra parsley before serving.

MAKE sure that when you roll the meatballs you make the mixture compact or they might break up as they cook. Push any pine nuts back into the polpette or they will catch and burn. When you add the sauce to the meatballs it will take away some of the colour so they need to be well browned first.

SERVES 6

INGREDIENTS

160 ml olive oil

1 onion, finely chopped

50 g pine nuts, roughly chopped

3 garlic cloves, finely chopped

40 g parsley, roughly chopped, plus
    extra, to serve

15 g basil or rosemary, chopped

1 teaspoon fennel seeds, ground

50 g fresh breadcrumbs

200 g ricotta

25 g Parmesan, grated

grated zest of 1 large lemon

500 g minced veal

SAUCE

100 ml red wine

800 g tin chopped tomatoes

Bollito misto with salsa verde

SERVES 8

INGREDIENTS

1 x 800 g cotechino sausage

1 x 1.25 kg small beef tongue

3 parsley sprigs

4 baby carrots

1 celery stalk, sliced

2 onions, roughly chopped

10 peppercorns

2 bay leaves

1 x 1.25 kg beef brisket

1 large tomato or 1 tablespoon
  tomato purée

1 x 900 g chicken

12 whole baby turnips

18 small pickling or pearl onions

SALSA VERDE

1½ tablespoons fresh white
  breadcrumbs

1 tablespoon milk

1 hard-boiled egg yolk

2 anchovy fillets

1 tablespoon capers

5 tablespoons finely chopped
  parsley, mint and basil

1 garlic clove, crushed

75 ml extra virgin olive oil

mostarda di Cremona

This mixture of candied fruit in a mustard-flavoured syrup is a speciality of Cremona that is traditionally served with boiled meats.

Bollito misto, boiled meats, is a tradition in northern Italy where cows and pigs are plentiful. It is, in particular, a speciality of Piedmont, where some of the more exclusive restaurants serve up to seven different meats with an array of sauces.

PUT the cotechino sausage in a pan of boiling water, reduce the heat, cover the pan and simmer for about 1½ hours, or until the sausage is tender (this will depend on the brand). Leave in the cooking liquid until ready to use.

MEANWHILE, bring a stockpot or very large saucepan of water to the boil. Add the tongue, parsley, carrots, celery, chopped onion, peppercorns, bay leaves and 1 teaspoon salt. Bring back to the boil, skim the surface and add the beef brisket and tomato. Cover, reduce the heat and simmer for 2 hours, skimming the surface from time to time.

TO make the salsa verde, process or pound (in a mortar and pestle) everything together except the olive oil. Then whisk in the oil.

ADD the chicken, turnips and onions to the stockpot and simmer for another hour. Top up with boiling water if necessary to keep the meat always covered. Add the cotechino for the last 20 minutes of cooking.

TURN off the heat and remove the tongue. Peel, trim and slice it, then arrange the slices on a warm platter. Slice the cotechino and beef and joint the chicken. Arrange all the meats on the platter and surround them with the carrots, turnips and onions. Moisten with a little of the cooking liquid then take the platter to the table. Serve with the salsa verde and *mostarda di Cremona*.

THE cooking time for your cotechino may vary. Some brands need a couple of hours, others a much shorter time. The ingredients in the sausage need to cook for long enough to make them all blend together and become tender.

TONGUE needs to be peeled before it is eaten. You might need to let it cool down a bit before you can handle it.

Vitello tonnato

Vitello tonnato is served cold. Traditionally it was always prepared in advance and the platter, sauce and all, chilled overnight to let the flavours develop. You will probably find it easier to prepare the meat and sauce the day before and then assemble on a chilled platter before serving.

SERVES 4

INGREDIENTS

1.25 kg boneless rolled veal roast

500 ml dry white wine

500 ml chicken stock

2 garlic cloves

1 onion, quartered

1 carrot, roughly chopped

1 celery stalk, roughly chopped

2 bay leaves

3 cloves

10 peppercorns

SAUCE

95 g tin tuna in olive oil, drained

15 g anchovy fillets

185 ml olive oil

2 egg yolks

2 tablespoons lemon juice

parsley sprigs, to serve

capers, rinsed and dried, to serve

thin lemon slices, to serve

PUT the veal, wine, stock, garlic, onion, carrot, celery, bay leaves, cloves and peppercorns in a stockpot or very large saucepan. Add enough water to come two-thirds of the way up the veal and bring to the boil. Reduce the heat, cover the pan and simmer for 1¼ hours, or until tender.

LEAVE to cool for 30 minutes, then remove the veal from the pan and strain the stock. Pour the stock into a saucepan and boil rapidly until reduced to about 250 ml.

TO make the sauce, purée the tuna with the anchovy fillets in a blender or small food processor with 3 tablespoons of the olive oil. Add the egg yolks and 1 tablespoon of the lemon juice and process until smooth. With the motor running, slowly pour in the rest of the oil. Gradually add the reduced stock until the sauce has the consistency of a thin mayonnaise. (If you are making the sauce by hand, chop the tuna and anchovy finely, mix in the egg yolks and lemon juice and then whisk in the stock.) Blend in the remaining lemon juice to taste, and season well. Chill until ready to serve.

TO serve, thinly slice the cold veal and arrange in overlapping slices down the centre of a serving platter. Spoon the sauce over the top and garnish with the parsley, capers and lemon slices.

serving

Serve vitello tonnato either as part of an antipasto platter or as a meat course. The sauce has quite a strong flavour and needs to be tempered with slightly less strongly flavoured dishes.

Venetian-style liver

SERVES 4

INGREDIENTS

800 g calf's liver, very thinly sliced

2 tablespoons olive oil

60 g butter

2 large white onions, thinly sliced

1 tablespoon finely chopped flat-
   leaf parsley

lemon wedges, to serve

Liver *(fegato)* is the most popular offal eaten in Italy. While calf's liver is generally eaten in the north, pig's liver is preferred in the south and central Italy. In Venice, this traditional dish of liver and onions is often served with polenta.

buying

If you buy your calf's liver unsliced, make sure you slice it thinly. Calf's liver has a particularly good flavour but you could use lamb or pig's liver if necessary.

TRIM the liver of any straggly bits. Heat the olive oil and half the butter in a large frying pan and add the onion. Cover the pan and cook over low heat for 30–40 minutes, stirring from time to time, until the onion is very soft and golden. Season well with salt and pepper and transfer to a bowl.

MELT the remaining butter in the frying pan, increase the heat and fry the liver quickly to brown on both sides. Return the onion to the pan and cook, stirring often, for 1–2 minutes, or until the liver is browned on the outside but still a little pink in the middle—if you prefer your liver well cooked then keep going until it is brown all the way through.

REMOVE from the heat, stir in the parsley and check for seasoning. Serve with lemon wedges.

Bistecca alla Fiorentina

The best steak to be found in Italy is in Tuscany. The most famous is the steak Florentine: a T-bone steak grilled over charcoal and served in the simplest of ways—with a drizzle of extra virgin olive oil, a wedge of lemon and a good sprinkling of salt and pepper.

HEAT a griddle or barbecue grill and season the steak with salt and pepper. Brush the meat very lightly with olive oil to prevent too many flames appearing and cook at a fierce heat, turning once, to your taste (ideally rare or medium rare).

TEST the steaks by pressing them and comparing this to the feeling of pressing the flesh at the base of your thumb. Rare meat will feel as your thumb feels when relaxed; for medium meat hold your thumb halfway across your palm; for well-done meat, hold your thumb all the way across your palm. This method is more accurate than timing as your heat source may be variable or your steak thinner or thicker.

REMOVE from the grill and serve on a large plate with a drizzle of good-quality extra virgin olive oil, some salt and pepper and a wedge of lemon. A simple salad and potatoes, either roasted or fried, are perfect accompaniments, although usually the meat is too large to serve with anything else on the plate.

buying

As T-bone steaks are quite large, one steak will probably be enough to serve two, or ask your butcher for two smaller steaks. Buy good-quality steak from a reputable butcher and make sure it is wrapped in greaseproof paper and not clingfilm, which will make it sweat. Keep in the fridge or a cool place but bring to room temperature 15 minutes before cooking so that the meat is not too cold. The shock of hitting the heat will not be so extreme and the meat will be more tender.

SERVES 4

INGREDIENTS

2 x 1 kg T-bone or sirloin steaks, about 3 cm thick
extra virgin olive oil
lemon wedges, to serve

TEST for rareness by pressing the steak with your finger.

NOW compare the feel of the meat with the feel of the flesh at the base of your thumb when your thumb is relaxed. Meat that feels like this is rare.

Sausages cooked with lentils

SERVES 4

INGREDIENTS

3 tablespoons olive oil

8 Italian sausages

1 onion, chopped

3 garlic cloves, thinly sliced

2 tablespoons finely chopped
  rosemary

800 g tin tomatoes

16 juniper berries, lightly crushed

1 teaspoon freshly grated nutmeg

1 bay leaf

1 dried chilli

200 ml red wine

100 g green lentils, such as
  Castelluccian or Puy lentils

Umbria is the fertile heart of Italy and the tiny lentils that come from Castelluccio are regarded as the country's best. Traditionally they are eaten on New Year's Eve to bring prosperity in the coming year.

buying

The sausages for this recipe can be either smoked or spiced but they do need to be firm. Buy good-quality sausages made with natural casings if you can. The natural casings are less likely to split as they cook than artificial ones.

HEAT the olive oil in a large saucepan and cook the sausages for 5–10 minutes, browning well all over. Remove the sausages and set aside. If the sausages burn the saucepan, wash it briefly before carrying on. If the pan is only slightly browned, this will enhance the flavour, so don't worry about cleaning it.

REDUCE the heat to low, add the onion and garlic to the pan and cook until the onion is soft and translucent, but not browned. Stir in the rosemary, then add the tomatoes and cook gently until the sauce has thickened.

ADD the juniper berries, nutmeg, bay leaf, chilli, red wine and 400 ml water. Bring to the boil, then add the lentils and the cooked sausages. Stir well, cover the saucepan and simmer gently for about 40 minutes, or until the lentils are soft. Stir the lentils a few times to prevent them sticking to the base of the pan and add a little more water if you need to cook them for a bit longer. Remove the bay leaf and chilli to serve.

Umbria

This small central region is the verdant 'green heart of Italy'; home to hearty simple food that is influenced by the lush pastures and many forests and woodlands of the area. Umbria is famous for its pork and cured meats: the region's pigs are particularly fine tasting as they are left to graze on wild fennel and acorns. Norcia, one of Umbria's better-known towns, gives its name to the *norcineria* (the pork butcher's shop) and *norcini*, the butchers themselves, as it was from here that the most skilled men came. Porchetta is a local speciality: a whole pig stuffed with herbs and roasted whole that is often found at markets. Slices are served in bread rolls and eaten as a snack.

Other local products are outstanding—the truffles, lentils, wild mushrooms and great pecorino cheeses—and renowned throughout Italy. The black truffles are shaved over fresh pasta or used as a flavouring in salamis and cheeses. Game is popular and usually simply stewed or roasted. The lakes and rivers of landlocked Umbria produce freshwater fish such as carp, eel and trout.

Umbria also enjoys pizza, torte and polenta dishes. The original pizzas *(pizza rustica)* are sometimes no more than a savoury bread, but can be filled with cheese and *salumi*.

Umbrian wines include Orvieto, Rosso di Montefalco and both red and white wines from the Colli di Trasimeno.

Lenticchie di Castelluccio

Castelluccio in Umbria is home to Italy's most famous lentils, the *lenticchie di Castelluccio*. These small grey-brown lentils are organically grown on the plains, the *Piano grande*, that surround the hilltop town. The lentil plants have pale blue flowers, which blend in with the wildflowers that also grow on the plateau.

Castelluccio lentils are used in the soups and braised dishes of the area or are simply cooked in water and then dressed with olive oil and lemon juice.

Fritto misto

Fritto misto means 'mixed fried food' and can refer to anything fried in batter, from fish to vegetables or offal, as here. Offal plays an important part in Italian cooking and this recipe uses calves' brains and sweetbreads, which are the thymus glands.

SERVES 4

INGREDIENTS

350 g fresh calves' sweetbreads

350 g fresh calves' brains

2 tablespoons vinegar or half
  a lemon

1 bay leaf

BATTER

50 g plain flour

2 teaspoons olive oil

3 egg whites

oil, for deep-frying

2 tablespoons capers, rinsed and
  squeezed dry

16 sage leaves

lemon wedges, to serve

MAKE sure that you prepare your offal properly to get rid of any blood. It needs to be soaked in regular changes of water. After it has been blanched, carefully pull off any membranes. If you don't have a deep-fat fryer for cooking, use a heavy-based deep frying pan or saucepan filled no more than one-third full. If you don't have a thermometer, test the oil with a piece of bread to check it is hot enough.

TO prepare the sweetbreads and brains, place them in cold water and leave to soak for at least 6 hours or overnight, changing the water several times until the water is clear and free of any blood. Rub your hands over the brains and sweetbreads to release any pockets of blood that might be trapped around them.

PLACE the offal in a saucepan, cover with cold water and add the vinegar or lemon, the bay leaf and a pinch of salt. Simmer for 3 minutes, remove from the heat and drain. Rinse in cold water and remove any outer skin or membrane. Cut or break the sweetbreads and brains into small chunks about 4 cm wide.

TO prepare the batter, put the flour in a bowl and make a well in the centre. Pour in the olive oil and a pinch of salt. Mix together with a wooden spoon or whisk, incorporating the flour from the edges into the centre so that it forms a paste. Add 75-100 ml warm water and mix well, beating out any lumps. The consistency should be like thick cream. Leave to rest for at least 10 minutes. Whisk the egg whites in a clean dry bowl with a pinch of salt until they form soft peaks and fold them gently into the batter.

TO cook the offal, heat the oil in a deep-fat fryer or fill a deep frying pan one-third full and heat to about 180 °C (350°F), or until a piece of bread turns golden brown when dropped in the oil. If the oil starts to smoke, it is too hot.

DIP the sweetbreads and brains into the batter, coating all sides, and fry in the hot oil until golden brown. Fry in batches to make sure that the temperature of the oil doesn't drop too much. Remove with a slotted spoon or tongs and drain on paper towels.

ADD the capers and sage to the oil and fry quickly until crisp. Remove with a slotted spoon and scatter over the offal. Season with salt and serve immediately with the lemon wedges.

capers

Capers *(caperi)* are the flower buds of a shrub that grows in Sicily and on the islands of Lipari and Pantelleria. They are preserved by curing in either vinegar or salt, with both varieties needing to be rinsed before use. You will find that small capers have more flavour than the larger ones.

farro

Farro was used as far back as Roman times for making bread and is now grown in Umbria, Tuscany and Lazio. It can be found in Italian or health food shops and is sometimes labelled as 'spelt'. Today farro is mainly used for making soups or stews. If you can't find it, use barley.

Wild boar with juniper berries and farro

SERVES 6

Wild boar are mostly found in northern Italy and around the hills of Umbria. This stew is based on a traditional recipe for cooking the boar slowly overnight in a pizza oven. The method has been adapted to suit slow-cooking in a conventional oven.

PREHEAT the oven to 150°C (300°F/Gas 3). Cut the wild boar into cubes and put in a heavy-based casserole with a tight-fitting lid.

MAKE a bouquet garni by tying together the herbs with the rosemary sprigs in the middle and a bay leaf and sage sprig on either side. Add to the casserole.

PRICK the chestnuts with a fork and boil for 25 minutes, or until tender. Drain, peel and roughly chop them. (If you are using ready-prepared chestnuts, just roughly chop them.) Add to the casserole with the onion, carrot, celery, garlic, juniper berries, farro and wine. Season with salt and pepper. Pour in about 1 litre water and briefly mix together.

BRING to a gentle simmer on the stovetop, then cover and cook in the oven for about 3 hours until the meat is tender. Check every hour or so that the meat is cooking at a very gentle simmer, not boiling.

REMOVE from the oven and leave to rest for half an hour. As wild boar can be fatty, skim the surface to remove any fat. Alternatively, allow the stew to cool completely and the fat to solidify, then scrape it off with a spoon. The stew is best left in the fridge overnight and reheated the next day.

IF you are using fresh chestnuts, you will need to soften them by cooking before you can peel their skins off (see page 11).

INGREDIENTS

800 g wild boar, leg or shoulder

3 rosemary sprigs

2 bay leaves

2 sage sprigs

350 g chestnuts or 200 g tinned or frozen cooked peeled chestnuts

1 onion, chopped

2 carrots, chopped

2 celery stalks, chopped

2–3 garlic cloves, sliced

1–2 teaspoons juniper berries, lightly crushed

2 tablespoons farro or barley

200 ml red wine

cooking

Depending on how well-fitting your casserole lid is and how quickly the stew cooks, you may need to add more water during the cooking time or reduce the liquid at the end by simmering the stew uncovered on the stovetop.

verdure e legumi

vegetables

cipolline

These baby onions are either round or slightly flattened in shape. They are mostly used for pickling or braising in sweet and sour sauces, but can also be used whole in stews or soups.

rocket

Rocket *(rucola)* is a salad leaf with a hot, peppery flavour. It is mainly used in salads but can also be chopped and used in pasta sauces and on pizzas.

fennel bulb

The sweet aniseed flavour of fennel *(finocchio)* goes particularly well with fish and it is often used as a flavouring when cooking whole fish. The bulb can also be used raw in salads or braised whole as a vegetable. Baby fennel bulbs are also available: they are more tender then the bigger ones and can be quartered and used like crudités for dipping in sauces.

cavolo nero

Meaning 'black cabbage', this is a dark green cabbage that turns almost black when cooked. It has long curled leaves and is a classic ingredient in the soup la ribollita.

courgettes

Courgettes *(zucchini)* are small squash with dark green, yellow or pale green skins. They vary in shape from the long ones shown here to round balls. In Sicily, there is a variety that is grown to about 1 metre long. Courgettes are eaten as a vegetable, usually fried or baked, as well as in dishes such as soups and pasta sauces. Orange and yellow courgette flowers are often dipped in batter or stuffed and deep-fried as a starter.

peppers

Peperone are a favourite ingredient in Italy and are available in red, green and yellow, as well as more esoteric colours such as black. They can be grilled or roasted and peeled for antipasto, stuffed, used in soups and ragùs and eaten raw in salads.

pumpkin

Pumpkin *(zucca)* is used in both savoury and sweet dishes in Italy. The name zucca actually means 'all squash' so varieties often have their own names. Pumpkin is used to fill pasta, baked as a vegetable, put in soups, candied or used in breads and cakes.

aubergines

A particular favourite in southern Italy, aubergine *(melanzana)* is used in many recipes. Different varieties range widely in size and colour, from dark and pale purple to white. Aubergines are at their most delicious fried or cooked with tomatoes or cheese.

vegetables

leeks

Like onions, leeks *(porro)* are used as a flavour base for dishes as well as being served as a vegetable in their own right. Baby leeks can be eaten raw like spring onions but larger ones need to be cooked, often in soups and gratins.

carrots

Carrots *(carota)* are a year-round vegetable in Italy. Most are orange but some are yellow or even purple in colour. Carrots are used to give flavour to soups and stews and are eaten raw as crudités and in salads. They are also used in fresh pickles such as *giardiniera*.

cauliflower

Cauliflower *(cavolfiore)* is made into pickles, pasta sauces and soups and baked in gratins. Several colours are available, including green and purple varieties.

peas

Although most often used as a vegetable accompaniment, peas *(piselli)* are very good in risottos such as risi e bisi, soups and pasta dishes.

borlotti beans

These beans are eaten in both their fresh and dried forms in Italy and are especially popular in the centre and northern regions. Both the fresh and dried beans are used in soups and are the main feature of pasta e fagioli.

chicory

Used both as a salad leaf and vegetable, chicory *(cicoria)* has a refreshing bitterness. The leaves are crunchy and good for scooping up dips. They can be halved or quartered then grilled or braised, and have a robust enough flavour to be served with rich meats.

asparagus

Asparagus *(asparago)* is available in green, white and purple varieties. It is best eaten in season and should be prepared with the minimum of fuss. The best way to cook it is by steaming or gentle grilling. It also features in primavera sauces for pasta and risottos. Choose asparagus that has undamaged tips and firm stalks. Unless your asparagus is particularly young and tender, you will need to snap off the tough woody end of the stalk before use.

radicchio

A type of chicory, radicchio has a dark red bitter leaf which is either curled into a ball like a cabbage or has a longer looser structure. Radicchio, like chicory, can be used as a salad leaf or grilled or braised as a vegetable accompaniment.

vegetables

beans

Beans *(fagiolini)* come in several varieties: green beans, yellowish white beans, and green and red beans. All are interchangeable in recipes. Beans are used as a *contorno* (vegetable side dish), in soups or braised dishes.

tomatoes

Almost synonymous with Italian cooking tomatoes *(pomodori)* are used as a main flavour for many dishes. Surprisingly, they are not indigenous to the country and were brought from South America in the sixteenth century. Available fresh, tinned, dried, puréed or roasted.

potatoes

Potatoes *(patata)* are not eaten as a staple as in the rest of Europe but tend to be relegated to use as a vegetable instead. They are popular roasted, fried, in gratins and as a thick purée of mash.

spinach

Spinach *(spinaci)* can be used both as a salad leaf and cooked as a vegetable. It purées easily and can be stirred into dishes or used to colour pasta or bread doughs. Dishes that feature spinach are called *alla fiorentina*. It is also cooked in fillings for pasta, soups, pasta sauces and risottos.

celery

Celery *(sedano)* is widely used in Italy as a basic ingredient in soffritto and to flavour a multitude of soups and ragùs. It is also eaten raw in salads or as crudités or can be braised or baked as a vegetable. White celery has been blanched as it is grown and may be more tender.

chillies

Chillies *(peperoncini)* are especially popular in the south of Italy where they are served as a condiment as well as being used to flavour many dishes. Chillies can be used fresh or dried but you need to check how hot they are first.

garlic

Garlic *(aglio)* is one of the mainstays of Italian cuisine. It is often used as a background flavouring, but can also be cooked whole or used in quantity in recipes such as pesto. It is important to use fresh unsprouted garlic for a good flavour.

lettuce

Used as a salad leaf, there are many varieties of lettuce *(lattuga)* available. Red leaves tend to be more bitter than the sweeter green varieties. Make sure lettuces are crisp when you buy them.

herbs

basil

One of the most common herbs used in Italian cuisine, basil *(basilico)* adds a fresh flavour to cooked dishes and salads. It loses its flavour easily so add it at the end of cooking, tearing rather than chopping the leaves, to prevent the cut edges blackening.

thyme

Available in both wild and cultivated forms, thyme *(timo)* is used in many Italian recipes. It makes a good flavouring for stuffings, roast meats and stews. It has a strong flavour so don't be tempted to use more than specified.

oregano

A popular herb, especially in the south of Italy, oregano *(origano)* is used both fresh and dried, but is much more commonly seen dried. It goes well with tomato sauces and other stronger tasting vegetables and is often used when roasting meats.

mint

Mint *(mentha)* comes in several varieties, peppermint being the most commonly used for cooking. It is found in cooked dishes and stuffings for pasta, meat and poultry, as well as salads or cold dishes.

rosemary

Rosemary *(rosemarino)* is a bush herb that is available all year round. It has rather coarse leaves, which, if not finely chopped, should be left on the stem so they can be easily spotted on the plate. Rosemary goes well with roast meats, especially lamb, and barbecued or grilled fish. The stems can be used as basting brushes or as skewers for kebabs.

parsley

Flat-leaved parsley *(prezzemolo)* is also known as Italian parsley and is used as a flavouring in many dishes. The curly variety is sometimes seen in Italy but is only ever used as a garnish.

sage

Sage *(salvia)* has a robust flavour that holds its own with equally strong flavoured meats such as liver and pancetta. The leaves are also wonderful fried with butter and served as a simple pasta sauce.

fennel fronds

These are the leaves of the fennel plant, which, much like the bulb, have an aniseed flavour. The fronds are chopped and used in salads or to flavour fish dishes.

chillies

There is no way to tell if a chilli is hot other than by tasting it. Size and colour bear no relation to heat, although round chillies are often reasonably hot. Chillies from the same bush may also vary in heat, so check them before you use them.

buying vegetables

Always choose plump fresh vegetables that do not look wrinkled or limp. If possible, buy vegetables in season: root vegetables are better in winter; salads and asparagus are best in spring and summer; and wild mushrooms in autumn. Bear in mind that smaller or baby vegetables may not yet have developed their flavour, however appealing they look.

storing

Vegetables should be kept in an environment as close to their natural one as possible. Potatoes need to be in the dark to prevent them sprouting. Tomatoes (technically fruit) should be stored at room temperature so they continue to ripen. Root vegetables should be stored loose and everything else should be in bags. All vegetables should be in the vegetable crisper as the other areas of the fridge can be too cold for them and destroy their texture. Mushrooms are best kept in the paper bag in which they are bought.

chopping chillies

WHEN you chop a chilli, you expose your flesh to the part of the chilli (the membrane) that holds the capsaicin. Because of this you may want to wear rubber gloves to stop the volatile oils getting on your fingers.

CUT the chilli in half with a sharp knife. Cut out the membrane and scrape out any seeds. Cut off the stalk.

LAY each chilli half cut side down on the board and make cuts lengthways (quite close together), reaching almost as far as the stalk end, then cut across the other way to give little squares.

peeling tomatoes

REMOVE the stems of the tomatoes and score a cross in the bottom of each one with a knife, cutting just through the skin. Blanch in boiling water for 30 seconds or so.

TEST one tomato to see if the skin will come off easily, otherwise leave them to soak for a few seconds more. Don't leave them for too long or they might start to cook.

TRANSFER the tomatoes to a bowl of cold water and then peel the skin away from the crosses—it should slip off very easily.

peeling and deseeding cucumbers

HALVE the cucumber horizontally. If your cucumber is long, cut it in half first as long pieces are difficult to cut evenly.

PEEL both halves with a potato peeler or a small sharp knife. A swivel peeler is the easiest thing to use as it removes the least amount of flesh with the skin.

SCRAPE out the seeds with a teaspoon and then allow the cucumber pieces to drain with the seeded side down. Cut as directed by the recipe.

degorging aubergines

CUT the aubergines into pieces and layer in a colander, sprinkling each layer with salt. This will help to draw out any bitter juices. It also stops the flesh from soaking up too much oil if you are frying them.

LEAVE for about 20 minutes to let the aubergines degorge their bitter juices, then rinse them thoroughly under cold running water.

SQUEEZE each piece of aubergine dry, making sure you have got rid of all the water.

preparing herbs

IN most recipes basil leaves will be torn rather than chopped. This prevents the cut edges from blackening. Basil should be torn at the last minute, just before use, as its flavour goes quickly. Herbs should be kept as dry as possible so they keep their colour when torn or chopped.

HERBS should be chopped with a large knife, sharp enough to slice cleanly without tearing. To roughly chop, arrange the herbs into a long pile, parallel to the knife blade.

KEEP the blade end of the knife on the board and rock the handle up and down and backwards and forwards.

TO finely chop herbs, keep chopping the pile of herbs as before or grip the blade at each end and chop blade backwards and forwards across the pile, scraping the herbs together every so often.

A mezzaluna (two-handled knife) is the ideal instrument for chopping herbs. Some come with a special board with a dip in it. Rock the blade backwards and forwards over the herbs, scraping the pile back together occasionally.

TO shred (chiffonade) larger leaves such as basil, lay the leaves on top of each other in a pile, then roll the pile up like a fat cigar and slice finely. A sharp knife will prevent the basil from bruising.

preserving

In Italy, vegetables to be used in the off season are far more likely to be preserved in oil or brine or dried than frozen. Bottled tomatoes, beans and peas can all be easily used and peeled peppers in oil save you having to prepare them yourself. Use as you would for fresh vegetables but only cook for the briefest time just to heat through. Dried vegetables such as beans, peppers, porcini mushrooms and tomatoes just need to be soaked until they are plump before using. Vegetables are also pickled and used as accompaniments or antipasto.

salad leaves

Salad leaves can often be bought by the handful and may be already mixed—one of the best mixes is misticanza. This is a Roman term for wild mixed leaves and it usually contains both herbs, such as mint and rocket, and leaves like sorrel and dandelion. The mix varies according to the individual sellers.

herbs

For the freshest herbs, buy those in pots that can be kept on a windowsill and picked as you need them. Basil, oregano, thyme and mint grow very well like this. For most Italian recipes herbs can be roughly chopped with a large kitchen knife. Basil leaves are better torn rather than chopped so that the cut edges of the leaves don't blacken, but, if they do need chopping, larger leaves can be rolled and shredded (chiffonaded), as shown. Some herbs such as mint release their aroma best when they are lightly crushed.

Panzanella

INGREDIENTS

900 g ripe tomatoes, peeled (see
page 172) and quartered

3 garlic cloves, crushed

30 g basil, torn, plus a few whole
leaves for garnishing

50 ml red wine vinegar

300 ml extra virgin olive oil

1 day-old 'country-style' loaf, such
as ciabatta, crust removed, cut into
4 cm cubes

1 small cucumber, peeled, deseeded
(see page 172)

2 red peppers, peeled (see page 10)
and cut into 2 cm strips

2 yellow peppers, peeled (see page
10) and cut into 2 cm strips

50 g capers, rinsed and dried

100 g black olives, pitted and halved

30 g anchovies, cut in half
lengthways

Recipes for this colourful Italian bread salad vary but the basic idea uses up leftover bread by soaking it in tomato juice and olive oil, throwing in a few herbs and vegetables along the way. It is important that you use ripe tomatoes and a good-quality olive oil.

TO crush garlic with a knife, put the peeled clove on a board with a pinch of salt. The abrasive nature of the salt helps break down the garlic. Coat the blade in the salt and scrape it against the garlic in a downwards motion. Keep scraping until the garlic is reduced to a paste.

HOLD each tomato quarter over a large bowl and squeeze out the seeds and juice. Add the garlic, half the basil, the vinegar and 200 ml of the olive oil. Taste for seasoning.

ADD the bread to the bowl along with the tomato quarters. Leave for at least 30 minutes. If the bread is quite hard, it may need more liquid; if so, add more olive oil and vinegar in the same proportions.

JUST before serving, thinly slice the cucumber and add to the bowl. To serve, divide half the salad among six plates. Top with half the peppers, then sprinkle with half the capers, half the olives and anchovies and the remaining basil. Put the last of the bread mixture on top and repeat with the remaining peppers, capers, olives, anchovies. Garnish with basil leaves and drizzle with the remaining olive oil just before serving. The salad can be left for up to 2 hours but serve it at room temperature, not from the fridge.

Caponata

Originally a classic Sicilian dish, caponata is now enjoyed throughout Italy. It is often served warm or at room temperature as part of an antipasto platter or to accompany meat. The dish can be prepared in advance—the flavours will only improve.

SERVES 6

INGREDIENTS

2 large aubergines, cut into 3 cm
  cubes
3 large celery stalks, finely chopped
3 tablespoons extra virgin olive oil
1 large onion, finely chopped
50 g pine nuts
4 garlic cloves, thinly sliced
400 g tomatoes, peeled (see page
  172), or 1 x 400 g tin chopped
  tomatoes
olive oil, for shallow-frying
1 teaspoon dried oregano
3 tablespoons capers, rinsed and
  dried
4 tablespoons red wine vinegar
12 green olives, pitted and chopped

PUT the aubergines in layers in a colander, sprinkling salt on each layer. Leave the aubergines to degorge (give off any bitter juices) for about 20 minutes, then rinse in cold water and squeeze dry with your hands. Put the aubergines in a large bowl.

BLANCH the celery in boiling water for 1 minute then plunge into cold water, drain and set aside. (Blanching dilutes the flavour of the celery a little as it can be quite overpowering.)

HEAT the extra virgin olive oil in a saucepan over low heat and cook the onion and pine nuts until the onion is soft and the pine nuts are light brown. Add the garlic and cook for another minute. Add the celery and tomatoes and cook until the sauce has thickened.

POUR a generous amount of olive oil into a deep frying pan. To test the oil is deep enough, hold a teaspoon upright in the pan: the oil should reach a quarter of the way up the spoon. Add enough aubergines to just cover the base of the pan and cook over medium heat until golden brown and soft on both sides. Remove from the pan and place in a colander to drain off any oil. Repeat until all the aubergines are cooked.

ADD the oregano, capers and red wine vinegar to the tomato sauce. Bring to the boil and simmer gently until thickened. Remove from the heat and add the aubergines and olives. Stir briefly and season with salt and pepper. Leave to rest for at least 15 minutes before serving.

DEGORGING aubergines not only rids them of any bitter juices, but it also stops them soaking up too much oil when they are fried. Make sure you both rinse and dry them well before cooking.

red wine vinegar

Aceto (vinegar) is made by turning alcohol into acetic acid using a bacteria or a bacterial fungi called a vinegar mother. Vinegar is used both as a preservative and to flavour food. It adds a sharp taste and helps to bring out other flavours. Red wine vinegar *(aceto di vino rosso)* can be made from a mixture of grapes or just one variety, provided it is good quality.

Insalata di rinforzo

INGREDIENTS

50 g carrots

150 g green beans

½ red onion

600 ml white wine vinegar

1 tablespoon sea salt

1 tablespoon sugar

1 bay leaf

300 g cauliflower florets

DRESSING

80 ml extra virgin olive oil

2 tablespoons lemon juice

1 tablespoon finely chopped parsley

1 tablespoon chopped capers

1 garlic clove, halved

4 anchovy fillets, halved lengthways

85 g small black olives, such as
   Gaeta or Ligurian

1 tablespoon roughly chopped
   flat-leaf parsley

½ tablespoon extra virgin olive oil

Meaning 'reinforced salad', this Neapolitan Christmas dish is supposed to last until Epiphany on January 6. The salad is topped up (reinforced) with fresh ingredients when the quantity begins to dwindle.

CUT the carrots into batons about the size of your little finger. Cut the beans into similar lengths and slice the onion thinly.

PUT the vinegar, sea salt, sugar and bay leaf in a saucepan with 500 ml water and bring to the boil. Cook the carrots for about 3 minutes, or until crisp but tender, and transfer to a bowl with a slotted spoon. Add the beans to the pan and cook for 2 minutes, then add them to the bowl. Add the onion and cauliflower to the pan and cook for 3 minutes, or until the cauliflower just starts to soften. Drain, add to the bowl and allow the vegetables to cool.

TO make the dressing, mix together the olive oil, lemon juice, parsley, capers and garlic and season well. Pour over the cooled vegetables and toss gently.

TO serve, toss the anchovy fillets, olives, parsley and oil through the salad.

TO chop parsley, remove the leaves from the stalks and make them into a long pile parallel to the knife blade. Using the whole blade of your knife, chop up and down through the pile, keeping the point of the knife on the board. After every few chops, scrape the pile back together.

Borlotti beans with tomatoes, parsley and mint

SERVES 4

This bean salad can be made with fresh, dried or tinned borlotti beans. As the beans are cooking, a little olive oil is added—this not only gives flavour to the beans but also softens their skins. The tomato, chilli, mint and parsley are simply stirred through just before serving.

IF using fresh beans, there is no need to soak and precook them. If using dried beans, soak them in cold water for at least 6 hours or overnight. Drain the beans, put them in a saucepan, cover with water and bring to the boil. Drain again, rinsing away any foam that has appeared on the surface of the water. If using tinned beans, simply rinse well and drain before mixing with the olive oil and vinegar below.

TO cook the fresh or dried beans, cover with water and bring to the boil, add the garlic, bay leaf and 1 tablespoon of the olive oil. Reduce the heat and simmer gently for about 20–30 minutes for fresh beans and about 40 minutes for dried, or until tender. Do not salt the beans during cooking as this will toughen the skins. Drain the beans, keeping the garlic.

REMOVE the skin from the garlic and mash with a fork (they will be quite soft after cooking and will easily break up). While the beans are still hot, mix in the rest of the oil, the vinegar and salt and pepper. Stir in the tomato, chilli and herbs just before serving.

preparing

TO prepare this dish a little ahead of time, the beans can be cooked and mixed with the garlic, oil, vinegar, salt and pepper and left in the fridge for a couple of hours. If you want to prepare the dish the day before, don't add the vinegar until closer to the serving time.

INGREDIENTS

250 g fresh borlotti beans, 200 g
  dried beans or 800 g tinned beans

3 garlic cloves, unpeeled

1 bay leaf

4 tablespoons extra virgin olive oil

3 tablespoons red wine vinegar or
  balsamic vinegar

2 tomatoes, peeled (see page 172)
  and finely chopped

½ large mild red chilli, finely
  chopped (see page 172)

3 tablespoons roughly chopped mint

3 tablespoons roughly chopped
  parsley

Grilled vegetable salad

SERVES 6

INGREDIENTS

1 yellow pepper, grilled and peeled
(see page 10)

1 red pepper, grilled and peeled (see
page 10)

2 medium aubergines, sliced
diagonally

4 courgettes, sliced diagonally

DRESSING

2 garlic cloves

1 heaped teaspoon sea salt

150 ml extra virgin olive oil

juice of 1 small lemon or
3 tablespoons red wine vinegar

½ red chilli, finely chopped (see
page 172)

15 g basil, torn

6 peppercorns, crushed

Summer in the south brings with it a glut of vegetables, and this simple salad is an easy way to make the best use of them. You can make it a day in advance and leave it to soak up the dressing, but add the herbs at the last minute and serve at room temperature.

CUT the yellow and red peppers into wide strips and set aside.

PREHEAT a griddle, chargrill or barbecue to very hot. Place a few aubergine slices on the griddle and cook over medium-high heat, turning once, until the aubergines are soft and cooked. Cook all the aubergines in this way, stacking them up on top of each other once they're cooked, to help them steam a little and soften. Cook the courgette slices in the same way until dark golden brown and add to the aubergines.

TO make the dressing, smash the garlic cloves with the sea salt in a mortar and pestle. Alternatively, crush the garlic with a little salt using the flat blade of your knife. To do this, coat the knife blade in the salt and scrape it against the garlic in a downwards motion until it forms a paste. Mix together the garlic, olive oil, lemon juice, chilli, basil and peppercorns.

PLACE all the vegetables in a flat dish and pour over the dressing. Mix briefly to avoid breaking up the aubergines and leave to marinate for at least 30 minutes.

THE vegetables can be prepared a day in advance and left to marinate in the dressing overnight but mix in the basil just before serving.

WHEN grilling vegetables, don't brush the griddle or vegetables with oil or the oil will burn and taste bitter. If the griddle is hot enough the vegetables won't stick. When the first set of lines is marked on the vegetables, pick them up and move them 90 degrees so the marks sit across the grill and allow them to mark again. Turn over and repeat on the other side.

Abruzzo e Molise

Although geographically positioned closer to central Italy, these regions have the culinary feel of the south. Abruzzo and Molise were joined until 1963 and have much in common. They are not particularly prosperous and rely on inexpensive ingredients in their cooking, imaginatively using all parts of the animal in food preparation. Both have cold mountainous regions, large areas of national park and coastlines on the Adriatic Sea. They also both have a history of transhumance: the movement of flocks of sheep, cattle or goats to higher pastures during the summer months and then back down again before the winter. Although this is a coastal area with abundant fish and seafood, it is more renowned for its lamb, mutton and kid dishes.

Vegetables are widely grown and eaten in both regions, particularly potatoes in Abruzzo and asparagus in Molise. Herbs such as oregano are abundant and very high-quality saffron is produced. The food is usually spiced up with hot chillies *(peperoncini)* and the region's olive oil is exported worldwide.

Pasta, both fresh and dried, is eaten—a fact that sums up the region's straddling of the centre and south of the country. Many pasta factories can be found in the area and one of the best-known dried pasta manufacturers, De Cecco, is based in Fara San Martino in Abruzzo. *Maccheroni alla chitarra* is a speciality—a fresh pasta shaped by rolling a sheet of dough over wires stretched across a box and often served with a mutton sauce. A soup, *minestrone de Teramo,* also known as *virtù*, contains seven different types of pasta as well as seven other ingredients such as vegetables and legumes.

Confetti

These are sugared almonds, reputed to be the best in the world. They are not thrown at the bride and groom in Italy, but given to them in a tiny muslin bag, always with an odd number of almonds in the bag, and kept as a souvenir of the wedding. But confetti are not only for weddings in Italy: they come in myriad colours, each signifying a different thing. Birthdays and anniversaries are celebrated by colour: pink for one; yellow for ten; silver for twenty-five; and gold for fifty. Even university graduations are celebrated with different colours according to the subject: red for medicine; purple for business; and black for engineering. Confetti are also turned into flowers, birds, butterflies and other novelties by being wired together and decorated.

Braised fennel with olives

SERVES 4

INGREDIENTS

2 large fennel bulbs

4 tablespoons extra virgin olive oil

1 red onion, halved and thinly sliced

3 garlic cloves, sliced

4 small sprigs of rosemary, chopped

100 ml white wine

50 g black olives, pitted and halved

The fennel bulb is one of Italy's favourite vegetables, although such is its mild sweet flavour and delicious aroma that it was once served at the end of a meal. Fennel takes well to braising, sautéeing or use in gratins. This dish can be served hot or at room temperature.

black olives

Black olives are cured ripe olives. Like green olives, they can be brine-cured but as they are picked ripe they are less bitter than green and can also be salt-cured, or salt-cured then sun-dried. Choose the best quality olives you can afford and pit them yourself. Very black olives, which are sold pitted in cans, are often chemically cured dyed green olives.

SLICE the fennel into thick wedges, cutting from top to bottom but keeping them joined at the root. Cut off and reserve any fronds. Heat the olive oil in a large frying pan and cook the fennel and onion over medium heat for about 10 minutes, stirring occasionally until lightly browned.

ADD the garlic and half the rosemary, season with salt and pepper and stir briefly to prevent the fennel and garlic from burning. After a few minutes, add the wine, put the lid on and gently cook for another 10–15 minutes, or until tender but still holding together. Lift the lid occasionally to make sure the fennel is not burning.

ONCE the fennel is soft it is cooked. If all the liquid has evaporated and the fennel is still not cooked, add a little more wine or water. Alternatively, if there is still a lot of liquid left and the fennel is almost cooked, lift the lid to allow the liquid to reduce a little. The fennel should be moist but not dry.

ADD the olives and the rest of the chopped rosemary just before the end of cooking time. Serve sprinkled with any reserved fennel fronds.

cooking

You can also make this dish with baby fennel. Simply cut them in half and cook them in the same way. Serve them rounded side up.

Oven-roasted tomatoes

Tomatoes are an integral ingredient in Italian cooking and their Italian name, *pomodoro*, means 'golden apple'. Here, they are simply topped with some herbs and oil and then slowly roasted in the oven. Serve with grilled chicken or as a light meal on their own with bread and cheese.

SERVES 6

INGREDIENTS

12 large ripe tomatoes

150 ml extra virgin olive oil

3 garlic cloves, chopped

2 tablespoons finely chopped thyme
   or rosemary

6 tablespoons finely chopped parsley

SLICE the tomatoes in half horizontally. Put them on a lightly greased baking tray or in a very shallow gratin dish and season with salt and pepper. Preheat the oven to 175°C (350°F/Gas 4).

MIX together the oil, garlic, thyme and parsley. Drizzle 2 teaspoons over the top of each tomato, then bake for 2–3 hours. The tomatoes should be caramelised and crisp on top and quite shrivelled, with all the liquid having reduced inside them. If the tomatoes are cooking too quickly and are starting to overbrown or burn, turn the heat down. If there is a lot of oil (the oil collects around the tomatoes), baste the tomatoes as they cook to keep the tops moist.

preparing

CHOP herbs with a knife or a mezzaluna (a two-handled knife). Some mezzalunas come with a special board with a dip in it; otherwise use any board. Rock the blade backwards and forwards through the herbs, scraping them back into a pile occasionally.

Chicory, radicchio and pancetta al forno

450 g white chicory

1 large radicchio

150 g pancetta or smoked bacon,
  thinly sliced

50 g fresh breadcrumbs

50 g Parmesan, grated

1½ tablespoons finely chopped
  thyme

1 garlic clove, finely chopped

570 ml double cream

A dish referred to as 'al forno' means that it has been baked or roasted in the oven. There are many varieties of radicchio but the burgundy and white varieties are often seen in Italy and include radicchio di Treviso and rosso di Verona.

PREHEAT the oven to 180°C (350°F/Gas 4). Slice the chicory in half lengthways (or if they are quite large, slice them into quarters). Divide the radicchio into six or eight wedges, depending on its size.

LIGHTLY butter a shallow 2.5 litre gratin dish. Place the chicory and radicchio in the dish in one layer, alternating the colours.

MIX together the pancetta, breadcrumbs, Parmesan, thyme and garlic and season well. Sprinkle over the chicory and radicchio.

POUR the cream over the top, cover with foil and bake for 50–60 minutes. Take the foil off the dish for the last 20 minutes to crisp up the pancetta and breadcrumbs. Leave to rest for about 10 minutes before serving.

Cannellini bean and gremolata salad

Dried beans are popular throughout Italy and make an appearance in many dishes, from soups to pastas or as accompaniments to meat and fish. Creamy white cannellini beans are used here to make a salad that can be served either warm or cold.

SERVES 6

INGREDIENTS

350 g dried cannellini or flageolet
    beans
3 garlic cloves, unpeeled
1 bay leaf
2 tablespoons extra virgin olive oil
3 red or yellow peppers, peeled (see
    page 10) and cut into strips
drizzle of extra virgin olive oil and
    1 tablespoon chopped parsley,
    to serve

DRESSING

4 tablespoons extra virgin olive oil
juice of 1 large lemon

GREMOLATA

2 garlic cloves
1 heaped teaspoon sea salt
grated zest of 1 large lemon
4 tablespoons chopped flat-leaf
    parsley

SOAK the beans in cold water for at least 6 hours. Drain the beans, put them in a saucepan, cover with water and bring to the boil. Drain again, rinsing away any foam that has appeared on the surface of the water.

COVER the beans with water again and bring to the boil. Add the garlic, bay leaf and olive oil. Simmer gently for about 40 minutes, or until tender (older drier beans will take longer to soften). Do not salt the beans during cooking as this will toughen the skins.

MEANWHILE, make a dressing with the olive oil, lemon juice and salt and pepper. Drain the beans, remove the garlic and, while still hot, pour the dressing over the top and mix together.

TO make a gremolata, smash the garlic cloves with the sea salt in a mortar and pestle. Alternatively, crush the garlic with a little salt using the flat blade of your knife. To do this, coat the knife blade in the salt and scrape it against the garlic in a downwards motion until it forms a paste. Using a fork, mix the garlic with the lemon zest, parsley and salt and pepper.

JUST before serving, stir the gremolata through the beans. Spread the peppers over the beans and serve sprinkled with a little parsley and a drizzle of olive oil.

YOU will need the zest from the lemon for the gremolata and the juice for the dressing. Zest the lemon first, before cutting it in half to juice it. The cleanest way to grate lemon or other citrus zest is to cover the surface of the grater with a piece of greaseproof paper. The cutting edges break through the paper, so just grate as normal and then pull off the paper, bringing all the zest with it.

Artichoke frittata

SERVES 4

INGREDIENTS

175 g broad beans, fresh or frozen

400 g tin artichoke hearts, drained

3 tablespoons olive oil

1 onion, thinly sliced

6 eggs

2 tablespoons chopped parsley

45 g pecorino, grated

pinch of nutmeg

olive oil

Olive oil *(olio d'oliva)* is made by crushing the flesh of olives and extracting the oil. Extra virgin olive oil is cold pressed. This means the olives are crushed and the oil is drained out rather than being heated or chemically treated. 'Extra virgin' refers to an olive oil of outstanding flavour and aroma with a maximum acidity of 1 per cent; 'virgin' has an acidity no higher than 1.5 per cent; and 'olive oil' or 'pure olive oil' is made by using heat and/or pressing to extract the oil, which is then refined. 'Light' or 'extra light' oil is refined oil with a light colour and flavour. The colour of olive oil is derived purely from the type of olive used.

Almost an omelette, but flashed under the grill to finish off the cooking, the frittata varies from thin and pancake-like, to thicker with a golden crust and creamy centre. It is a favourite throughout Italy, but the artichoke frittata is a speciality of Trentino.

BRING a small saucepan of water to the boil and add a large pinch of salt and the broad beans. Boil for 2 minutes, then drain and rinse under cold water. Peel off the skins from the beans.

CUT the artichoke hearts from bottom to top into slices about 5 mm wide. Discard any slices that contain the tough central choke.

HEAT the oil in a 30 cm frying pan and fry the onion over low heat for 6–8 minutes, without allowing it to brown. Add the artichoke slices and cook for 1–2 minutes. Stir in the broad beans.

PREHEAT the grill. Lightly beat together the eggs, parsley, pecorino and nutmeg and season well with salt and pepper. Pour into the frying pan and cook over low heat until three-quarters set, shaking the pan often to stop the frittata sticking.

FINISH the top off under the grill and leave to cool before serving in wedges.

Braised artichokes with peas and broad beans

This is a great recipe to prepare in the spring months when all these ingredients are in season and at their best. Small peas and beans will be more succulent. Serve with roast pork or grilled fish, or as a topping for bruschetta.

IF your broad beans are not particularly young, take them out of their outer skins. These can get very tough and leathery when cooked and, though double podding takes time, it is worth it.

CUT each artichoke heart into 12 segments. Pod the broad beans and peas and blanch them for 1 minute in boiling water, then refresh in iced water. If the broad beans are very large and old you may also want to remove the pale green outer skin which can be very leathery.

HEAT the olive oil in a large saucepan or deep frying pan and add the artichoke, onion and pancetta. Cook gently for about 15 minutes, stirring frequently. Season with salt and pepper. Add the broad beans and peas and cook for 5 minutes. (If the broad beans are large, add them before the peas as they will need a minute or two longer.) Stir in the garlic, add the wine and cook for 10 minutes more, or until all the liquid has evaporated.

PIERCE the artichokes with a knife to see if they are tender. If they need more cooking, add a dash of water and cover. When cooked, add the mint, taste for seasoning and leave to stand for a few minutes to allow the flavours to develop.

SERVES 6

INGREDIENTS

750 g cleaned artichoke hearts

1 kg fresh broad beans in pods
(300 g podded weight)

400 g fresh peas in pods
(150 g podded weight)

3 tablespoons extra virgin olive oil

1 red onion, quartered and thinly
sliced

185 g smoked pancetta

2 garlic cloves, chopped

125 ml white wine

2 tablespoons chopped mint

cooking

Pea pods, if very fresh, can add a little sweetness to this dish, but only use a few. Scrape the inside of the pod to get rid of the slightly bitter membrane, then cut them up and add them with the peas.

Puglia

Orecchiette

Orecchiette

Orecchiette (little ears) are made from 80 per cent semolina flour and 20 per cent winter wheat flour. Today, they are generally made by machine but in Puglia they are still shaped by hand on a wooden board. Their curved saucer-like shape and slightly rough texture makes them ideal for holding sauce. Orecchiette are traditionally served with *cime di rapa*, the leafy green bitter tops of turnips.

Puglia is the flattest region in Italy (a country filled with mountains and hills) and is situated in its south-east corner. Over time it has had many invaders and the Greeks, Normans and Turks have all left their mark on the area. Wheat is grown on the flat lowland areas, vegetables grow prolifically and the sea surrounds a large percentage of the region. The north is meat-eating with a strong dairy culture (thousands of sheep from nearby Abruzzo and Molise were once driven to its pastures in the winter months), while the coastline yields prawns, squid, octopus and sea bream in abundance.

The cooking of the region is opulent with fruit and vegetables grown to perfection, particularly olives, herbs, almonds and fruit such as grapes, melons and figs. Dried vegetables are common, left out under the hot summer sun until they are completely desiccated. Pasta is generally made without egg and eaten with vegetable or legume sauces, with orecchiette being the 'local' shape. Cheeses include caciocavallo, scamorza and ricotta and the regional bread, pugliese, is now well known around the world. Puglia produces one-third of Italy's olive oil.

Antipasti here are among the best in Italy and are based on local vegetables and seafood. The region's ham, *capocollo*, is made in Martina Franca as is the veal and pork sausage, *cervellata*.

Aubergine parmigiana

Parmigiana is a deceptive name for this dish as it does not, in fact, hail from that city. Instead, its creation is claimed by nearly every region of Italy, but the use of mozzarella and tomatoes indicates that it is a dish from the south.

THINLY slice the aubergines lengthways. Layer the slices in a large colander, sprinkling salt between each layer. Leave for 1 hour to degorge (extract the bitter juices). Rinse and pat the slices dry on both sides with paper towels, then coat lightly with the flour.

PREHEAT the oven to 180°C (350°F/Gas 4) and grease a shallow 2.5 litre baking dish.

HEAT 125 ml of the olive oil in a large frying pan. Quickly fry the aubergine slices in batches over high heat until crisp and golden on both sides. Add more olive oil as needed and drain on paper towels as you remove each batch from the pan.

MAKE a slightly overlapping layer of aubergine slices over the base of the dish. Season with pepper and a little salt. Spoon 4 tablespoons of passata over the aubergine and scatter some of the basil over the top. Sprinkle with some mozzarella, followed by some Parmesan. Continue with this layering until you have used up all the ingredients, then finish with a layer of the cheeses.

BAKE for 30 minutes. Remove from the oven and allow to cool for 30 minutes before serving.

SERVES 8

INGREDIENTS

1.5 kg aubergines

plain flour, seasoned with salt and pepper

350 ml olive oil

500 ml tomato passata or tomato pasta sauce (see page 38)

2 tablespoons roughly torn basil leaves

250 g mozzarella, chopped

90 g Parmesan, grated

mozzarella

True mozzarella is made from buffalo milk: that made from cow's milk is called *fior di latte*. The curds *(mozzata)* are stretched and shaped into balls by hand (though some balls are now factory made). Mozzarella should be white, fresh-smelling and have tiny holes that weep whey when it is very fresh. It is available in a variety of sizes (from small ones like cherries to large 600 g balls) that are sold in their own whey and also as plaits.

Potato and tomato al forno

SERVES 4

INGREDIENTS

120 ml extra virgin olive oil

1 large red onion, halved and thinly
    sliced

3 garlic cloves, sliced

500 g ripe tomatoes, peeled (see
    page 172) and cut into large cubes

1 kg waxy potatoes, unpeeled, cut
    into thick slices or wedges

15 g rosemary or oregano, roughly
    chopped

16 black olives, pitted and chopped

4 tablespoons red wine vinegar

Forno means 'oven' in Italian and 'al forno' refers to any dish that is baked or roasted in the oven. Use pink fir apple or similar waxy potatoes for this recipe as they will hold their shape well when cooked.

PREHEAT the oven to 200°C (400°F/Gas 6). Heat half the olive oil in a pan and cook the onion and garlic until the onion is soft and translucent.

MIX together the tomatoes, onion, potatoes, herbs, olives, vinegar and the remaining olive oil and season well.

SPOON into a shallow 2.5 litre gratin dish and bake for 1–1½ hours, until the tomato juices and dressing have been absorbed by the potatoes and they are soft and golden on top. If the tops of the potatoes start to overbrown, cover them loosely with a piece of foil until they are cooked through—they should be tender to the point of a knife.

COOKING onion slowly (sweating) turns its starch to sugar and makes it very sweet. If you like, you can cover the onion with a circle of damp greaseproof paper (a cartouche). This helps it stay moist as it cooks and stops it from browning.

Potato and leek al forno

Although the potato has never become quite the staple in Italy that it is in other countries, with the Italians tending to favour pasta, rice or polenta, there are still many recipes in which the potato plays a starring role.

THINLY slice the potatoes with a mandolin or very sharp knife (they have to be the same thickness or they will not cook through evenly). Preheat the oven to 180°C (350°F/Gas 4). Heat the butter or oil in a saucepan and cook the leeks over low heat for about 10 minutes, or until soft. Season with salt and pepper. Add the garlic and herbs and cook for a couple of minutes.

GREASE a shallow 3 litre gratin dish with butter or oil. Arrange a layer of potatoes in the base of the dish and season with salt and pepper. Scatter with one-third of the leeks and a few dollops of mascarpone. Continue in the same way to make two more layers, finishing with a layer of potatoes (but not leeks as they will burn) and top with mascarpone. Pour the wine over the top and cover with foil.

BAKE in the oven for about 1 hour, removing the foil for the last 15 minutes to brown and crisp the top.

SLICING the potatoes on a mandolin gives fine, even slices. You can adjust the position of the blade to give the thickness you want. Slicing by hand requires a good long sharp knife and a very steady hand. Slice evenly downwards for the best effect.

SERVES 4

INGREDIENTS

1 kg waxy potatoes, unpeeled

3 tablespoons butter or olive oil

400 g leeks, trimmed, halved
and sliced

3 garlic cloves, thinly sliced

1 tablespoon chopped thyme or
rosemary

300 g mascarpone

250 ml white wine

SERVES 6

INGREDIENTS

150 g asparagus

4 tablespoons olive oil

1 onion, chopped

1 courgette, halved lengthways and
finely sliced

2 garlic cloves, chopped

100 g spinach, stalks removed if
necessary, roughly chopped

2 tablespoons chopped basil

75 g Parmesan, grated

250 g ricotta

250 g mascarpone

6 eggs

Vegetable torte

Vegetables in Italy have never been seen as mere accompaniments to meat and the country is rich in regional recipes for vegetable pies, both with and without pastry. Don't be constrained by the ingredient list: you can make this recipe with just about whatever is in season.

serving

The torte needs to be refrigerated for 3 hours before serving anyway, to give it time to firm up, so it is easy enough to prepare it a day in advance and serve it chilled. If so, use only 4 eggs and reduce the cooking time to about 40 minutes.

UNLESS it's very young, asparagus often has a tough woody end that needs to be removed. To find the natural breaking point, hold the asparagus at each end and bend it gently.

IT will snap at its natural breaking point, where the woody part ends. These tough pieces can be used to flavour stock.

WASH the asparagus and remove the woody ends (hold each spear at both ends and bend it gently—it will snap at its natural breaking point). Remove the spear tips of the asparagus and slice the remaining stems. Bring a small saucepan of salted water to the boil and cook the asparagus stems for about 2 minutes. Add the tips and cook for 1 minute. Drain the asparagus and set aside.

PREHEAT the oven to 180°C (350°F/Gas 4). Heat the olive oil in a saucepan and cook the onion until soft. Increase the heat and add the courgette. Cook until the courgette is soft and a little golden brown, stirring occasionally. Add the garlic and cook for 1 minute more. Add the spinach and mix briefly until just wilted and cooked.

REMOVE the pan from the heat, add the asparagus and basil, season with salt and pepper and set aside to cool.

GREASE a 20 cm springform tin with butter and dust with a tablespoon of the Parmesan. Mix the ricotta, mascarpone, eggs and 50 g Parmesan into the cooled vegetables and taste for seasoning.

SPOON into the tin and scatter with the remaining Parmesan. Place the tin on a tray (to catch any drips) and bake for 50–60 minutes. The top should be a light golden brown and the mixture should still wobble slightly in the centre. Cool for 30 minutes, then chill in the fridge for 3 hours, or until the torte has set.

Parmesan

The making of *Parmigiano Reggiano*, the Italian hard cheese that is also simply known as Parmesan, is strictly regulated. The cows can only be fed on grass and hay and the cheese is only made in certain areas of Emilia-Romagna such as Parma and Reggio Emilia. Parmesan is made with the milk collected over two days, half skimmed and half unskimmed. The curds are cut into very small pieces and the cheeses are formed in special moulds. Each rind is marked with the place and date of making, as well as with the words *Parmigiano Reggiano* (look for this when buying Parmesan). The cheeses are then aged in large rooms called cathedrals for up to a year before being tested (some are even further aged). Parmesan is traditionally not cut but broken into pieces with a special knife.

Marinated courgettes

SERVES 4

INGREDIENTS

500 g small courgettes

1 tablespoon olive oil

1 tablespoon finely chopped parsley

1 garlic clove, sliced

1 tablespoon balsamic or red
  wine vinegar

An important, but relatively modern, part of most Italian meals is the *contorno*, a side dish of vegetables served with the main course. *Contorni* can include potatoes, beans or cooked greens but only one or two are served with each meal. Salad, pasta and rice are never classed as *contorni*.

THINLY slice the courgettes diagonally. Heat the oil in a heavy-based frying pan and fry the slices on both sides until browned. Remove with a slotted spoon and drain.

PUT the courgettes in a non-metallic dish and add the remaining ingredients. Season well and leave for a few hours. Serve with grilled or roast meats or as an antipasto.

Sautéed spinach

SERVES 4

INGREDIENTS

1 kg spinach

2 tablespoons olive oil

1 garlic clove

Contorni are carefully chosen to flatter the meal they are to accompany. In the same way that baked tomatoes are the accepted accompaniment to grilled chicken, spinach that has been lightly fried in oil and garlic is often the choice to serve with saltimbocca.

WASH the spinach thoroughly and shake it dry, leaving just a little water clinging to the leaves. Heat the oil in a frying pan and add the garlic. Cook for a few seconds and then add the spinach. Cover the pan for a minute to create some steam. Remove the lid and turn up the heat, stirring the spinach until all the liquid has evaporated. Season before serving.

Green beans

Pasta should always be served *al dente*, but this does not necessarily apply to vegetables. Green beans cooked until soft will not retain their bright green colour, but they will have more flavour than if they are still crunchy. You can use the same cooking method for peas.

COOK the beans in boiling salted water for 5 minutes, then drain and refresh. Drain thoroughly.

HEAT the oil in a frying pan and add the beans. Toss them in the oil for a minute or two and then season well.

SERVES 4

INGREDIENTS

500 g green beans, topped
  and tailed
1 tablespoon olive oil

Mashed potato

Although it is not as popular a dish as in France and Britain, the Italians do eat mashed potato. It is usually served with meat, poultry or fish dishes that have a sauce to be soaked up. Keep the pieces of potato fairly large when you boil them, or your mash could become watery.

CUT the potatoes into large even pieces and cook them in boiling salted water for about 12 minutes, or until they are tender to the point of a knife.

DRAIN well. Put the milk in the saucepan and heat it briefly, then add the potatoes and mash until very smooth.

BEAT in the olive oil and Parmesan and season with salt, pepper and nutmeg.

SERVES 4

INGREDIENTS

1 kg floury potatoes
200 ml milk
4 tablespoons extra virgin olive oil
75 g Parmesan, grated
freshly grated nutmeg

pane e
pizza

bread flours

Flours used for bread-making vary from region to region. Most bread recipes can be made with strong bread flour as well as ordinary flour. The increased gluten content of strong flour will make the bread rise more, giving it a lighter texture. Ordinary plain flour will create a denser bread, more authentic in texture to the 'country-style' loaves found in Italy. This also produces better bread for toasting, if you are making bruschetta and crostini.

kneading

It is very important to knead bread dough properly. This generally means that it will take longer than you anticipated—sometimes up to 10 or 15 minutes. The more you knead the dough, the better the outcome will be. You can use the dough hook on a food mixer if you like.

finishes on bread

You can finish the tops of loaves in many different ways. A dusting of flour will give a rustic look, a wash of milk or milk and egg produces a shinier finish and a pure egg glaze will turn the top dark shiny brown, as will a sugar and water glaze. Sesame seeds and poppy seeds can be added to a glazed surface. Scoring a cross in the top of the loaf with a sharp knife also looks attractive.

bread dough

TO make the starter, mix 185 ml lukewarm milk and 2 teaspoons honey in a large bowl with 3 tablespoons warm water. Sprinkle 7 g fresh yeast or 1 teaspoon dried yeast over the top and stir to dissolve.

LEAVE in a draught-free spot to activate. If the yeast does not bubble and foam in 5 minutes it is dead, so throw it away and start again.

ADD 125 g plain flour and whisk to form a thick paste. Cover loosely with clingfilm and leave overnight at room temperature to develop.

TO make the dough, sprinkle 7 g fresh yeast or 1 teaspoon dried yeast over the starter. Break up the starter by squeezing it between your fingertips.

GRADUALLY add 250 ml water, combining it with the starter. Mix in 2½ teaspoons salt and 500 g plain flour with your fingers until the mixture comes together to form a soft dough.

TURN out the dough onto a lightly floured work surface and knead for 10 minutes or until it is smooth and elastic and a finger indent pops out quickly.

PLACE the dough in a lightly oiled bowl and cover with a damp tea towel. Leave to rise in a draught-free place for 1–1½ hours or until doubled in size.

KNOCK back the dough by punching your fist into the middle of it. This deflates the air bubbles.

TURN out the dough onto a lightly floured surface and knead for 1–2 minutes until it is very smooth and all the air bubbles have been knocked out. The dough is now ready to use.

pizza base

MIX 2 teaspoons flour in a large bowl with 3 tablespoons lukewarm water. Sprinkle 7 g fresh yeast or 1 teaspoon dried yeast over the top and stir to dissolve.

LEAVE in a draught-free spot to activate. If the yeast does not bubble and foam in 5 minutes it is dead, so throw it away and start again.

PUT 600 g plain flour, the yeast, 2 teaspoons sea salt, 300 ml water and 1 tablespoon olive oil in a large bowl or in a food mixer with a dough hook.

MIX to form a dough, turn out onto a floured surface and knead for about 5 minutes. For pizzas, the dough does not have to be kneaded as well as it does for bread as it will be rolled out thinly and doesn't need to rise.

PUT the dough back in the bowl and smear with a film of oil to prevent it drying out. Cover with a tea towel and leave in a draught-free spot for about 2 hours or until doubled in size.

KNOCK back the dough by punching your fist into the middle of it. This deflates the air bubbles. Turn the dough out onto a lightly floured work surface and divide into four or six portions.

DUST with a little flour and roll into small balls. Try to make the surface as smooth as possible so that when the dough is rolled out it will not bubble too much.

PUT the balls on a tray or board dusted with a little flour and cover with a tea towel. Leave to rest for between 30 minutes and 2 hours.

HEAVILY dust the work surface with flour to prevent the dough sticking, then flatten each ball into a circle. Finish off with a rolling pin to make a thin crust about 2 mm thick, leaving a small ridge around the edge to hold the filling.

yeast

Because yeast is such an active ingredient there is no exact recipe for its use. You can use fresh yeast or dried for any recipe, with fresh usually being double the weight of dried. Sourdoughs are made with natural yeasts produced by starters, such as beer, fermented potatoes or fruit. Easy-active yeast can also be used and does not need 'activating' (leaving until spongy to make a starter) before use. It is simply added to the flour and liquid to make a dough. Easy-active yeast should be used within 6 months of purchase and not kept in a damp or overheated place.

baking

Breads and pizzas are baked at very high temperatures and are best cooked in a pizza oven or on a pizza stone in an ordinary oven to give them a crisp base. If you have a pizza oven or stone, place the bread in a well-greased bowl then, after the second rise, empty the dough straight onto the preheated stone or oven base without shaping it. This creates a firmer based crust. Make sure your stone has time to heat up properly. If you don't have a pizza oven or stone, turn your oven to very hot and preheat a baking tray with a thick base. When making pizzas, spread the topping on the base on a work surface and then slide the whole thing onto the hot stone or tray already in the oven. If you're not confident doing this, you can construct and bake the pizza on a cold tray, but the base won't be as crispy.

shaping pizzas

Bear in mind that bread dough rises in the oven. This means that if you want a pizza with a thin crust you will need to roll the base very thinly. Leave a small ridge around the edge to stop the filling running out.

MAKES 1 large loaf

INGREDIENTS

STARTER

250 g plain white flour

7 g fresh yeast or 1 teaspoon dried
   yeast

15 g fresh yeast or 2 teaspoons
   active dried yeast

2 teaspoons sea salt

3 tablespoons extra virgin olive oil

450 g plain white flour

100 g rye flour (or plain wholemeal
   flour)

Country-style bread

This recipe requires a starter to give a nuttier flavour. The starter is a mixture of yeast, flour and water that has been left to ferment for longer than when you are making an ordinary loaf of bread. A little rye flour has been added as well—a North Italian slant.

TO make the starter, put the flour, yeast and 150 ml lukewarm water in a large bowl or in a food mixer with a dough hook attachment. If using fresh yeast, mix with the warm water first. Mix into a dough, using your hands or the dough hook, and then knead for about 5 minutes, either using the dough hook or with your hands on the work surface, until the dough is soft and smooth.

PUT in a bowl, cover with clingfilm and leave in a warm place (about 20°C) for about 12 hours or overnight. The starter is meant to ferment, so if it is too cold, the yeast will not react sufficiently. The starter should be bubbly when it is ready.

TO make the bread, put the starter in a large bowl or in a food mixer with a dough hook and add 300 ml water, the remaining yeast, salt and oil and mix well to break up the starter into a thick batter. Add the flours and knead into a soft dough for about 10 minutes with the dough hook or your hands. The dough should be soft and smooth and, when you press your finger into it, the indent will pop out quickly. Place in a lightly oiled bowl and cover with a tea towel. Leave in a draught-free spot for about 2 hours, or until doubled in size. The temperature does not need to be as warm as it needs to be for the starter and a slow rise makes better bread.

GREASE a metal baking tray. Remove the dough from the bowl and gently form it into a round. Tuck the outside of the bread underneath to make an even ball shape. Place on the baking tray, stretching out into an oblong shape if you prefer. Cover with clingfilm and leave to rise for another 1-1½ hours.

PREHEAT the oven to 220°C (425°F/Gas 7). When the bread has risen for the second time, dust the top with flour. Spray a little water into the oven and bake the loaf on the top shelf for 30-40 minutes, or until the bread is brown on top and sounds hollow when tapped on the base. If the oven is very hot, the temperature might need to be reduced a little to prevent the bread burning before it is cooked through. Cool completely on a wire rack before serving.

cooking

Spraying a little water into the oven at the beginning of cooking will create some steam and help a good crust to form on the bread.

Bread rolls

MAKES 10–14 rolls

INGREDIENTS

1 quantity bread dough (see
   page 198)

plain flour, for dusting

The same dough can be used to make a variety of bread rolls. This recipe gives instructions for making four different styles: round rolls; *ciambellini* (made by rolling a dough rope and then joining the ends together); cylindrical; and oval bread rolls.

PREHEAT the oven to 200°C (400°F/Gas 6).

TO make round rolls, divide the dough into 14 pieces. Take each piece and roll it into a neat ball: the best way to do this is to cup the palm of one hand above dough and roll it in a circular movement on the work surface. Put the rolls on an oiled baking tray in a loose circle, spacing them about 2-3 cm apart—as they rise, they will join together again. Cover with a damp cloth and leave to rise for 10–15 minutes. Dust the tops with flour and bake for 35 minutes, or until the rolls are golden and risen and sound hollow when tapped on the base. Cool on wire racks.

TO make ciambellini, divide the dough into 12 pieces. Roll each one out into a rope about 20 cm long, then join the two ends together firmly. Put the rings on an oiled baking tray, cover with a damp cloth and leave to rise for 10-15 minutes. Dust the tops of the rolls with flour and bake for 20-30 minutes (spray the inside of the oven with a fine water mist when you put them in), or until they are golden and risen and sound hollow when tapped on the base. Cool on wire racks.

TO make cylinders, divide the dough into 12 pieces. Roll each piece into a ball then, using a rolling pin on a floured surface, roll the ball into a 1-cm thick circle. Hold the far end of the dough to stop it shrinking and, with your other hand, roll up the front end of the dough to resemble a scroll. Use a rolling pin to gently roll out the roll—this is just to flatten it as it will rise further. Put the rolls on an oiled baking tray, cover with a damp cloth and leave to rise for 10-15 minutes. Dust the tops of the rolls with flour and bake for 20-30 minutes (spray the inside of the oven with a fine water mist when you put them in) or until they are golden and risen and sound hollow when tapped on the base. Cool on wire racks.

TO make oval rolls, divide the dough into 10 pieces. Roll each one into the shape of a lemon and put them on an oiled baking tray. Taking a wooden spoon, press the handle lengthways down into each roll to form a deep mark—you will need to go the whole way down or the mark will bounce out as the roll rises. Cover with a damp cloth and leave to rise for 10-15 minutes. Dust the tops of the rolls with flour and bake for 20-30 minutes (spray the inside of the oven with a fine water mist when you put them in) or until they are golden and risen and sound hollow when tapped on the base. Cool on wire racks.

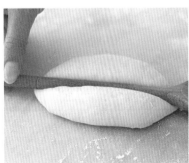

THE various shapes of the bread rolls produce a variety of crusts. The round rolls are arranged in a circle to bake, giving them soft edges where they join up. Ciambellini have a large crust surface and the cylinder rolls will have a layered crumb. For the oval rolls, you must make sure the central indent is deep enough to still be seen after cooking.

Focaccia

MAKES 1 focaccia

INGREDIENTS

15 g fresh yeast or 2 teaspoons dried yeast

1 teaspoon sugar

400 g strong white flour

100 ml extra virgin olive oil

large pinch of salt

20–24 small rosemary sprigs

coarse sea salt

Focaccia is an Italian flat bread made from yeasted bread dough. The dough is rolled flat, dimpled with fingermarks and then drizzled with lots of olive oil and salt. Originally it was cooked over an open fire, which provided the inspiration for its name, from the Latin *focus*, meaning 'fireplace'.

cooking

You can flavour the focaccia with chopped herbs, grated cheese, olives or pine nuts. Sprinkle them into the dimples just before baking, but remember that if you make the pieces too small they may burn.

PUT the yeast in a bowl with the sugar and stir in 250 ml lukewarm water. Leave in a draught-free spot to activate. If the yeast does not bubble and foam in 5 minutes it is dead, so throw it away and start again.

PUT the flour, 50 ml of the olive oil and the salt in a large bowl or in a food mixer with a dough hook attachment and pour the yeast mixture into the middle. Knead the dough for about 5 minutes, either using the dough hook or with your hands on the work surface, until it forms a soft and slightly sticky ball.

PUT the dough in a lightly greased bowl and smear with a film of oil to prevent it drying out. Cover with a tea towel and leave to rise in a warm place for about 2 hours or until doubled in size.

KNOCK back the dough to its original size by punching it with your fist. Press the dough into a greased 20 x 30 cm baking tray. Cover with a damp cloth and leave to rise for 30 minutes.

PREHEAT the oven to 220°C (425°F/Gas 7). Press deep dimples all over the surface of the dough with your fingertips. Put a rosemary sprig in each dimple. Bake for about 20 minutes, or until golden brown. As soon as the focaccia comes out of the oven, drizzle it with the remaining oil and sprinkle with coarse salt. Serve warm.

yeast

Yeast is a naturally occurring, microscopic, single-celled organism. It feeds on carbohydrates, breathes air and gives off carbon dioxide and alcohol. Yeast is used in bread-making and brewing, and also to make the rinds on cheeses. When yeast is used in bread-making, it converts the natural sugars in the flour to bubbles of carbon dioxide. These bubbles are trapped in the elastic mesh formed in the dough by the gluten—as the bubbles expand, they stretch the mesh and the bread rises. The process of baking kills the yeast and sets the dough around the bubbles.

Grissini

These Italian bread sticks originated in Turin but are now popular all over the country. Serve with antipasto or wrap in strips of prosciutto and eat as a snack. Hand-made grissini vary in thickness, look somewhat knobbly and are usually the length of the baker's arm.

PUT 310 ml warm water in a bowl and stir in the malt and yeast. Leave in a draught-free spot to activate. If the yeast does not bubble and foam in 5 minutes it is dead, so throw it away and start again. Sift the flour and salt into another bowl, add the yeast and the oil and mix until the dough clumps together.

FORM into a ball and knead on a lightly floured surface for 5–6 minutes, or until the dough is smooth and elastic. Put the dough on a lightly oiled tray and squash out to fill the shape of the tray. Brush with oil to stop it sticking and slide the tray into a plastic bag. Leave for 1 hour until doubled in size.

PREHEAT the oven to 230°C (450°F/Gas 8) and lightly oil two baking trays. Sprinkle the dough with semolina. Cut the dough into four portions along its length, then slice each one into five strips. Pick up each strip by both ends and stretch out to at least 20 cm long, remembering that the dough will shrink when you put it down. Try to keep the grissini as evenly shaped as you can so that they cook at the same rate.

ARRANGE the grissini on the trays, spacing them out a little. Dust lightly with flour. Bake for 20 minutes, or until crisp and golden. Cool slightly on the trays and then on wire racks.

SQUASH the dough out to fill the tray and cover with a plastic bag. Leave for 1 hour, then shape the grissini by both rolling and pulling them. Don't worry if they are not even—grissini made by non-commercial methods are always slightly lumpy. Shape the dough well to start with, then slice it into the right sized strips. Give each of these a brief roll if they look too square and then stretch them out. Remember, they will shrink back a little.

MAKES 20

INGREDIENTS

1 tablespoon malt syrup

15 g fresh yeast or 2 teaspoons dried yeast

500 g plain flour

1½ teaspoons salt

2 tablespoons olive oil

fine semolina, for dusting

MAKES 1 x 30 cm pizza

INGREDIENTS

120 g ripe plum tomatoes

3 basil leaves

2 garlic cloves, crushed

1 tablespoon tomato passata

2 teaspoons extra virgin olive oil

1 x 30 cm pizza base (see page 199)

3 tablespoons extra virgin olive oil

150 g mozzarella, chopped

9 small basil leaves

Pizza Margherita

This classic pizza was invented in 1889 by Raffaele Esposito in honour of Queen Margherita. The Queen heard so much of the fabled pizzas of Naples that she requested one to eat when she visited the city.

CORE the tomatoes and purée in a food processor with the basil leaves (or chop the tomatoes and basil very finely and stir together). Stir in the garlic, passata and olive oil and season well. Leave for at least 30 minutes to allow the flavours to blend.

PREHEAT the oven to very hot and put a baking tray or pizza stone in the oven to heat up. Drizzle the pizza base with 2 tablespoons of the oil and spread with the tomato sauce. Scatter with the mozzarella and drizzle with the remaining olive oil. Slide onto the hot tray or stone (if you're not confident doing this, you can construct and bake the pizza on a cold tray, but the base won't be as crisp).

COOK for 2–12 minutes (this will depend on how hot your oven is), or until the base is light brown and crisp and the topping is cooked. Before serving, drizzle with a little more oil and scatter the basil over the top.

cooking

If you are planning to make more than one pizza, make sure your oven is at its highest setting and cook no more than two at a time. Swap them around on the shelves halfway through so they both cook quickly.

Campania

Situated on the south-west coast of Italy, Campania is famous for many things, among others, the city of Naples, Mount Vesuvius, Pompeii, the Amalfi Coast, the island of Capri and pizza. This is the region whose cuisine most people think of as synonymous with Italian food: tomatoes, mozzarella, basil, spaghetti and the ubiquitous pizza.

Seafood is available all along the picturesque coast, especially *vongole* (clams) and *cozze* (mussels), which are eaten either as antipasti or tossed through spaghetti. Buffalo graze on the coastal plains to produce milk for the region's second most famous product, soft fresh *mozzarella di bufala* (the cow's milk version is called *fior di latte*). Other cheeses include ricotta made from the leftover mozzarella whey and locally made pecorino. Pasta tends to be dry and is often cut into spaghetti, vermicelli or ziti. The rich volcanic soil makes the region perfect for growing vegetables, particularly the tomatoes that were introduced in the sixteenth century from Peru. The local San Marzano tomatoes are made into rich sauces for pasta, pizza and baked dishes such as aubergine parmigiana.

Naples is also well known for its coffee—espresso sweetened with sugar—lemon and coffee granitas and crunchy ricotta-filled pastries. The lemon liqueur, *limoncello*, comes from the Amalfi coast and Strega, a liqueur made with 70 herbs and spices, is made in Benevento. The best-known wine from Campania is Lacrima Christi.

Pizza

Pizza first existed as a bread to accompany meals. The original topping for a *pizza bianca* (white pizza) was garlic, lard, salt and anchovies. The arrival of the tomato from South America gave rise to a whole new era in pizza-making and the pizza became a meal in itself, the dough base topped with tomato, mozzarella and other ingredients. In 1889, a Naples pizza-maker called Raffaele Esposito created the Margherita (also called the Napoletana) in honour of Queen Margherita who was visiting the city. With the royal seal of approval, the pizza went from strength to strength. The true Neapolitan pizza has a thin crust and is baked on the floor of a very hot wood-fired oven for 1 to 2 minutes. It is cut into quarters and eaten with the hands.

MAKES 1 x 30 cm pizza

INGREDIENTS

1 x 30 cm pizza base (see page 199)

2 tablespoons extra virgin olive oil

1 potato, very thinly sliced

100 g Taleggio, cut into small pieces

10 g rocket

extra virgin olive oil, for drizzling

Potato and rocket pizza

Although rocket *(rucola* or *rughetta)* is mostly used as a salad leaf, its tasty, slightly peppery flavour also works well as a flavouring for pasta sauces or, as here, to enliven a simple and delicate potato pizza.

PREHEAT the oven to very hot and put a baking tray or pizza stone in the oven to heat up. Drizzle the pizza base with oil. Cover with a layer of potato, leaving a thin border, sprinkle with the Taleggio and season. Slide onto the hot tray or stone (if you're not confident doing this, you can construct and bake the pizza on a cold tray, but the base won't be as crisp).

COOK for 2–12 minutes (this will depend on how hot your oven is), or until the potato is cooked. Drizzle with oil and scatter with rocket.

MAKES 1 x 30 cm pizza

INGREDIENTS

100 g fresh wild mushrooms, such as
  chanterelles or porcini, trimmed
  but left whole

3 tablespoons extra virgin olive oil

1 x 30 cm pizza base (see page 199)

1 tablespoon chopped thyme

2 small garlic cloves, chopped

extra virgin olive oil, for drizzling

Wild mushroom pizza

If chanterelles or porcini are proving difficult to come by, you can always substitute the same amount of chopped field mushrooms. If you're feeling decadent, add a drizzle of truffle oil to them to add flavour.

PREHEAT the oven to very hot and put a baking tray or pizza stone in the oven to heat up. Toss the mushrooms in a tablespoon of the oil.

DRIZZLE the pizza base with oil and scatter with thyme and garlic. Top with the mushrooms and season. Slide onto the hot tray or stone (if you're not confident doing this, you can construct and bake the pizza on a cold tray, but it won't be as crisp).

COOK for 2–12 minutes (this will depend on how hot your oven is), or until the base is crisp and the topping cooked. Drizzle with oil.

Sausage and tomato pizza

You can use any type of sausage for this pizza but you will find that Italian sausages do have more flavour. The tinned tomatoes can be replaced with fresh tomatoes, as long as they are really ripe and flavourful. Core and purée them in a food processor.

PREHEAT the oven to very hot and put a baking tray or pizza stone in the oven to heat up.

MIX the tomatoes to a pulp in a food processor or push through a sieve. Remove the sausage skins and break the meat into pieces.

SPREAD the tomato pulp over the pizza base. Scatter with the sausage pieces, oregano and olives, and season. Slide onto the hot tray or stone (if you're not confident doing this, you can construct and bake the pizza on a cold tray, but the base won't be as crisp).

COOK for 2–12 minutes (this will depend on how hot your oven is), or until the base is light brown and crisp and the topping is cooked. Before serving, drizzle with a little extra virgin olive oil.

MAKES 1 x 30 cm pizza

INGREDIENTS

200 g tin chopped tomatoes

2 Italian sausages

1 x 30 cm pizza base (see page 199)

½ teaspoon dried oregano

8 black olives

extra virgin olive oil, for drizzling

tomatoes

Tomatoes (pomodori), although not indigenous to Italy, have become one of the flavours most associated with Italian cooking. All kinds of tomatoes are used in Italy but the ones most favoured for making tomato sauces come from around Naples and are a plum-shaped type called San Marzano. If you are using fresh tomatoes to make a sauce, make sure they are very ripe, even verging on overripe.

Calzone

EACH RECIPE MAKES

1 x 25 cm calzone

INGREDIENTS

cornmeal

½ quantity pizza dough (see
  page 199)

1½ tablespoons olive oil

**MOZZARELLA AND
PROSCIUTTO CALZONE**

170 g mozzarella, cut into
  2 cm cubes

2 thin slices prosciutto, cut in half

1 artichoke heart, marinated in oil,
  drained and cut into 3 slices from
  top to bottom

**POTATO, ONION
AND SALAMI CALZONE**

2 tablespoons vegetable oil

1 small onion, very thinly sliced

75 g small red potatoes, unpeeled,
  very thinly sliced

75 g mozzarella, cut into
  2 cm cubes

60 g sliced salami

2 tablespoons grated Parmesan

A speciality of Naples, calzone differs from other pizzas in that the base is folded over to enclose the topping. This recipe gives instructions for two different fillings—each will make one calzone, enough to feed two people for a light meal or one hungry person.

PREHEAT the oven to 230°C (450°F/Gas 8). Lightly oil a baking tray and dust with cornmeal. On a lightly floured surface, roll out the dough to form an 18 cm circle. Using the heels of your hands and working from the centre outwards, press the circle out to a diameter of about 30 cm. Transfer to the baking tray. Lightly brush the entire surface with the oil.

TO make the mozzarella and prosciutto calzone, spread the mozzarella cheese over half the dough circle, leaving a narrow border around the edge. Roll the prosciutto into little tubes and arrange on top of the cheese. Top with the artichoke slices and season well.

FOLD the other side of the circle over the filling to make a half-moon shape. Match the cut edges and press them firmly together. Fold them over and press into a scrolled pattern to thoroughly seal in the filling. Brush the surface with a little extra olive oil, then transfer to the oven. Bake for about 20 minutes, or until the crust is golden.

TO make the potato, onion and salami calzone, heat the oil in a frying pan and add the onion. Cook for 1 minute, then scatter the potato on top. Cook, stirring, for 3–4 minutes, until beginning to brown. Season, then spread over half the dough circle, leaving a narrow border around the edge. Scatter with the mozzarella, followed by the salami slices and Parmesan.

FOLD the other side of the circle over the filling to make a half-moon shape. Match the cut edges and press them firmly together. Fold them over and press into a scrolled pattern to thoroughly seal in the filling. Brush the surface with a little extra olive oil, then transfer to the oven. Bake for about 20 minutes, or until the crust is golden.

THE most important thing to remember when making calzone is that the base must be thin enough to cook through, but not so thin that it will break easily. You must also make sure that the edges are sealed properly so no filling escapes when the pizza is cooked. A scrolled pattern prevents this happening.

dolci

sponge cake

You can use the instructions opposite for any of the recipes that specify '1 quantity sponge cake'. If you are short of time, buy a Madeira or pound cake or even a pandoro instead. Each will work equally well.

alcohol for desserts

You can use any number of liqueurs or sweet wines for making desserts but bear in mind that if you use one with a strong flavour it will change the taste of the whole dish. You only need to add a little alcohol—if you use more than the recipe recommends you may overpower the whole dish.

fruit

When buying fruit for desserts, bear in mind what it will be used for. Fruit for poaching needs to be firm enough to hold up to the cooking time. Fruit to be eaten raw needs to be completely ripe. Check that the fruit you are using actually has flavour—sometimes fruit such as strawberries and peaches can look perfect but have little taste.

custard

The custard recipe opposite is a standard technique but you will find there are many variations on custard making. Usually custard is cooked over very low heat without letting it come to the boil—this would cause the eggs in it to scramble and congeal. However, when a custard (such as zuppa inglese) contains cornflour it needs to be brought to the boil.

sponge cake

GREASE a 25 cm round cake tin or loaf tin with a little butter. Line the base of the tin with greaseproof paper. Grease the paper and then lightly dust with flour.

CREAM together 150 g butter and 175 g caster sugar until pale and creamy by beating it with a wooden spoon or with an electric whisk.

ADD 3 room-temperature eggs, one at a time, beating each one in thoroughly. The last egg may make the mixture curdle, but don't worry if this happens.

SIFT 250 g plain flour, a pinch of cinnamon and 1 teaspoon baking powder into the bowl and lightly fold everything together. Add 50 ml milk, folding it in gently, to make the mixture soft enough to fall easily off a spoon.

SPOON into the cake tin, filling it no more than three-quarters full or the cake may ooze over the sides of the tin as it cooks.

BAKE for 30-40 minutes at 180°C (350°F/ Gas 4), or until a skewer inserted into the middle comes out clean. Turn out onto a wire rack to cool.

making custard

WHISK the egg yolks and caster sugar in a large bowl until pale and foamy. Pour the milk over the egg yolk mixture and whisk quickly to combine.

POUR into a saucepan and cook over very low heat, stirring, to just thicken. Do not boil or the eggs will scramble. When the white film starts to disappear from the surface, remove from the heat and keep stirring until completely thickened.

DIP the wooden spoon into the custard. Draw a line through the custard on the back of the spoon—if the line stays and the custard does not run through it, then it is ready; if not, cook a little longer.

sweet pastry

RUB 100 g unsalted butter into 200 g plain flour with your fingertips until the texture resembles fine breadcrumbs.

STIR in 50 g caster sugar, 1 egg and 1 egg yolk and mix with the blade of a knife to form a dough.

TIP the dough out onto a lightly floured work surface and bring together with your hands to form a ball. Wrap in clingfilm and rest for a minimum of 30 minutes or, preferably, overnight.

lining a tart tin

GREASE a metal loose-based tart tin. Lightly dust the work surface with flour and roll out the pastry until large enough to fit the tin. (If your kitchen is very warm, simply press the pastry into the tin instead of rolling it out first.)

ROLL the pastry over the rolling pin and transfer it to the tin. Drape it over the tin, then gently fit into the base and side of the tin, pressing it into the flutes.

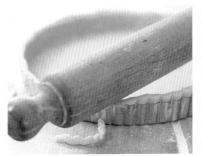

TRIM the edge with a sharp knife or by rolling a rolling pin across the top, then gently push the pastry a little way above the edge of the tin.

blind baking

LINE the pastry shell with a circle of crumpled greaseproof paper and baking beads (if you don't have baking beads, use uncooked dried beans instead).

BLIND bake the pastry at 200°C (400°F/ Gas 6) for 12 minutes, or until lightly cooked. Remove the greaseproof paper and the beads.

RETURN the pastry to the oven for 5 minutes—it should look completely dry. If you are using a very liquid filling, brush the pastry with a beaten egg while it is still hot as this will close up any tiny holes.

pastry

The secret to making pastry is not to overwork it and to chill it thoroughly if you do. Pastry should be made with the tips of your fingers and then only kneaded enough to bring it together. It should be chilled thoroughly before it is cooked to set the fat.

tart tins

Metal loose-based tart tins are the best to use. Metal because it conducts heat well and loose-based because then you can push a filled cooked tart out of the tin without breaking it. If you use a ceramic quiche or tart dish, you will have to serve it from the dish and you might find it sticks.

blind baking

Blind baking starts cooking the pastry before the filling is put in. This stops the side collapsing as it cooks and also prevents the base becoming soggy. If you are putting a liquid filling into the base, make sure you don't prick holes all the way through.

patching pastry

If your pastry starts to crack or you blind baked a tart with holes in it, then patch these up with small thin pieces of dough and put it back in the oven for just long enough for the new pastry to set. Or simply glaze it with a beaten egg.

Tiramisu

Tiramisu means 'pick me up' in Italian—a reference, no doubt, to the generous shot of brandy in this rich dessert. It was created in the nineteen sixties in a Treviso restaurant and has rapidly become popular in many other countries.

SERVES 4

INGREDIENTS

5 eggs, separated

180 g caster sugar

250 g mascarpone

250 ml cold very strong coffee

3 tablespoons brandy or sweet
  Marsala

44 small sponge fingers

80 g dark chocolate, finely grated

BEAT the egg yolks with the sugar until the sugar has dissolved and the mixture is light and fluffy and leaves a ribbon trail when dropped from the whisk. Add the mascarpone and beat until the mixture is smooth.

WHISK the egg whites in a clean dry glass bowl until soft peaks form. Fold into the mascarpone mixture.

POUR the coffee into a shallow dish and add the brandy. Dip some of the sponge finger biscuits into the coffee mixture, using enough biscuits to cover the base of a 25 cm square dish. The biscuits should be fairly well soaked on both sides but not so much so that they break up. Arrange the biscuits in one tightly packed layer in the base of the dish.

SPREAD half the mascarpone mixture over the layer of biscuits. Add another layer of soaked biscuits and then another layer of mascarpone, smoothing the top layer neatly. Leave to rest in the fridge for at least 2 hours or overnight. Dust with the grated chocolate to serve.

preparing

It is important that the coffee you use for soaking the sponge fingers is very strong or the overall flavour of the tiramisu will be too weak. The best coffee to use is espresso.

grappa

This grape-based spirit is made from the crushed fruit used for wine-making. Grappa is usually drunk at room temperature after a meal as a digestive, but it can also be added to dishes such as zuppa inglese.

Zuppa inglese

The name of this pudding, which is similar in construction to the English trifle, does not literally translate to 'English soup', as might be assumed. The *zuppa* has the same linguistic background as the English 'sops' and refers to bread (or, in this case, cake) soaked in wine.

TO make the custard, whisk the egg yolks with the sugar until pale and fluffy. Add the cornflour and flour and mix well. Heat the milk with the vanilla pod and bring just to the boil. Pour into the egg mixture, whisking as you do so. Pour back into the saucepan and gently bring to the boil, stirring all the time. Once the mixture is just boiling, take it off the heat and stir for another few minutes. Pour into a bowl and cover the surface with clingfilm to prevent a skin forming.

SLICE the sponge into 2 cm strips. Place a couple of pieces on each plate (you need to use deep plates) and brush with about 100 ml of the alcohol. Leave to soak for at least 10 minutes.

PUT the raspberries and blackberries in a saucepan with the remaining alcohol and the caster sugar. Gently warm through so that the sugar just melts, then set aside to cool. Spoon over the sponge, then pour the custard over the top of the fruit and serve immediately with the cream.

cooking

When you heat milk, make sure that you use a heavy-based saucepan. The protein in milk coagulates and burns very easily, so keep stirring as it comes to the boil. Stirring will also prevent a skin forming—once a skin has formed, it cannot be stirred back into the milk.

SERVES 6

INGREDIENTS

CUSTARD

6 large egg yolks

100 g caster sugar

2 tablespoons cornflour

1 tablespoon plain flour

600 ml milk

½ vanilla pod or 1 teaspoon vanilla extract

1 quantity sponge cake (see page 220)

150 ml clear alcohol, such as grappa or kirsch

200 g raspberries

350 g blackberries

2 teaspoons caster sugar

500 g lightly whipped fresh cream, to serve

Baked apples

SERVES 6

INGREDIENTS

6 cooking apples

75 g unsalted butter, chilled

6 small cinnamon sticks

100 g pistachio nuts or pine nuts

3 tablespoons brown sugar

100 g raisins or sultanas

200 ml grappa

The advantage of this simple but elegant dessert is that the apples can be prepared and baked in advance and then gently warmed through just before eating. Take care not to overcook the apples or they will collapse. Serve with ice cream or crème fraîche.

PREHEAT the oven to 175°C (350°F/Gas 4). Remove the cores from the apples with a sharp knife or corer and put them in an ovenproof dish.

DIVIDE the butter into six sticks and push it into the cores of the apples. Push a cinnamon stick into the middle of each apple and scatter with the nuts, sugar and raisins. Finally, pour over the grappa.

BAKE for 30–35 minutes, basting the apples occasionally with the juices in the dish until they are soft when tested with a skewer.

Baked figs

SERVES 4

INGREDIENTS

16 figs, halved

50 g hazelnuts

150 ml sweet Marsala

2 tablespoons honey

grated zest of 1 lemon and juice of ½ lemon

200 g mascarpone

Originally from Syria, figs are now grown in many areas of Italy, including Puglia, Calabria and Sicily. They are a versatile fruit—they can be eaten fresh with Parma ham, their soft, sweet flesh can be minced and used in cakes, or they can be baked until soft and golden, as here.

PREHEAT the oven to 190°C (375°F/Gas 5). Arrange the fig halves in a buttered gratin dish large enough to fit them all snugly.

TOAST the hazelnuts in the oven for 8 minutes, then chop them finely. Drizzle the Marsala and honey over the figs. Mix the lemon zest, hazelnuts and mascarpone together and spoon a little onto each fig. Sprinkle with the lemon juice.

BAKE for about 25–35 minutes, or until the juices have reduced into a syrup and the figs are soft. Serve the figs with the juices poured over.

Fruit poached in red wine

When poaching fruit, it is best to use varieties that hold their shape when cooked instead of breaking down to a soft mush. Good apples for poaching include Granny Smiths, Braeburns, Cox's, Russets or Pink Ladies. Good cooking pears include Conference, Beurre Bosc and Anjou.

PUT the pears and apples in a large saucepan. Add the sugar, vanilla pod, cinnamon sticks, red wine and dessert wine and bring to the boil. Reduce the heat and gently simmer for about 5-10 minutes, or until just soft.

ADD the plums, stirring them through the pears and apples, and bring the liquid back to a simmer. Cook for another 5 minutes or until the plums are soft.

REMOVE the saucepan from the heat, cover with a lid and leave the fruit to marinate in the syrup for at least 6 hours. Reheat gently to serve warm or serve at room temperature with cream or ice cream and a biscuit.

cooking

Make sure that you cook the fruit at a gentle simmer. If it cooks too fast, the pieces will break up.

SERVES 6

INGREDIENTS

3 pears, peeled, quartered and cored

3 apples, peeled, quartered and cored

50 g sugar

1 vanilla pod, cut in half lengthways

2 small cinnamon sticks

400 ml red wine

200 ml dessert wine or port

700 g red-skinned plums, halved

apples

Apples *(mela)* are grown in the north of Italy, especially Trentino, Alto Adige and Campania. They are one of the country's most popular fruit, with many different varieties now being cultivated. Apples can be baked, poached, used in pies and tarts and also made into apple paste *(cotognata)* and jam *(confettura)*.

Zuccotto

INGREDIENTS

1 quantity sponge cake baked in a
  loaf tin (see page 220)

125 ml grappa, maraschino
  or brandy

50 g almonds

100 g dark chocolate, chopped

500 g mascarpone

2–4 teaspoons icing sugar

50 g raspberries or 6 strawberries,
  hulled and cubed, or segments
  from 1 orange, drained

icing sugar and cocoa powder, to
  dust

Zuccotto is a traditional Florentine dessert, its shape inspired by the rounded roof of the local *duomo*. It consists of a sponge filled with layers of chocolate, mascarpone, fruit (traditionally candied fruit) and nuts. You can use a ready-made Madeira or sponge cake to save time.

preparing

Zuccotto is best prepared a day in advance to give the flavours a chance to develop. For best results, remove from the fridge an hour before serving—you want the cake to be slightly soft and almost mousse-like in the centre, rather than too solid.

LINE the bowl with triangles of cake, arranging the pieces so they point into the centre of the bowl in a star shape. Fill the gaps with more pieces of sponge. When you have filled the zuccotto with the chocolate mascarpone, trim the cake flush with the top of the bowl. When the zuccotto is full, fit the rest of the sponge pieces tightly together to cover the top.

LINE a round 1 litre pudding bowl with clingfilm, letting the clingfilm hang over the edge of the bowl. Cut about three-quarters of the cake into 1.5 cm slices. Cut each slice into two triangles and arrange them around the bowl, leaving no gaps. The easiest way to do this is to make a star shape in the bottom of the bowl and then work outwards. The sponge should come right to the top of the bowl or even higher.

USING a pastry brush, soak the sponge with the grappa or other alcohol. Start at the top and work down towards the centre, as the grappa will run down the side of the sponge. Reserve 2 tablespoons of grappa.

TO make the filling, toast the almonds under a hot grill for 2–3 minutes or until they start to brown. Keep watching to make sure they don't burn and turn them over if they need it. Alternatively, toast them in the oven at 190°C (375°F/Gas 5) for 10 minutes. Cool them completely and then roughly chop.

GENTLY melt the chocolate in a heatproof bowl set over a saucepan of simmering water, making sure that the bowl does not touch the water and that the water does not get into the bowl or the chocolate will seize. You can also melt the chocolate in a microwave. Mix half the mascarpone into the warm chocolate and spoon into the cake-lined bowl. Spread the mixture up the side of the bowl, leaving a hollow in the middle. Trim the top of the cake flush with the edge of the bowl.

MIX the remaining mascarpone with the icing sugar and almonds, then fold in the fruit. Spoon this into the middle of the cake. Arrange the rest of the cake on top, fitting it snugly, and brush with the rest of the grappa.

COVER with clingfilm and leave in the fridge for at least 2 hours. If the bowl is well sealed the zuccotto will last up to 2 days before serving. To serve, unmould the zuccotto and dust with icing sugar. For a traditional look, dust the top with alternate segments of cocoa powder and icing sugar.

candied fruit

Candied fruit *(canditi)* is used mainly in desserts and baking. Fruit such as cherries, strawberries, chestnuts, pineapple, apricots and varieties of citrus are candied in sugar syrup, both as a preservative and to turn them into a sweetmeat.

Cassata

Strangely, there are two Italian desserts sharing the same name. One is an ice-cream dessert. The other, hailing from Sicily, is a cake made with ricotta and candied fruit and covered in marzipan that is traditionally coloured green. This, obviously, is the cake cassata.

USE clingfilm to line a 20 cm round cake tin with sloping sides (a *moule à manqué* would be perfect). Cut the cake into 5 mm slices to line the tin, reserving enough pieces to cover the top at the end. Fit the slices of cake carefully into the tin, making sure there are no gaps. Brush the Marsala over the cake in the tin, covering it as evenly as possible and reserving a little for the top.

PUT the ricotta in a bowl and beat until smooth. Add the sugar and vanilla extract and mix well. Mix in the candied fruit and chocolate. Spoon the mixture into the mould, smooth the surface and then cover with the remaining slices of cake. Cover with clingfilm and press the top down hard. Put the cassata in the fridge for at least 2 hours, then unmould onto a plate.

KNEAD enough green food colouring into the marzipan to tint it light green. Roll out the marzipan in a circle until it is large enough to completely cover the top and side of the cassata. Melt the jam in a saucepan with 1 tablespoon of water and brush over the cassata. Position the marzipan over the top and trim it to fit around the edge.

MIX the icing sugar with a little hot water to make a smooth icing that will spread easily. Either pipe the icing onto the cassata in a decorative pattern, or drizzle it over the top in a crosshatch pattern. Serve immediately.

preparing

Make sure that the cake slices you are using for lining the tin are thin enough to be flexible so they fit easily into the curve of the tin.

MAKES 1 x 20 cm cake

INGREDIENTS

1 quantity sponge cake (see page 220)

4 tablespoons sweet Marsala

350 g ricotta

75 g caster sugar

½ teaspoon vanilla extract

100 g mixed candied fruit (orange, lemon, cherries, pineapple, apricot), finely chopped

50 g dark chocolate, chopped

green food colouring

250 g marzipan

2 tablespoons apricot or strawberry jam

100 g icing sugar

LINE the tin with cake pieces very carefully so that there are no gaps for the filling to squeeze through. Trim the sponge flush with the top of the tin.

COVER the cassata with a layer of marzipan, smoothing it over the side to get rid of any folds. Trim the bottom edge neatly.

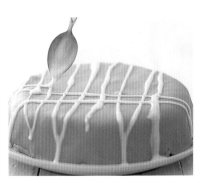

DEPENDING on how creative you are feeling, you can either pipe or drizzle the icing onto the cassata. If you're not confident piping, drizzling in a crosshatch pattern is neatest.

INGREDIENTS

1 quantity sweet pastry (see
   page 221)
200 g dried apricots
100 ml brandy or grappa
icing sugar, to dust

ALMOND FILLING

180 g softened unsalted butter
180 g caster sugar
180 g flaked blanched almonds
2 eggs
1 teaspoon vanilla extract
1 heaped teaspoon plain flour

Apricot and almond tart

This recipe uses dried apricots but works just as well with fresh when they are in season. If you're using fresh apricots, don't bother peeling them and there is no need to soften them with alcohol as you would dried.

WHEN the tart cooks, the filling will puff up and cover the apricots, so make sure you don't push the apricots too far into the mixture if you want the pattern to stand out.

GREASE a 25 cm loose-bottomed metal tart tin. Lightly dust the work surface with flour and roll out the pastry until large enough to fit the tin. Line the tin and trim the edges with a sharp knife. If there is any leftover pastry, roll it thinly and cut into strips to lattice the top of the tart, or use it to make another smaller tart.

REST the pastry in the fridge for 15 minutes or, if time is short, in the freezer until the pastry is firm. Preheat the oven to 200°C (400°F/Gas 6).

LINE the pastry shell with crumpled greaseproof paper and baking beads. Blind bake the pastry for 12 minutes, then remove the greaseproof paper and, if the pastry still looks wet, dry it out in the oven for 5 minutes. Leave to cool for a few minutes. Reduce the oven to 180°C (350°F/Gas 4).

WHILE the pastry is cooling, put the dried apricots and brandy in a saucepan and cook over low heat for about 5 minutes, or until most of the liquid has evaporated and just coats the apricots. Leave to cool.

TO make the almond filling, use a food processor to cream the butter and sugar until light and pale. Add the almonds, eggs, vanilla and flour and briefly blend until just combined. If you overbeat it, the mixture may separate. You can use a whisk or wooden spoon to mix, but you will need to coarsely chop the almonds first or the filling won't be well mixed and can become greasy.

SPOON the filling into the pastry shell, then position the apricots in the tart shell, arranging them in two circles, one inside the other. Bake for 30–40 minutes, or until the filling is set and the top golden brown. If the top starts to get too brown cover it loosely with foil.

LEAVE the tart to cool and sprinkle with icing sugar just before serving. Serve with crème fraîche or cream.

preparing

Most of the stages for this tart (making and lining the tart tin with pastry, cooking the apricots and making the almond filling) can be done ahead of time and then the tart baked when you need it.

figs

Grown in southern Italy and Sicily, figs *(fici)* are best left to ripen on the tree and then eaten very fresh as they soon deteriorate. There are different varieties and shapes of fig but all are interchangeable in recipes. Make sure they are ripe when you buy them.

Fig and raspberry cake

Unlike many other recipes that are best left for the flavours to blend and develop, this cake is best eaten fresh on the day it is made. Serve slightly warm from the oven as a dessert with cream. You can use either fresh or dried figs but you need to plump up the dried ones first (see note below).

PREHEAT the oven to 180°C (350°F/Gas 4). Cream the butter and sugar in a bowl until light and pale. Add the eggs and beat again. Sift the flour over the bowl and fold in with the baking powder and a pinch of salt. Chill for 15 minutes until firm enough to roll out.

LIGHTLY grease a 23 cm springform tin. Divide the dough in two and roll out one piece large enough to fit the base of the tin. Cover with the figs, orange zest and raspberries. Roll out the remaining dough and fit it over the filling. Lightly brush the dough with water and sprinkle with sugar.

BAKE for 30 minutes, or until the top and bottom of the cake is cooked. Poke a skewer into the cake to see if it is ready—there should be no wet cake mixture clinging to the skewer. Serve with cream or mascarpone.

preparing

If fresh figs are not available, you can use the same amount of dried figs but you need to rehydrate them first. Simmer them in orange juice for 5 minutes until they are plumped up and soft.

SERVES 6

INGREDIENTS

185 g unsalted butter

185 g caster sugar

1 egg

1 egg yolk

335 g plain flour

1 teaspoon baking powder

4 figs, quartered

grated zest of 1 orange

200 g raspberries

2 tablespoons sugar

Toscana

One of the better-known regions of Italy, Tuscany has both beautiful countryside and cities steeped in history. This is an area where the quality of the ingredients are allowed to speak for themselves and cooking is kept to a minimum: grilled steaks and simply prepared vegetables and legumes. The world's best extra virgin olive oils come from Tuscany and are used for cooking or simply poured over food before serving. From a culinary point of view Tuscans eat lots of meat, the bistecca alla fiorentina is probably the largest steak in the world and feeds at least two people. Hams made from local pigs, sausages, salami and grilled meats of all descriptions are also enjoyed but, despite this, the Tuscans are known as *i mangiafagioli* or 'bean-eaters' due to their love of fagioli and borlotti beans.

Tuscan bread, *pane Toscano*, is unsalted. As well as an accompaniment to meals it is used as an ingredient in panzanella and pappa al pomodoro and soups such as la ribollita and *acquacotta*. It is also grilled to make crostini and bruschetta. Ribbons of pappardelle pasta are often dressed with sauces made from hare, duck and wild boar (the Tuscans strongly believe in hunting wild food in their lush countryside). Seafood is abundant on the coast, where stews are made containing many different types of fish.

Siena has a reputation for sweets, especially panforte and almond-honey biscuits called *ricciarelli*. Florence is the home of the zuccotto and elsewhere small dry biscuits such as cantucci or biscotti are eaten, dipped in the sweet dessert wine, Vin Santo.

Panforte

Panforte is a medieval recipe from the twelfth or thirteenth century, a speciality of Siena where nearly every shop seems to feature it. This rich cake is sold in huge wheels of both blonde and dark panforte (the latter made by adding cocoa) and will keep for about two weeks.

BUTTER and line the base of a 20 cm springform tin with rice paper. Cut a few thin strips to line the side as well. Preheat the oven to 150°C (300°F/ Gas 3) and lightly brown the hazelnuts and almonds on a baking tray for 6–8 minutes. Check often as the nuts can burn very quickly. Allow to cool.

GRIND the whole spices together in a spice grinder or mortar and pestle. Put the nuts in a metal or china bowl with the spices, figs, cocoa, candied peel, lemon zest and flour and mix together.

PUT the sugar, honey and butter in a heavy-based saucepan to melt, briefly stirring the butter into the sugar as it just starts to melt. Do not stir again or the sugar will crystallise. Bring to the boil and cook until the syrup reaches 120°C (245°F) on a sugar thermometer, or a little of it dropped into cold water forms a soft ball when moulded between your finger and thumb.

IMMEDIATELY pour the syrup into the nut mixture and mix well, working quickly as it will soon cool and stiffen. Pour into the tin and smooth the top with a spatula.

BAKE for about 15 minutes. Unlike other cakes, this will not colour or seem very firm, even when cooked, but will begin to harden as it cools. Allow to cool a little in the tin until it is firm enough to enable the side of the tin to be removed. If the mixture is still quite soft when cooled, place in the fridge to set. To serve, dust the top heavily with icing sugar.

cooking

If the mixture does cool down too quickly and is difficult to pour into the tin, warm it again briefly over a pan of hot water or in a microwave. Do not let it boil or the cake will be very brittle once finally cooled.

MAKES 1 x 20 cm cake

INGREDIENTS

4 small sheets rice paper

100 g skinned hazelnuts

100 g blanched almonds

1 teaspoon each whole coriander seeds, cloves, nutmeg and black peppercorns

1 teaspoon ground cinnamon

50 g finely chopped dried figs

1 tablespoon cocoa

200 g roughly chopped candied orange and lemon peel

grated zest of 1 lemon

50 g plain flour

150 g sugar

4 tablespoons clear honey

2 tablespoons unsalted butter

icing sugar, to dust

LINE the base of the tin with rice paper. The use of an edible paper is essential as the cake is so sticky that it is almost impossible to remove all the paper once it is cooked.

SERVES 4

INGREDIENTS

450 ml double cream

4 tablespoons caster sugar

2 tablespoons grappa (optional)

vanilla extract

3 leaves or 1¼ teaspoons gelatine

250 g berries, to serve

Panna cotta

Meaning 'cooked cream', panna cotta is a rich creamy dessert set with leaf or powdered gelatine. Generally, gelatine leaves will give better results, although they may be harder to find. Whichever you choose, take care to use the amount specified or your panna cotta may end up rubbery.

PUT the cream and sugar in a saucepan and stir over gentle heat until the sugar has dissolved. Bring to the boil, then simmer for 3 minutes, adding the grappa and a few drops of vanilla extract to taste.

IF you are using the gelatine leaves, soak them in cold water until floppy, then squeeze out any excess water. Stir the leaves into the hot cream until they are completely dissolved. If you are using powdered gelatine, sprinkle it onto the hot cream in an even layer and leave it to sponge for a minute, then stir it into the cream until dissolved.

POUR the mixture into four 125 ml metal or ceramic ramekins, cover each with a piece of clingfilm and refrigerate until set.

UNMOULD the panna cotta by placing the ramekins very briefly in a bowl of hot water and then tipping them gently onto plates. Metal ramekins will take a shorter time than ceramic to unmould as they heat up quickly. Serve with the fresh berries.

cooking

Sponging (soaking) the powdered gelatine before stirring it into the hot cream helps dissolve it through the mixture more thoroughly and stops it clumping into hard balls.

Italian orange biscuits

These light crumbly citrus biscuits can be served up anytime with a cup of coffee, but they are also a perfect crunchy accompaniment to ice cream and zabaglione. They will keep for several days in an airtight container.

PUT the flour, semolina, sugar, butter, orange zest, eggs and a pinch of salt in a food processor and mix until smooth. Chill in the fridge for 15 minutes.

PREHEAT the oven to 190°C (375°F/Gas 5). Grease a baking tray and place a teaspoon of the mixture on the tray. Lightly moisten your fingers with a little water and press the mixture down to flatten it. Don't use too much water or it will affect the texture of the biscuits. Leave space between the biscuits as the biscuits will expand during cooking.

BAKE for about 15 minutes, or until the edge of the biscuit is dark golden brown. Remove from the oven, scoop off the tray with a metal spatula and cool on a wire rack. If you are baking the biscuits in batches, make sure the tray is greased each time you use it. When cooled, store in an airtight container.

MAKES 45

INGREDIENTS

175 g plain flour

200 g semolina or fine polenta

100 g caster sugar

100 g unsalted butter, softened

2½ teaspoons grated orange zest

2 eggs

SERVES 8

INGREDIENTS

150 g flaked or whole almonds

1 slice pandoro sweet cake or
  1 small brioche (about 40 g)

300 g dark chocolate

2 tablespoons brandy

150 g unsalted butter, softened

150 g caster sugar

4 eggs

1 teaspoon vanilla extract (optional)

200 g mascarpone

cocoa powder, to dust

Chocolate and almond torte

This rich chocolate torte is ideal for parties as it can be cooked in advance and stored in the fridge—allow it to come to room temperature for at least one hour before you want to serve it. Use the best-quality dark chocolate you can get your hands on.

cooking

You can use flaked or whole almonds in the recipe, but not ground almonds. The texture is too fine and the freshness of the almonds diminishes rapidly once they are ground.

PREHEAT the oven to 170°C (325°F/Gas 4). Toast the almonds in the oven for 8–10 minutes until golden brown, keeping a close eye on them.

PUT the almonds and pandoro in a food processor and process until the mixture resembles coarse breadcrumbs. Alternatively, finely chop the nuts and pandoro and mix them together. Grease a 23 cm springform tin with a little butter. Tip some of the mixture into the tin and shake it around so that it forms a coating on the bottom and side of the tin. Put the remaining nut mixture aside.

GENTLY melt the chocolate and brandy in a heatproof bowl set over a saucepan of simmering water, making sure that the bowl does not touch the water and that the water does not get into the bowl or the chocolate will seize. You can also melt the chocolate in a microwave. Stir occasionally until the chocolate has melted. When melting chocolate, be careful not to overstir or the cocoa butter in the chocolate can separate. It is also possible to burn chocolate when cooking, so take care. Cool slightly.

CREAM the butter and sugar in the food processor or with a wooden spoon for a few minutes until light and pale. Add the melted chocolate, eggs, vanilla and mascarpone. Add the remaining nut mixture and mix well. Tip into the tin.

BAKE for 50-60 minutes or until just set. Leave to rest in the tin for about 15 minutes before taking out. Dust with a little cocoa when cool and serve with crème fraîche.

Ricotta cake with almonds and candied peel

A by-product of cheese-making, ricotta is a fresh, slightly sweet cheese created by skimming off milk solids left in the whey. It is low in fat, has a delicate light texture and is a versatile ingredient in both sweet and savoury dishes.

PREHEAT the oven to 180°C (350°F/Gas 4). Toast the almonds on a baking tray in the oven for 8–10 minutes until golden brown.

PUT the almonds and pandoro in a food processor and process until the mixture resembles coarse breadcrumbs. Alternatively, finely chop the nuts and pandoro and mix them together. Grease a 20 cm springform tin with a little butter. Tip some of the mixture into the tin and shake it around so that it forms a coating on the bottom and side of the tin. Put the remaining nut mixture aside.

WHISK the eggs and sugar for several minutes until pale and a little frothy. Add the orange and lemon zest, ricotta, candied peel and the remaining nut mixture and mix together very briefly.

POUR into the tin and bake for 40–50 minutes, or until the cake feels just firm to the touch. Cool in the tin. Dust with icing sugar before serving at room temperature.

preparing

To save having to clean fiddly citrus zest out of your grater, stick a piece of greaseproof paper against the grater before you use it. When you pull off the paper all the zest will come with it.

SERVES 6

INGREDIENTS

150 g flaked or whole almonds

50 g pandoro sweet cake

6 eggs

100 g caster sugar

grated zest of 1 orange

grated zest of 1 lemon

500 g ricotta

200 g candied peel, chopped

icing sugar, to dust

Blood orange granita

Granitas are popular all over Italy, but particularly in the south and Sicily where they are very refreshing in the hot months. Granitas are often flavoured with coffee or lemon, but this recipe uses blood oranges, which are in abundance in the south after Christmas.

SERVES 6

INGREDIENTS

100 g caster sugar

400 ml blood orange juice (about 5 oranges)

2 tablespoons Grand Marnier, vodka or rum

grated zest of 2 oranges

oranges

Oranges *(arancia)* were first cultivated in Sicily around 1,000 AD. These oranges were introduced by the Arabs and were bitter varieties. Now, sweet oranges are grown extensively and bitter oranges are used for their oil. Oranges are used in both sweet and savoury dishes.

HEAT the caster sugar with 100 ml of the orange juice in a saucepan until the sugar dissolves. Add the rest of the orange juice, the Grand Marnier and the orange zest and stir well.

POUR into a plastic or metal freezer box. The juice should be no deeper than 3 cm so that the granita freezes quickly and breaks up easily. Freeze overnight.

REMOVE the granita from the freezer and rake over it with a fork to break up the ice crystals. Return to the freezer and leave to chill for at least another 2 hours to solidify.

SERVE by raking the crystals again and then spooning into chilled bowls. Granita melts very quickly so a chilled bowl will help it keep its shape a little longer.

USE a fork to rake over the granita and separate it out into ice crystals—the texture should be reasonably coarse. Refreeze and then rake the crystals again just before serving.

preparing

It is easier to zest the oranges before you juice them. Make sure only the top layer of zest is taken from the orange and not the bitter white pith that lies just beneath it.

Sicilia

Sicily, like most of Italy's other islands, has a long history of invasion and at various times the Greeks, Romans, Arabs, Normans and Spanish have all passed that way. These conquerors left in their wake a legacy of foodstuffs such as rice, almonds and couscous that have been incorporated into the local diet. The most important of these was the sugar introduced by the Arabs, and the island's *dolci* are considered Italy's best. As well as these imports, Sicily has a few distinctive flavourings of its own. The island is famed for its citrus fruit, salt is produced at Trappani, olives are abundant and grapes are used for both wine and to make raisins, a common ingredient in the regional cuisine. The local capers add a savoury quality to many dishes and the sea gives up anchovies, tuna, swordfish and sardines in abundance. *Involtini*, fish fillets rolled around a filling, is a speciality.

Pasta, possibly the icon of Italian cooking which has travelled furthest in the world, was first introduced in Sicily. The cuisine of Sicily is based mainly on *cucina povera*: dried pasta is eaten with sauces such as Norma, or dressed with fried breadcrumbs or *ricotta salata*. Antipasto has no history here but dishes such as arancini or marinated sardines take on that role perfectly. Cheeses include caciocavallo and canestro as well as the local pecorino.

The well-known dishes of Sicily include caponata and cassata alla siciliana. Sorbets, gelati and granitas are essential in the summer heat. Sweets and pastries are produced by both speciality shops and convents and monasteries. The *pasticceri* have inherited the sweet tooth of the Arabs, with lots of nuts and candied fruit used, and the cannoli are famed. *Pasta reale* (marzipan) is coloured and shaped into tiny intricate edible decorations.

Marsala

Marsala, a fortified wine, was invented in 1773 by John Woodhouse, an Englishman, and named after the small Sicilian town that today remains the centre of production. The wine was originally not for local consumption but made for export to London and the British Empire. Marsala is DOC regulated and must be aged in wooden casks, where it can rest for up to a decade before being bottled. *Marsala fine* is aged for one year and can be sweet, semi-dry or dry. *Superiore* is aged for over two years, while *vergine* or *solera* is aged in wood for five years if it is dry or ten years if it is *stravecchio*, very mature.

Cinnamon gelato

SERVES 8

INGREDIENTS

1 vanilla pod

550 ml double cream

550 ml milk

2 cinnamon sticks

6 egg yolks

100 g caster sugar

Gelato is the Italian name for an ice cream made with egg custard and sugar. It is important that you use fresh, very aromatic cinnamon sticks for this recipe, otherwise the flavour will not be strong enough.

SPLIT the vanilla pod down the middle, leaving it joined at one end, and put in a saucepan with the cream, milk and cinnamon sticks. Bring just to the boil, then remove from the heat and leave to infuse for 1 hour.

WHISK the egg yolks and caster sugar in a large bowl until pale and creamy. Pour the milk over the egg yolk mixture and whisk quickly to combine.

POUR the custard back into the saucepan and cook over very low heat to just thicken it, stirring continuously with a wooden spoon. Remove from the heat and dip the spoon into the custard. Draw a line on the back of the spoon—if the line stays and the custard does not run through it, then it is ready, if not cook a little longer. Do not boil the custard or the eggs will scramble.

SCRAPE the vanilla seeds from the pod and mix them into the custard. Strain into a bowl, removing the vanilla pod and cinnamon sticks, and leave to cool. Churn in an ice-cream machine following the manufacturer's instructions. Alternatively, pour into a metal or plastic freezer box and freeze, whisking every 30 minutes to break up the ice crystals and give a creamy texture. Once set, keep in the freezer until ready to serve.

THE custard is thick enough when it holds its shape on the back of a spoon. Run a finger through it to see if the line stays clean. When whisking the ice cream, the outside will freeze the fastest, so stir this back into the middle.

Peach and Campari sorbet

This sorbet is best made when peaches are in season and at their most sweet and flavoursome. (White peaches in particular give the ice a lovely colour.) The rest of the time you can use other summer fruits or even citrus fruit, which also go very well with Campari.

SERVES 6-8

INGREDIENTS

5 tablespoons caster sugar

5 tablespoons Campari, grappa or
 brandy

1. 5 kg ripe peaches

juice of 2 large lemons

Campari

An *apéritif* made with herbs, alcohol, sugar and red food colouring, Campari has a bitter aromatic flavour that flatters sweet fruit such as peaches. If you find it too bitter, cut down the amount you use and add peach or orange juice to make up the measure.

HEAT the sugar and Campari in a small saucepan over low heat until the sugar has dissolved.

BLANCH the peaches in boiling water, refresh in cold water, then peel. Cut the flesh off the stones and chop. Purée the peaches in a food processor or blender, or push the flesh through a sieve. Pour the purée into a bowl (you should have about 1 litre), add the Campari and lemon juice and mix thoroughly. Taste a little to check the balance between sweetness and bitterness. If too sweet, add more fruit purée or lemon juice; if too bitter, add more sugar dissolved in water.

CHURN in an ice-cream machine following the manufacturer's instructions. Alternatively, pour into a metal or plastic freezer box and freeze, whisking every 30 minutes to break up the ice crystals and give a creamy texture. Sorbet will not be as creamy as ice cream as it does not contain dairy products but the ice crystals should be very fine. Once set, keep in the freezer until ready to serve.

cooking

Churn or freeze the mixture immediately so that the peaches don't have a chance to oxidise and change colour.

Praline semifreddo

SERVES 6

Meaning 'semi-frozen', this Italian light ice cream has a smooth creamy texture that never sets completely. Semifreddo can also refer to any chilled or partly frozen dessert, possibly containing ice cream, sponge cake, cream and fruit.

INGREDIENTS

200 g blanched almonds

200 g caster sugar

600 ml double cream

2 eggs, separated

100 g icing sugar, sifted

2 tablespoons Mandorla (almond-flavoured Marsala) or brandy

MELT the sugar carefully in a heavy-based saucepan, making sure that you heat the pan evenly. Tip the sugar from side to side so it colours evenly and doesn't burn. When you have stirred in the almonds, the mixture will be very hot, as will the baking tin you tip it into. Handle the praline very carefully until it is cold.

TO make the praline, put the blanched almonds in a hot frying pan and dry-fry until well browned all over, then set aside. Melt the sugar in a saucepan over medium heat until golden, tipping the saucepan from side to side so the sugar melts evenly. Remove from the heat and immediately stir in the almonds. Pour into a greased baking tray (be careful as it will be very hot) and smooth out with the back of your spoon. Leave to cool completely.

FINELY crush the praline in a food processor or by pounding it with a rolling pin or in a mortar and pestle. Pour the cream into a large bowl and whisk until soft peaks form.

BEAT the egg yolks with a quarter of the icing sugar until pale. Whisk the egg whites in a clean dry glass bowl until stiff peaks form, then gradually add the rest of the icing sugar and whisk until glossy stiff peaks form. Gently fold the egg yolks into the cream, then fold in the egg whites. Fold in the praline and Mandorla.

LINE six 250 ml metal dariole moulds with two long strips of foil each, leaving the ends of the strips to overhang the edge (these can be used as handles to lift out the semifreddos when set). Spoon in the mixture, level the surface and tap each mould on the bench a few times. Cover the surface with more foil and freeze for at least 24 hours. To unmould, leave at room temperature for 5 minutes, then lift out with the foil handles.

Zabaglione

Zabaglione *(zabaione)* is one of the lucky accidents of the culinary world. It came into being in the seventeenth century when a chef in the court of Savoy mistakenly poured sweet wine into an egg custard. Today it is eaten on its own or served as a sauce over fruit, cake or pastries.

SERVES 4

INGREDIENTS

6 egg yolks

3 tablespoons caster sugar

125 ml sweet Marsala

250 ml double cream

WHISK the egg yolks and sugar in the top of a double boiler or in a heatproof bowl set over a saucepan of simmering water. Make sure that the water does not touch the base of the bowl or the egg may overcook and stick. It is important that you whisk constantly to move the cooked mixture from the outside of the bowl to the centre.

WHEN the mixture is tepid, add the Marsala and whisk for another 5 minutes, or until it has thickened enough to holds its shape when drizzled off the whisk into the bowl.

WHIP the cream until soft peaks form. Gently fold in the egg yolk and Marsala mixture. Divide among four glasses or bowls. Cover and refrigerate for 3–4 hours before serving.

Marsala

A fortified wine made originally by the British in Sicily, Marsala comes in different degrees of sweetness. The dry is served as an *apéritif* or used in savoury dishes, while the sweet is enjoyed as a dessert wine or added to *dolci* such as zabaglione.

ZABAGLIONE is thickened by gently cooking the egg mixture in a double boiler or bowl set over simmering water. Before the mixture is heated it is dark yellow and thin.

WHEN the zabaglione is ready it will be thick enough to hold its shape if you drizzle it off the whisk back into the bowl. However, it will not be as thick as whipped cream or meringue.

Coffee granita

SERVES 6

INGREDIENTS

200 g caster sugar

1.25 litres very strong
  espresso coffee

The south of Italy is famed for its cold *dolci*: granitas, sorbets and gelati, and Naples in particular is well known for its coffee granitas, traditionally served topped with whipped cream. A granita is an Italian water ice with a coarse texture, the crystals broken up by stirring with a fork.

HEAT the caster sugar with 25 ml hot water in a saucepan until the sugar dissolves. Simmer for 3 minutes to make a sugar syrup. Add the coffee and stir well.

POUR into a plastic or metal freezer box. The mixture should be no deeper than 3 cm so that the granita freezes quickly and breaks up easily. Stir every 2 hours with a fork to break up the ice crystals as they form. Repeat this two or three times. The granita is ready when almost set but still grainy. Stir a fork through it just before serving.

Affogato

SERVES 4

INGREDIENTS

4 scoops vanilla ice cream

4 shots of liqueur such as grappa,
  nocino, frangelico or amaretto

4 shots very hot fresh espresso
  coffee

Affogato literally means 'poached' or 'drowned'. Here it refers to the scoop of vanilla ice cream with a shot of liqueur poured over it that is then 'drowned' in a cup of hot espresso. This is served both as a coffee and a dessert.

LINE up four coffee cups on their saucers. Put a scoop of ice cream into each one and pour a shot of liqueur over each.

POUR a shot of espresso over the ice cream and serve immediately.

IF you like, serve the liqueur and coffee separately and let people pour them over the ice cream themselves.

coffees

espresso

An espresso is made from a small quantity of coffee through which water is forced under pressure. This produces a dark rich coffee topped with an orange-brown *crema* (foam). In the United States an espresso is known as a 'single'. In Australia it is known as a 'short black'.

latte macchiato

Latte macchiato is a glass of foamed milk with a shot of espresso poured in through the foam. Usually served in a long glass.

caffè latte

This is an espresso topped up with three times its volume of steam-heated milk. In different countries a latte can have a foam or be served separated into stripes of coffee and milk. It may be served in a glass or cup.

caffè freddo

This iced coffee is based on a shot of sweetened espresso and served in a decorative glass.

macchiato

A macchiato is an espresso 'stained' with a drop of cold or hot foamed milk and usually served in a small cup or glass.

caffè corretto

This espresso has been 'corrected' with a shot of alcohol such as grappa.

ristretto

Caffè ristretto, 'restricted' coffee, is extra-strong espresso made with a little less water.

cappuccino

This is an espresso topped up with milk steamed to silky thickness and sometimes served with a dusting of cocoa powder. Cappuccinos are usually drunk before 11 am in Italy—they are considered too weak and milky to drink after meals or later in the day.

wines

barolo

Made in Langhe, Piedmont, from Nebbiolo grapes, this excellent wine is a deep red colour with a strong flavour best appreciated after ageing for up to 10 years. Good with game or to use for *brasato al Barolo*, beef braised in red wine.

bardolino

One of Italy's most exported wines, Bardolino is made from the same grapes and in the same region as Valpolicella. Light and often slightly sparkling, it can be served chilled with pasta or antipasto.

valpolicella

Made around Verona from Corvina, Rondinella and Molinara grapes, this is a popular, easy-drinking wine. It is worth searching out the excellent versions from the hills of Verona.

prosecco

A sparkling wine made in the Veneto from Prosecco grapes. This wine comes in both *frizzante* and *spumante* (light and fully sparkling) versions and can be sweet or dry. Add peach juice to make a bellini cocktail.

lambrusco

From Emilia-Romagna, this rich red, naturally fizzy wine is very different in Italy to the mass-produced export versions. Its acidity balances the region's rich foods.

soave

Made in the Veneto, Soave is very pale in colour with a greenish tinge and a light bouquet. Though much is mass-produced, there are some very good wines from the hilly *classico* area. A good accompaniment for risotto.

chianti

No longer usually found in straw-covered bottles, the quality of Chianti is now governed by DOCG regulations. Made largely from Sangiovese grapes, it is best drunk young.

frascati

A well-known white wine made in the hills near Rome from Trebbiano Toscano and Malvasia Bianca grapes. Mostly dry, it is good with Rome's famous meat dishes.

drinks

limoncello

This liqueur from the Amalfi coast in southern Italy is always served ice cold and is made from fresh lemons, sugar and alcohol.

amaretto

This sweet bitter-almond liqueur is drunk as a *digestif* after a meal, but you will also find it used in many sweet recipes as a flavouring.

vin santo

A Tuscan dessert wine made from Malvasia and Trebbiano grapes that are left out to dry in the sun before being pressed. The wine is aged for three to four years and is often served with *cantucci* (sweet biscuits) for dunking.

campari

Campari is a red spirit-based drink usually served as an *apéritif*. Its flavour is bitter and works well combined with soda water and citrus juices. Can also be used in sorbets to great effect.

punt e mes

This vermouth-based Milanese drink is flavoured with herbs. Serve straight with a slice of orange or mixed with soda.

grappa

Grappa is produced by distilling the skins, seeds and pulp that are left over from winemaking. It is usually drunk as a *digestif* after a meal.

nocello

This liqueur is made from an infusion of sugar, alcohol and green walnuts. It is also known as nocino.

marsala

Sicily's most famous wine. Comes in dry and sweet styles, as well as being flavoured with almonds or egg. Good as an *apéritif* or (the sweeter styles) with dessert.

peperoncini

The Italian name for chillies, these are popular in the cooking of the South, and are also served there as a condiment. The smallest are called diavolilli.

polenta

The name of the dish and also the ingredient itself, which is ground corn. The cornmeal comes in different grades of coarseness. Finer varieties are better in cakes, and coarse ones to accompany stews. There is also a white cornmeal.

porcini

The Italian name for a cep or boletus mushroom. Usually bought dried and reconstituted in boiling water, but available fresh in the spring and autumn.

prosciutto

The Italian name for ham. Prosciutto crudo is cured ham and includes Parma ham and San Daniele. Prosciutto cotto is cooked ham.

provolone

Curd cheese made from cows' milk. The curds are spun and worked into large pear- or tube-shaped cheeses, then immersed in brine and bound with string. Available fresh or matured and eaten as a table cheese or used in cooking.

radicchio

A salad leaf of the chicory family with slightly bitter red leaves. There are several varieties: radicchio di Castelfranco, di Chioggia and rosso di Verona are similar to a red cabbage with round leaves; radicchio di Treviso has longer, pointed leaves. Bear in mind the bitterness before adding too many leaves to a mixed salad; you may need sweeter green leaves to offset the flavour.

ricotta

Ricotta means 'recooked'. It is a soft cheese made by recooking the whey left over from making other cheeses and draining it in baskets. It is produced as a by-product of many different types of cheese and varies in fat content. Hard, salted versions are available and there is also a ricotta made from buffalo milk. Fresh ricotta cut from a wheel has a better texture and flavour than that sold in tubs.

risotto rice

Round-grained, very absorbent rice, cultivated in northern Italy. Risotto rice comes in four categories, classified not by quality but by the size of each grain. The smallest, Riso comune (common rice) is very quick to cook (12–13 minutes), and is ideal for rice pudding. Semifino rice includes varieties like vialone nano and cooks in about 15 minutes. Fino takes a minute longer and has more bite. The largest, Superfino, includes arborio and carnaroli and takes about 20 minutes.

seaweed

This can be bought fresh from some fishmongers or dried from specialist supermarkets, health-food shops and Japanese food shops. Look in the Japanese section. Soak dried seaweed to soften it.

semolina

Ground durum wheat available in different sized grains. Finer grains are used to make pasta, coarser grains are used to make semolina gnocchi. Semolina is also useful for dusting fresh pasta to stop it sticking together.

soffritto

The flavour base for many soups, stews and risottos. Soffritto is a mixture of fried ingredients like onion, celery, carrot, garlic, pancetta and herbs. It means literally to 'under-fry' and the mixture should be sweated rather than coloured.

squid/cuttlefish ink

Used to colour and flavour pasta and risotto. The ink is stored in a sac that can be removed from whole squid and cuttlefish or bought in sachets from fishmongers or delicatessens.

sweetbreads

The thymus glands of calves or lambs, these need to be soaked in several changes of cold water and then blanched in boiling water and trimmed before use.

taleggio

A mountain cheese originally from the Italian Alps near Bergamo, but now also made in other regions. Taleggio is a very good table and cooking cheese and should be eaten young—its flavour becomes more acidic with age. It is made in squares and has a pink-yellow crust and creamy centre.

tomatoes, tinned

Several types of tinned tomatoes are available. Whole ones often need to be chopped before use or broken down with the edges of a spoon as you cook them. Chopped ones are cut into small cubes. Most tinned tomatoes are a plum-shaped variety called San Marzano.

truffles

Both black and white truffles can be found in Italy. The black ones come from Umbria (especially around Norcia), Piemonte and Emilia-Romagna. The white ones come from Alba (considered the best), Emilia-Romagna, Le Marche, Tuscany and Umbria. Fresh truffles are very expensive but only a tiny amount is needed. Preserved truffles are also available, as is truffle oil. Truffles are best thinly shaved into slices—you can buy special small mandolins to slice them with.

vermouth

Martini and Cinzano produce the most famous vermouths, white wine infused with herbs. Vermouth is either sweet or dry and comes as rosso (sweet red); bianco (sweet white) or secco (dry white).

vin santo

A golden dessert wine eaten with cantucci biscuits. Now made all over Italy, but the best known is made in Tuscany.

wild mushrooms

Mushrooms such as porcini, slippery Jack, shaggy inkcaps, morels and horns of plenty, all of which grow wild. Available fresh when in season and dried at other times. Mixed packets or individual types can be bought.

zucchini

The Italian name for courgettes. Varieties include the common dark green ones, pale green ones known as 'white' and yellow ones. Some are long and thin, others are ball-shaped. Tiny 'baby' courgettes are also available as are their flowers.

kitchen equipment

baster
Very useful for basting poultry and meats. The pan juices are sucked into the tube of the baster by pressing on the bulb at the end, then the bulb is pressed again to release the juices all over the meat.

citrus zester
An easy way of removing citrus zest without the bitter white pith. Choose one with sharp cutting holes and a cannelle knife. Use it by running it along the outside of citrus fruits.

crinkle cutter
A wavy-edged roller cutter on a handle. Used for cutting crinkled edges to strips of pasta or ravioli.

fish tweezers
For removing pin bones. Special ones are available but eyebrow tweezers with flat ends can also be used. Tweezers are much easier to use for holding slippery bones than using your fingers.

griddle
A thick griddle or grill pan made of cast iron. A griddle can be used on top of the stove for grilling vegetables, meat or fish when a barbecue or open fire is not available. Choose a heavy one with a ridged surface.

mandolin
Not essential, but if you are not confident about thinly slicing zucchini or potatoes for example, it can do them perfectly and easily. Be careful, as the blades are very sharp.

mezzaluna
Perfect for chopping herbs, this is a semicircular knife blade which is designed to rock backwards and forwards across piles of herbs. Sold with a double or single blade and often with a wooden board with a shallow dip in it.

pasta machine
Useful for making fresh pasta which would otherwise have to be rolled by hand. There is a handy attachment for cutting ravioli.

pasta scoop
These are special strainers and come in various designs, some with a deep bowl that is excellent for scooping up long pasta such as spaghetti. These special scoops are not essential if you have metal tongs but it does make picking up and serving pasta easy.

pestle and mortar
Good for smashing garlic and grinding spices and peppercorns to a perfect consistency. Choose a heavy, deep one with a rough inner surface for better grinding ability.

pizza wheel
For slicing through pizza easily without tearing it. This is a sharp circular blade on a wooden or metal handle.

poultry shears
These easily cut through bones, sinew and flesh of poultry and are much easier to use than a knife. The blades are usually curved and pointed to make cutting much easier.

salad spinner
For drying salad leaves and herbs thoroughly. These consist of an outer container and a basket that sits inside the container which is spun by pulling a string or turning a knob on the lid. It is an important tool because if salad leaves aren't properly dried the dressing will run off and the flavours will tend to be watered down.

tortellini cutters
Square-shaped cutters with serrated edges, often with a handle to use for pressing down on sheets of pasta to make tortellini.

wooden tray
There are special trays available that are used for drying pasta but an ordinary wooden tray can be used. You can also improvise when drying pasta, using the backs of a couple of kitchen chairs spaced sufficiently apart.

index

bibliography

Carluccio, Antonio and Priscilla, *Complete Italian Food*, Quadrille Publishing Ltd., London, 1997
Del Conte, Anna, *Gastronomy of Italy*, Prentice Hall Press, New York, 1988
Freson, Robert, *Savouring Italy*, Pavilion Books Ltd., London,1994
Harris, Valentina, *Italian Regional Cookery*, BBC Books, London, 1990
Mariani, John, *The Dictionary of Italian Food and Drink*, Broadway Books, New York,1998
Millon, Marc and Kim, *The Food Lover's Companion to Italy*, Little, Brown and Co. (UK), London, 1996
Plotkin, Fred, *Italy for the Gourmet Traveller*, Kyle Cathie Ltd., London, 1997
Root, Waverley and the editors of Time-Life Books, *Foods of the World: The Cooking of Italy*, Time-Life International (Nederland) NV, 1969

Published by Murdoch Books® a division of Murdoch Magazines Pty Ltd.
First published in 2002

Murdoch Books® Australia
GPO Box 1203, Sydney, NSW 1045
Phone: (612) 4352 7000   Fax: (612) 4352 7026

Murdoch Books UK Limited
Ferry House, 51– 57 Lacy Road, Putney, London SW15 1PR
Phone: + 44 (0) 20 8355 1480   Fax: + 44 (0) 20 8355 1499

Design Concept: Vivien Valk
Designer: Alex Frampton
Creative Director: Marylouise Brammer
Food Editor: Lulu Grimes
Editorial Director: Diana Hill
Editors: Kim Rowney, Jane Price
Picture Librarian: Anne Ferrier
Photographer: Ian Hofstetter
Location photographer: Chris L. Jones
Stylist: Katy Holder
Stylist's Assistants: Jo Glynn, Valli Little
Recipe testing: Jo Glynn
Recipes written by Sophie Braimbridge

Chief Executive: Juliet Rogers
Publisher: Kay Scarlett
Production Manager: Kylie Kirkwood

PRINTED IN SINGAPORE by Tien Wah Press

National Library of Australia Cataloguing-in-Publication Data
Braimbridge, Sophie. Simply Italian. Includes index. ISBN 1 74045 184 8. ISBN 1 74045 197 X (pbk.).
1. Cookery, Italian. I. Title 641.5945

IMPORTANT: Those who might be at risk from the effects of salmonella food poisoning
(the elderly, pregnant women, young children and those suffering from immune deficiency
diseases) should consult their GP with any concerns about eating raw eggs.

ACKNOWLEDGMENTS

The Publisher wishes to thank the following for all their help in making this book possible:

AEG Kitchen Appliances; Breville Holdings Pty Ltd; Corso de' Fiori; Porter's Original Paints